PORSCHE
914 & 914-6

THE DEFINITIVE HISTORY OF THE ROAD & COMPETITION CARS

Also from Veloce Publishing

SpeedPro Series
4-Cylinder Engine – How to Blueprint & Build a Short Block for High Performance by Des Hammill
Alfa Romeo DOHC Engines High-Performance Manual by Jim Kartalamakis
Alfa Romeo Twin Cam Engines – How to Power Tune by Jim Kartalamakis
Alfa Romeo V6 Engine Hi-Performance Manual by Jim Kartalamakis
BMC 998cc A-Series Engine – How to Power Tune by Des Hammill
BMC/Rover 1275cc A-Series Engines – How to Power Tune by Des Hammill
Camshafts – How to Choose & Time them for Maximum Power by Des Hammill
Cylinder Heads – How to Build, Modify & Power Tune Updated & Revised Edition by Peter Burgess
Distributor-type Ignition Systems – How to Build & Power Tune by Des Hammill
Fast Road Car – How to Plan and Build New Edition by Daniel Stapleton
Ford SOHC 'Pinto' & Sierra Cosworth DOHC Engines – How to Power Tune Updated & Enlarged Edition by Des Hammill
Ford V8 – How to Power Tune Small Block Engines by Des Hammill
Harley-Davidson Evolution Engines – How to Build & Power Tune by Des Hammill
Holley Carburetors – How to Build & Power Tune New Edition by Des Hammill
Jaguar XK Engines – How to Power Tune New Edition by Des Hammill
MG Midget & Austin-Healey Sprite – How to Power Tune Updated Edition by Daniel Stapleton
MGB 4-Cylinder Engine – How to Power Tune by Peter Burgess
MGB – How to Give your MGB V8 Power Updated & Revised Edition by Roger Williams
MGB, MGC & MGB V8 – How to Improve by Roger Williams
MGB V8 Conversion by Roger Williams
Mini Engines – How to Power Tune on a Small Budget 2nd Edition by Des Hammill
Motorsport – Getting Started in by S S Collins
Nitrous Oxide Systems – How to Build & Power Tune by Trevor Langfield
Rover V8 Engines – How to Power Tune by Des Hammill
Sportscar/Kitcar Suspension & Brakes – How to Build & Modify Enlarged & Updated 2nd Edition by Des Hammill
SU Carburettors – How to Build & Modify for High Performance by Des Hammill
Suzuki 4WD for Serious Offroad Action – Modifying by John Richardson
Tiger Avon Sportscar – How to Build Your Own Updated & Revised 2nd Edition by Jim Dudley
TR2, 3 & TR4 – How to Improve by Roger Williams
TR5, 250 & TR6 – How to Improve by Roger Williams
V8 Engine – How to Build a Short Block for High Performance by Des Hammill
Volkswagen Beetle Suspension, Brakes & Chassis – How to Modify for High Performance by James Hale
Volkswagen Bus Suspension, Brakes & Chassis – How to Modify for High Performance by James Hale
Weber DCOE, & Dellorto DHLA Carburetors – How to Build & Power Tune 3rd Edition by Des Hammill

Those were the days ... Series
Alpine Trials & Rallies 1910-1973 by Martin Pfundner
Austerity Motoring by Malcolm Bobbitt
Brighton National Speed Trials by Tony Gardiner
British Police Cars by Nick Walker
BRM V16 by Karl Ludvigsen
Crystal Palace by S S Collins
Dune Buggy Phenomenon by James Hale
More Dune Buggies by James Hale
Motor Racing at Brands Hatch in the Seventies by Chas Parker
Motor Racing at Goodwood in the Sixties by Tony Gardiner
Motor Racing at Oulton Park in the 60s by Peter McFadyen
Three Wheelers by Malcolm Bobbitt

Enthusiast's Restoration Manual Series
Citroën 2CV – How to Restore by Lindsay Porter
Classic Car Bodywork – How to Restore by Martin Thaddeus
Classic Cars – How to Paint by Martin Thaddeus
Reliant Regal – How to Restore by Elvis Payne
Triumph TR2/3/3A – How to Restore by Roger Williams
Triumph TR4/4A – How to Restore by Roger Williams
Triumph TR5/250 & 6 – How to Restore by Roger Williams
Triumph TR7/8 – How to Restore by Roger Williams
Volkswagen Beetle – How to Restore by Jim Tyler
Yamaha FS1-E Moped – How to Restore by John Watts

Essential Buyer's Guide Series
Alfa GT Buyer's Guide by Keith Booker
Alfa Romeo Giulia Spider Buyer's Guide by Keith Booker
Jaguar E-Type Buyer's Guide by Peter Crespin
MGB, MGB GT Buyer's Guide by Roger Williams
Porsche 928 Buyer's Guide by David Hemmings
Triumph TR6 Buyer's Guide by Roger Williams
VW Beetle Buyer's Guide by Ken Cservenka & Richard Copping
VW Bus Buyer's Guide by Ken Cservenka & Richard Copping

Auto Graphics Series
Fiat & Abarth by Andrea & David Sparrow
Jaguar MkII by Andrea & David Sparrow
Lambretta LI by Andrea & David Sparrow

General
AC Two-litre Saloons & Buckland Sportscars by Leo Archibald
Alfa Romeo Berlinas (Saloons/Sedans) by John Tipler
Alfa Romeo Giulia Coupé GT & GTA by John Tipler
Alfa Romeo Tipo 33 Development, Racing & Chassis History by Ed McDonough
Anatomy of the Works Minis by Brian Moylan
Armstrong-Siddeley by Bill Smith
Autodrome by S S Collins & Gavin Ireland
Automotive A-Z, Lane's Dictionary of Automotive Terms by Keith Lane
Automotive Mascots by David Kay & Lynda Springate
Bahamas Speed Weeks by Terry O'Neill
Bentley Continental, Corniche and Azure by Martin Bennett
BMC Competitions Department Secrets by Stuart Turner, Peter Browning & Marcus Chambers
BMW 5-Series by Marc Cranswick
BMW Z-Cars by James Taylor
British 250cc Racing Motorcycles by Chris Pereira
British Cars, The Complete Catalogue of, 1895-1975 by Culshaw & Horrobin
Bugatti Type 40 by Barrie Price
Bugatti 46/50 Updated Edition by Barrie Price
Bugatti 57 2nd Edition by Barrie Price
Caravans, The Illustrated History 1919-1959 by Andrew Jenkinson
Caravans, The Illustrated History from 1960 by Andrew Jenkinson
Chrysler 300 – America's Most Powerful Car 2nd Edition by Robert Ackerson
Citroën DS by Malcolm Bobbitt
Cobra – The Real Thing! by Trevor Legate
Cortina – Ford's Bestseller by Graham Robson
Coventry Climax Racing Engines by Des Hammill
Daimler SP250 'Dart' by Brian Long
Datsun 240, 260 & 280Z by Brian Long
Datsun Fairlady Roadster to 280ZX by Brian Long
Dino: The V6 Ferrari by Brian Long
Ducati 750 Bible by Ian Falloon
Dune Buggy, Building a – The Essential Manual by Paul Shakespeare
Dune Buggy Files by James Hale
Dune Buggy Handbook by James Hale
Fiat & Abarth 124 Spider & Coupé by John Tipler
Fiat & Abarth 500 & 600 2nd edition by Malcolm Bobbitt
Ford F100/F150 Pick-up 1948-1996 by Robert Ackerson
Ford F150 1997-2005 by Robert Ackerson
Ford GT – Then and Now by Adrian Streather
Ford GT40 by Trevor Legate
Ford in Miniature by Randall Olson
Ford Model Y by Sam Roberts
Funky Mopeds by Richard Skelton
Grand Prix Racing, 1 1/2 litre 1961-1965 by Mark Whitelock
Honda NSX Supercar by Brian Long
Jaguar, The Rise of by Barrie Price
Jaguar XJ-S by Brian Long
Jeep CJ by Robert Ackerson
Jeep Wrangler by Robert Ackerson
Karmann-Ghia Coupé & Convertible by Malcolm Bobbitt
Land Rover, The Half-Ton Military by Mark Cook
Lea-Francis Story, The by Barrie Price
Lexus Story, The by Brian Long
Lola – The Illustrated History (1957-1977) by John Starkey
Lola – All The Sports Racing & Single-Seater Racing Cars 1978-1997 by John Starkey
Lola T70 – The Racing History & Individual Chassis Record 3rd Edition by John Starkey
Lotus 49 by Michael Oliver
Marketingmobiles: Promotional Vehicles of the World, The Wonderful Wacky World of by James Hale
Maxda MX-5 New Edition by Brian Long
Mazda MX-5/Miata 1.6 Enthusiast's Workshop Manual by Rod Grainger & Pete Shoemark
Mazda MX-5/Miata 1.8 Enthusiast's Workshop Manual by Rod Grainger & Pete Shoemark
Mazda MX-5 (& Eunos Roadster) - The World's Favourite Sportscar by Brian Long
Mazda MX-5 Miata Roadster by Brian Long
MGA by John Price Williams
MGB & MGB GT – Expert Guide (Auto-Doc Series) by Roger Williams
Micro Caravans by Andrew Jenkinson
Mini Cooper – The Real Thing! by John Tipler
Mitsubishi Lancer New Edition by Brian Long
Montlhéry – The story of the Paris autodrome by William Boddy
Motor Racing Reflections by Anthony Carter
Motorhomes, The Illustrated History by Andrew Jenkinson
Motorsport in colour, 1950s by Martyn Wainwright
MR2 – Toyota's Mid-engined Sports Car by Brian Long
Nissan 300ZX & 350Z - The Z-Car Story by Brian Long
Pass the Driving Test by Clive Gibson & Gavin Hoole
Pontiac Firebird by Marc Cranswick
Porsche Boxster by Brian Long
Porsche 356 by Brian Long
Porsche 911 Carrera by Tony Corlett
Porsche 911R, RS & RSR, 4th Edition by John Starkey
Porsche 911 – The Definitive History 1963-1971 by Brian Long
Porsche 911 – The Definitive History 1971-1977 by Brian Long
Porsche 911 – The Definitive History 1977-1987 by Brian Long
Porsche 911 – The Definitive History 1987-1997 by Brian Long
Porsche 911 – The Definitive History 1997 to 2004 by Brian Long
Porsche 911SC 'Super Carrera' by Adrian Streather
Porsche 914 & 914-6 by Brian Long
Porsche 924 by Brian Long
Porsche 944 by Brian Long
Porsche 993 'King of Porsche' by Adrian Streather
RAC Rally Action! of by Tony Gardiner
Rolls-Royce Silver Shadow/Bentley T Series Corniche & Camargue Revised & Enlarged Edition by Malcolm Bobbitt
Rolls-Royce Silver Spirit, Silver Spur & Bentley Mulsanne 2nd Edition by Malcolm Bobbitt
Rolls-Royce Silver Wraith, Dawn & Cloud/Bentley MkVI, R & S Series by Martyn Nutland
RX-7 – Mazda's Rotary Engine Sportscar (updated & revised new edition) by Brian Long
Singer Story: Cars, Commercial Vehicles, Bicycles & Motorcycles by Kevin Atkinson
SM: Citroën's Maserati-engined Supercar by Brian Long
Subaru Impreza: The Road & WRC Story by Brian Long
Taxi! The Story of the 'London' Taxicab by Malcolm Bobbitt
Triumph Motorcycles & the Meriden Factory by Hughie Hancox
Triumph Speed Twin & Thunderbird Bible by Harry Woolridge
Triumph Tiger Cub Bible by Mike Estall
Triumph Trophy Bible by Harry Woolridge
Triumph TR6 by William Kimberley
Turner's Triumphs, Edward Turner & his Triumph Motorcycles by Jeff Clew
Velocette Motorcycles – MSS to Thruxton Updated & Revised Edition by Rod Burris
Volkswagen Bus or Van to Camper, How to Convert by Lindsay Porter
Volkswagens of the World by Simon Glen
VW Beetle Cabriolet by Malcolm Bobbitt
VW Beetle – The Car of the 20th Century by Richard Copping
VW Bus, Camper, Van, Pickup by Malcolm Bobbitt
VW Bus – 40 years of splitties, bays & wedges by Richard Copping
VW Golf": Five Generations of Fun by Richard Copping & Ken Cservenka
VW – The air-cooled era in colour by Richard Copping
Works Rally Mechanic by Brian Moylan

First published March 2006 by Veloce Publishing Limited, 33 Trinity Street, Dorchester DT1 1TT, England. Fax 01305 268864/e-mail info@veloce.co.uk/web www.veloce.co.uk or www.velocebooks.com
ISBNs 1-84584-030-5/978-1-84584-030-3/UPC 636847-04030-7 (paperback); ISBNs 1-84584-014-3/978-1-84584-014-3/UPC 636847-04014-7 (hardback).
© Brian Long and Veloce Publishing 2006. All rights reserved. With the exception of quoting brief passages for the purpose of review, no part of this publication may be recorded, reproduced or transmitted by any means, including photocopying, without the written permission of Veloce Publishing Ltd. Throughout this book logos, model names and designations, etc, have been used for the purposes of identification, illustration and decoration. Such names are the property of the trademark holder as this is not an official publication.
Readers with ideas for automotive books, or books on other transport or related hobby subjects, are invited to write to the editorial director of Veloce Publishing at the above address.
British Library Cataloguing in Publication Data – A catalogue record for this book is available from the British Library. Typesetting, design and page make-up all by Veloce Publishing Ltd on Apple Mac.
Printed in India by Replika Press.

PORSCHE
914 & 914-6

THE DEFINITIVE HISTORY OF THE ROAD & COMPETITION CARS

Brian Long

VELOCE PUBLISHING
THE PUBLISHER OF FINE AUTOMOTIVE BOOKS

Introduction and acknowledgements

Launched in 1969, the 914 series experienced many problems and went through numerous changes before production came to an end in 1976. Constantly improved during its short life, time just ran out for the model, though it is interesting to note that, until the Boxster made its debut, the 914 remained Porsche's only mid-engined production car, although for some years the company's racing models had been built using this layout.

The 914 also had a fine competition history – something that is often overlooked or disparaged because it wasn't as brilliant as the 911's; by usual standards, though, it was indeed a fine history. There were also a large number of specials built on the 914 chassis, and both of these aspects have been covered in detail in this book.

The 914 series has often been cited as the forgotten Porsche, but a growing band of enthusiasts only have eyes for this model. The handling is, of course, a major factor which contributes toward the enjoyment of the type, but a large number of people like the styling, and the fact that, for so many years, this was the most affordable of all Porsches to own and run.

Now, times have changed and the model has appreciated and grown, not only in value, but in terms of awareness, too. The 914/6 has become particularly desirable, and it is hoped that this book will go some way toward explaining the 914's various merits.

Thanks, as always, must go to Klaus Parr of the Porsche Archives, and his team; in particular, his assistant Jens Torner. The vast majority of the material in this book has come from the factory and, like my 356 book, virtually all of it (including the colour photographs) is contemporary.

I would like to acknowledge Valentina Kalk at ItalDesign (Giugiaro); Dan Hopper at Porsche North America; Volkswagen in Japan (especially Dorothea Gasztner), and marque specialists Flat-Four; Mizwa Motors Corporation (the Porsche concessionaire for Japan); W Reddig at the AutoMuseum Volkswagen; Paul Buckett and his colleagues at Volkswagen GB, and Klaus Bohrer of the Club Porsche Espana. I would also like to thank my aunt, Emmy Whittle, for helping with the German translation.

Notes to the second edition

The original 914 book was published in 1997, and has been reprinted in paperback form twice since then, as well as translated into German. It was my second Porsche book, setting the basic format for those that followed. The 356 volume (the first in the series) has since been revised and expanded to better match the other titles, which now feature 192 pages in full colour. This left only the 914 title with 160 pages and a separate colour section, so the time has come to bring it up to date. I sincerely hope you enjoy the end result.

Brian Long
Chiba City, Japan

Contents

1 Porsche: a brief history 7
    The legendary 356 8
    356 developments 14
    Porsche in competition 14
    The last 356 16
    The Type 901 18
    Racing news 20
    911 update 20

2 A joint project 21
    The Karmann Ghia 22
    Links with Porsche 23
    Building on success 24
    Sharing resources 25
    The 914 is born 27
    A death in the family 29
    Final details of the 914 33
    Launch of the new model 36

3 The early production models 44
    The 914/4 in Europe 47
    The 914/4 in America 55
    The 914/6 59
    The 914/6 in Britain 62
    News from the USA 65
    The 1971 model year 67
    The 1972 model year 79
    The four-cylinder car in the USA 85
    Company news 87
    Review of the series to date 89
    Preview of the 1973 model year 90

4 End of the line 91
    The model in Europe 97
    The 914-2.0 107
    The 1974 model year 112
    Matters of the moment 121
    The 914 GT & Limited Edition 123
    Company news 127
    The 1975 model year 130
    The final year 134

5 The model in competition 137
    The 914/6 GT 137
    Motorsport in 1970 140
    Motorsport in 1971 146
    The twilight years 152
    SCCA racing in America 155
    A final note 160

6 914 specials 161
    The 914/8 161
    The Goertz prototype 162
    The Tapiro 169
    The Murene 171
    The Hispano-Aleman 173
    The 916 173
    Other specials 176
    VW Karmann 'Cheetah' 180

7 After the 914 181
    A final thought 181
    The 912E 182
    The 924 182
    The contemporary 911s 183
    The 928 & 944 184

Appendix I Concise buyer's guide .. 190
    Exterior trim 192
    Engine 192
    Transmission 193
    Suspension, steering and braking system..... 193
    Interior 196
    Heating system 196
    Spares today 196
    The best buy? 196

Appendix II Engine specifications 197

Appendix III Chassis specifications 199

Appendix IV Production details 201

Index 207

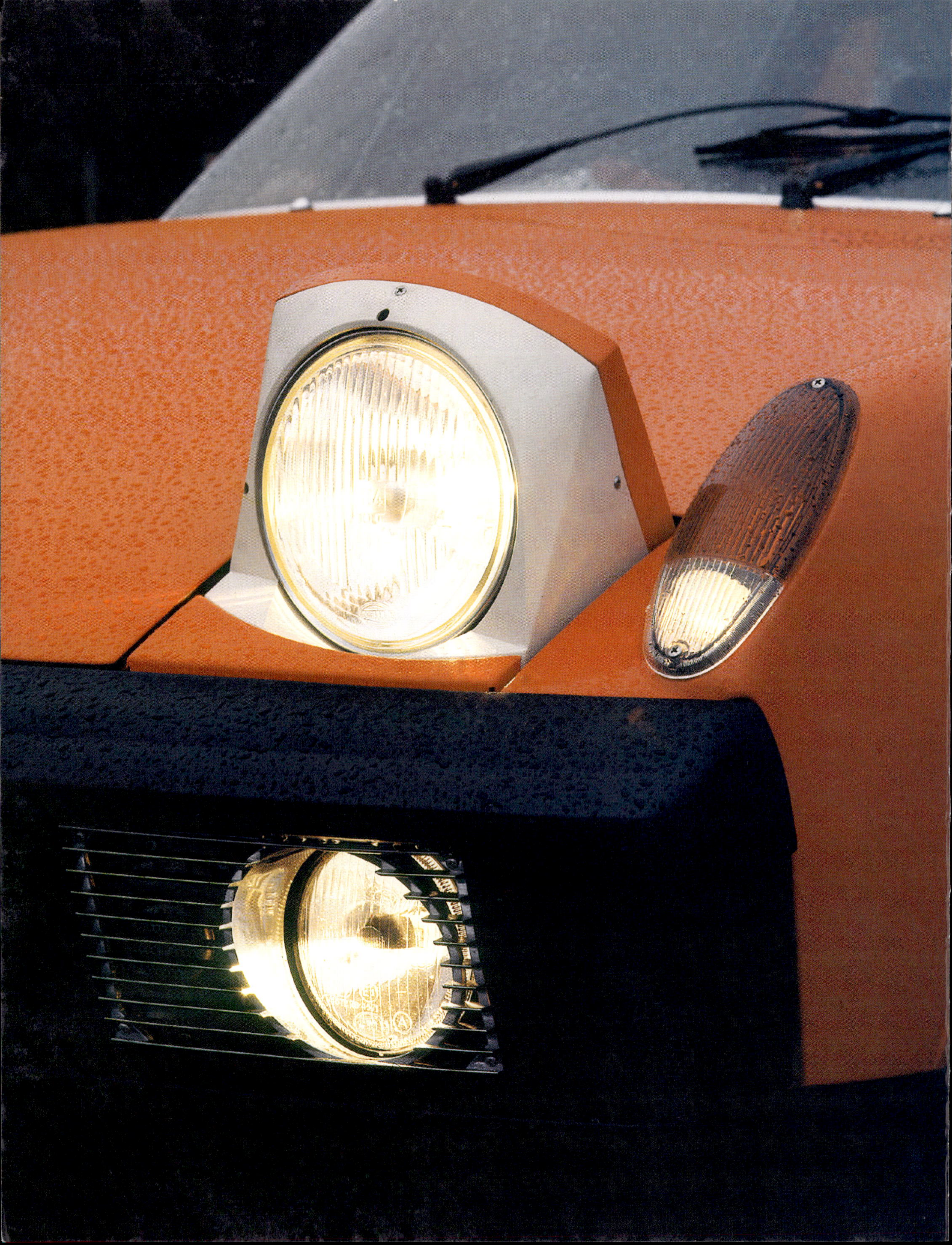

1
Porsche: a brief history

Professor Ferdinand Porsche had worked for Lohner, Austro-Daimler, Daimler (which soon after became Daimler-Benz) and Steyr, and in Germany had an unrivalled reputation as a designer. After leaving Steyr, he felt the time had come to set up his own company.

Registered in April 1931, a design studio was established in Stuttgart with a team of hand-picked engineers and designers, including Porsche's son, Ferry. Born on 19 September 1909, Ferry inherited much of his father's natural flair for engineering and, although he wanted to become a racing driver, his father soon put a stop to these aspirations. This is perhaps fortunate for, without him, the Porsche company, as it exists today, would never have evolved, and neither would the vehicles recognized as 'true' Porsches.

Adolf Hitler was very supportive of German industry, and financed the Mercedes-Benz and Auto Union racing programmes to show the world the strength of German engineering. The highly-successful Auto Union V16 Grand Prix car was a Porsche design, of course, but it was the Volkswagen project which provided the basis for the Porsche success story. The Volkswagen was also financed by the Nazi party; a blessing at the time, but one which would cause problems later.

Just as Hitler was passing the final plans for the Volkswagen, the Second World War broke out. During the hostilities, Porsche and his team were moved to the Austrian village of Gmünd, and there they produced many designs, including those for a number of tanks. Because of his so-called "links" with the Nazi leader, Professor Porsche was arrested and interrogated by the Allied authorities following the war, but was promptly released.

After this, Porsche went to Renault and, whilst

The first vehicle to bear the Porsche name - the Lohner-Porsche. This example set a number of records and is seen here in September 1900 with E W Hart of England at the wheel.

Ferry Porsche (centre left) discussing a new design with his father (centre right). Just one year after this picture was taken in the design office attached to the Reutter works, Professor Porsche died. However, Ferry proved himself to be a fine, entrepreneurial leader.

there, he and his son-in-law, Anton Piech, were arrested and imprisoned by the French on war criminal charges, with bail set at one million francs. (Ferry Porsche had also been imprisoned for a short time but his sister, Louise, had managed to negotiate his release.) However, the Porsche offices in Stuttgart were occupied by the United States Army, and Ferry Porsche had little chance of raising the ransom money repairing ex-Army Volkswagens.

By an amazing stroke of luck, Ferry Porsche was approached by Carlo Abarth (the famous engine tuner) and Piero Dusio, a rich Italian industrialist, who, among other things, wanted to build a Grand Prix car. The Cisitalia, as it was known, drew heavily on prewar Auto Union designs and was very complex. Sadly, the project was destined to fail, as escalating costs put a potentially successful car beyond even Dusio's wealth. It did, however, provide Ferry Porsche with enough money to free his father. The Professor was allowed back to Austria in August 1947 but died less than four years later. His health had never been the same following imprisonment, but at least he lived to see his son develop a new car bearing the family name.

The legendary 356

Already, Porsche's sports car was making a name for itself. Design work had begun in Gmünd after Ferry Porsche decided that his small company should contruct a vehicle based on Volkswagen components. Given the design number Type 356, the first drawing was dated 17 July 1947, just one month after the project was instigated.

The first chassis was completed in March 1948 and fitted with a prototype open body two months later. The spaceframe chassis on Number One was well-designed, but unsuitable for cost-effective series production as it was very labour-intensive to build.

The engine was a tuned 1131cc Volkswagen unit mounted back-to-front to give good weight distribution but, unfortunately, took up too much space to allow for any more than two seats. A number of other problems were encountered with this set-up and, from the second car on, the engine was mounted in traditional Volkswagen fashion on a sheet steel platform chassis.

Number One was taken to the European Grand Prix in Switzerland to allow journalists to test the car,

How the legend began. This is Porsche Number One, driven here by Otto Huslein, (Managing Director of the Gmünd works) in 1948.

An early 356 coupé, pictured in 1953. Note the bumper mounted on the body and the split windscreen. The 356 quickly established itself in rallying, although it's interesting to note that the works always used the alloy Gmünd coupés as they were lighter than the Stuttgart-built machines.

and it was at this meeting that Porsche met Rupprecht von Senger, who was particularly enthusiastic about the project. Von Senger and his partner agreed to buy the next four cars produced, and also proved very helpful in getting supplies from Wolfsburg to Gmünd.

The second car was a coupé, completed in August 1948. Aerodynamics were very good and the combination of a seamless body construction and lack of openings at the front meant the Porsche was capable of some very high speeds for such a small-engined car.

Announced during the summer of 1948, the car's public debut was scheduled for the Geneva Show in 1949. It wasn't long before a 1086cc capacity was adopted, allowing the cars to compete in the 1100cc Class at international level. In the meantime, in mid-September 1948, Porsche sealed a deal with Volkswagen securing the supply of parts, as well as use of the Volkswagen dealer and service network.

The Gmünd cars were completely handbuilt, their aluminium bodies beaten into shape, as there simply wasn't the money available to tool up. According to Ferry Porsche, 46 cars were built at Gmünd between June 1948 and March 1951. However, figures vary wildly between sources, with most quoting 50 or 51 vehicles.

Serious production began early in 1950 when the firm moved back to Stuttgart. The Porsche site was still being used by the Americans at the time, so the factory belonging to Porsche's neighbours – the Reutter body works – was used initially. Reutter had already been given the contract to build new steel bodies for Porsche in November 1949, and an area was set aside for the motor manufacturer.

The first steel-bodied Porsche was completed in April 1950. There were a number of minor differences compared to the Gmünd alloy cars, but they were indeed subtle. In fact, mild and constant updating was to become a feature of Porsche production through the years, with the company preferring to introduce new models that were evolutions of the outgoing vehicle. Even competition Porsches were largely based on production cars during these early days.

At the 1950 Paris Show, an ailing Ferdinand Porsche held talks with Max Hoffman and others to try and get the 356 into America. By the end of 1950, he had become gravely ill and died a national hero in January 1951.

In the meantime, in December that year a small design and management office was purchased near the Reutter works, and a racing shop was attached with just enough room for two cars and four mechanics. It was at this stage in the proceedings that the company was registered as Dr Ing h c F Porsche KG.

The mid-engined Porsche 550 Spyder pictured with Karl Kling and Hans Herrmann. The event was the 1953 Carrera Panamericana – a dangerous race that, in the future, lent its name to a famous line of Porsche models.

The Stuttgart concern had a staff of 108 at the time, with planned production of around ten cars per month. In the event, this target was easily doubled, and nearly 300 Porsche 356s were built in the year. The 500th German-built 356 was driven out of the works in March 1951 and, just five months later, the 1000th 356 left the factory.

By March 1951, 1283cc engines were available, and a 1488cc unit followed in October. Although the 1100 power unit continued until the end of 1954, there were fewer sales of smaller capacity models, especially in America, a market that was already very important to the company.

In September 1952, the 1500 gave a refined 55bhp, while the roller-bearing engines giving 70bhp became known as the 1500 Super. Other important revisions carried out during 1952 included dropping the old two-piece windscreen, although the distinct V-shape remained until 1955. Stronger bumpers, now moved further away from the body, were also a feature.

The original Porsche factory was supposed to have been handed back in September 1950 but, due to the alert caused by the Korean War, the American authorities held on to it. With no sign of the old factory being returned, another works was built in 1952, next door to Reutter. By November 1952, the first cars were starting to roll out of the new Werk II.

From November 1953, a roller-bearing version of the 1.3 litre engine – called the 1300 Super – was made available. Launched at the Paris Salon, this 60bhp unit was shortlived, remaining in production for only six months; all pushrod roller-bearing engines were phased out by the end of 1957.

During 1952, Dr Ernst Fuhrmann began to design the powerful Carrera engine. In order to keep the physical size of the unit to a minimum, he devised an ingenious system incorporating no fewer than nine shafts, 14 bevel gears and two spur gears to operate the dohc per bank arrangement. The beauty of this system lay in the fact that the engine's overall dimensions were little changed from the standard four-cylinder power unit. The first engine was up and running in April 1953. It was right virtually from the start and testing took place in the new Porsche 550 at the Nürburgring in August.

Based on the original Porsche Number One, the Type 550 made its debut in May 1953 for the Eifelrennen at the Nürburgring. On this occasion, the mid-engined car was powered by a 1500 Super unit, but nonetheless narrowly beat the Borgwards to take a maiden Class victory. It provided the Porsche concern with the foundation stone on which to build a racing legend.

By the early part of 1954, the first batch of customer cars was being completed by Wendler of Reutlingen. The 1500 Super engine was used, but tuned to bring up power to around 100bhp. The official designation was 550/1500RS, but Max Hoffman coined the name Spyder, and it was this moniker that stuck in the public's mind. Excellent results at Le Mans, on the Carrera Panamericana, the Mille Miglia (the 1954 event was the international debut of the 550 Spyder with the Carrera engine), the Tour de France Automobile, Tourist Trophy, and numerous tracks across Europe and America secured the Spyder a place in racing history.

A Carrera engine was installed in one of the works Gmünd coupés entered for the 1954 Liège-Rome-Liège Rally, held that particular year in August. Ferry Porsche's theory was that if the car could survive such a tough event, it could safely be used in a production car – the decision was made easier after Herbert Linge and Helmut Polensky won outright!

In 1954, staff numbers increased to 493, but

One of the first Porsche Speedsters (left) with a 356A coupé. The 356A was introduced at the 1955 Frankfurt Show, distinguished from its predecessor by the smoother windscreen shape.

only 1934 cars were produced – 44 fewer than in the previous year. However, on 15 March 1954, the 5000th German-built Porsche was completed (two years later the figure reached 10,000) and exports now accounted for 60 per cent of production.

John von Neumann, Porsche's West Coast distributor, was the inspiration behind the Speedster. The Speedster was exactly what Hoffman needed to boost sales Stateside, selling at $2995 in basic form. Based on the Cabriolet but with minimal equipment (such as a cheap hood, low and flimsy windscreen, and detachable sidescreens instead of wind-up windows), it was introduced into America in September 1954. In all, a total of 4854 Speedsters were produced (both 356 and 356A types together) and it became the darling of the racing set.

Back in 1951 at the Earls Court Show, two Porsche 356s – a coupé and a cabriolet – were put on display by Connaught Cars Ltd, becoming the first German cars to be shown in England since the end of the war. Before long, AFN Ltd of Isleworth (the concern behind Frazer-Nash) became the agent, with imports starting seriously in 1954. Prices ranged from £1842 to £2378;

Announced at the 1959 Frankfurt Show, the 356B brought with it higher mounted bumpers and a slightly different wing line, allowing the car to meet regulations for all American states. The Karmann hardtop model (seen here) was introduced shortly after, but was never as popular as Porsche had hoped. It must be said that the styling does look a little uncomfortable compared to the smooth lines of Erwin Komenda's original.

12

quite expensive given that a Jaguar XK120 cost around £1600 at this time, and the almost unlimited choice of even cheaper British sports cars.

The 356A was introduced at the Frankfurt Show in September 1955. There were subtle changes to the body, and suspension improvements made the car feel more stable going into corners. The 356s were still being successfully used in rallying, with the Liège-Rome-Liège event virtually a Porsche benefit. The racing side of competition was left almost exclusively to the Spyders, although there were Class wins on both the Mille Miglia and Targa Florio.

The 1582cc engine came in 1955, with two versions listed – the 1600 and 1600 Super, giving 60 and 75bhp respectively. The 1300 and 1300 Super continued unchanged in most markets, but had been dropped in America earlier in the year and were phased out completely by the end of 1957. The 1500GS Carrera engine was made available for the new 356A range and, like the other power units, could be specified in the updated coupé, cabriolet or Speedster bodyshells.

On 1 December 1955, the old works was at last handed back to its rightful owner. Called Werk I, the management – along with the Design, Experimental and Racing Departments – moved there, together with the Repair Shop. Towards the end of 1955, three out of every four cars produced by Porsche (which, by now, employed around 600 people) were exported, with the majority finding their way to American shores.

There were fewer changes to the cars now as production increased; teardrop tail lights replaced the twin round items in March 1957, but by far the biggest changes came when the T-2 body was introduced at the 1957 Frankfurt Show. Following the event, the Carrera became available in two versions: a De Luxe (GS) model with different carburation and an improved heater, and the GT. The 110bhp GT was catalogued as a Speedster or coupé only and was intended solely for competition use.

In August 1958, the Speedster was superceded by the Convertible D (the D being added in recognition of the coachbuilder, Drauz of Heilbronn) with a more

After a short break the Carrera again became available as a road car with the launch of the Carrera 2. It was announced in September 1961 alongside the face-lifted 356B models, but didn't enter production until April the following year.

To meet the ever-increasing threat from Alfa Romeo and Lotus, Porsche exploited the FIA rules to the limit and had a new Carrera made ready in order to retain its position at the top of the 1600 Class. A total of 25 chassis were reserved by Porsche for the Abarth-Carrera project, although eventually only 20 of the lightweight Zagato-bodied cars were built. Four or five were prepared for works drivers in 1960, with Class wins duly coming on the Targa Florio, and at Le Mans, Sebring and the Nürburgring.

At the Frankfurt Show in September 1961, the T-6 body made its debut. A number of new features distinguished the latest model, such as larger front and rear windows on the coupé, a new engine cover with two grilles fitted across the range, and a larger front hood featuring a squarer-shaped leading edge (which in turn gave more luggage space).

serviceable hood, a better windscreen, padded seats and wind-up side windows. It was much more in line with Ferry Porsche's ideals.

356 developments
The 356B made its public debut at the 1959 Frankfurt Show, distinguished by the elevated position of the headlights in a new wing line, and higher, stronger bumpers. The standard 1.6 litre 60bhp engine of the 356A was retained, as was the Super, which was now known as the Super 75 in order to differentiate it from the new Super 90. This 90bhp unit was available from March 1960, and was considered powerful enough to render the Carrera model unnecessary. For the time being at least, a Carrera was not listed.

The 356B initially came with three body styles: the Convertible D was renamed the Roadster, with the coupé and cabriolet making up the range. In August 1960, they were joined by the shortlived Karmann hardtop coupé. A third factory (Werk III) had been built at Zuffenhausen towards the end of 1959 to cope with the workload and, by 1960, turnover was around DM 90,000,000 a year.

At the same time as the T-6 356B was introduced, the Carrera returned to the line-up. Named the Carrera 2, it had a two-litre version of the Carrera engine and was sold to the public from the following April. The Carrera 2 introduced disc brakes to the Porsche marque for the first time and, with 130bhp on tap, a top speed of 124mph (198kph) was possible. The 50,000th German-built Porsche left the line in April 1962, but shortly afterwards the Karmann hardtop coupé and the Roadster were discontinued due to falling sales.

Porsche in competition
On the competition front, the Wendler-bodied 550A had been introduced in April 1956. Gone was the ladder chassis of the old Spyder, replaced by a lighter but stiffer spaceframe, and the model incorporated a low-pivot swing axle rear suspension. The 550A gave

Porsche its first taste of victory on the Targa Florio, and there were many Class wins.

The Type 718 prototype was built up over the winter of 1956/57. Based on the one-off Type 645, it was a lighter machine again, constructed around a spaceframe chassis and some 125mm (five inches) lower than the old 550 Spyder. An improved suspension, superior braking and 142bhp resulted in a far better car. The mid-engined 718 RS became the 718 RSK through further suspension changes (though later reverted the RSK name stayed).

Formula Two returned in 1957, the new regulations dictating that 1.5 litre engines running on pump fuel would form the basis for the series. Porsche entered a couple of races and actually won the F2 Class at the Nürburgring Grand Prix with a 550A.

The RSK had made only two appearances at the race track in the 1957 season, but, by the early part of 1958, the definitive 718 RSK had arrived. On the 1959 Targa Florio, Edgar Barth and Wolfgang Seidel took Porsche's second victory on the classic event, followed home by three other Porsche drivers.

As early as 1953, Ferry Porsche had hinted that Porsche might become involved in Grand Prix racing. During October 1958, the CSI announced that Formula One would run with 1.5 litre cars with a minimum weight of 500kg (1100lb) for 1961; the rules seemed ideally suited to Porsche.

In the meantime, the company continued to field the RSK in Formula Two races. A programme was instigated so that Porsche would have an open-wheeled F2 car for 1959, using it as a testbed for the proposed F1 machine for 1961. It was running by April 1959, very much the same as the Type 718 under the skin save for the new narrow chassis frame and detail changes that this necessitated.

The German car was improved as the season progressed and Stirling Moss was sufficiently impressed to test it, with the result that Rob Walker was loaned one of the new works F2 cars for Moss' use during the 1960 season. Porsche won the 1960 Formula Two Championship.

The company's F1 debut came at Brussels on 9 April 1961, but the cars consistently failed to achieve

Porsche's success on the tracks was amazing, especially considering how similar the competition and production models were. Here is Graham Hill, at speed, in the Porsche 718 W-RS Spyder. The strength of the Porsche team can be gauged by the fact that Hill, good though he was, was totally overshadowed by the likes of Edgar Barth, Heini Walter, Herbert Linge and Jo Bonnier. Even Team Manager Huschke von Hanstein recorded some excellent results during this period.

Porsche even tried its hand at Formula One racing, when a change in the regulations allowed the company to enter without the need for masses of development work. However, the venture was rewarded with only one Formula One victory.

the desired result: Dan Gurney's victory in the 1962 French Grand Prix was Porsche's only win in a World Championship event. Formula One proved too expensive and, despite having invested a small fortune in developing the flat-eight engine, Porsche decided to cut its losses and withdraw gracefully from the Grand Prix scene.

The RS60, which followed on from the RSK, had a larger windscreen to comply with new FIA regulations for 1960. Otherwise, the RS60 was basically the same as the 718, except for the slightly longer wheelbase and more powerful engine. The similar-looking RS61 followed for the 1961 season.

The last 356

Introduced in July 1963, the 356C was essentially a stop-gap model until the new 911 became established. More refined than its predecessors, the body was very much the same as that of the 356B (offered in coupé and cabriolet forms, with the option of a detachable steel hardtop for the latter); the main changes were mechanical. There were new 75 and 95bhp engines, a modified rear suspension, and disc brakes were standard across the range. However, the basic layout of four air-cooled cylinders, horizontally opposed in pairs, remained unchanged throughout the 17 year lifespan of the 356. The body changed little, though all

The 356C arrived in 1963 and brought with it disc brakes across the range. This was to be a shortlived model (available as either a coupé or cabriolet), as the replacement for the 356 was almost ready to enter production. This picture was taken at the 1964 Geneva Show.

16

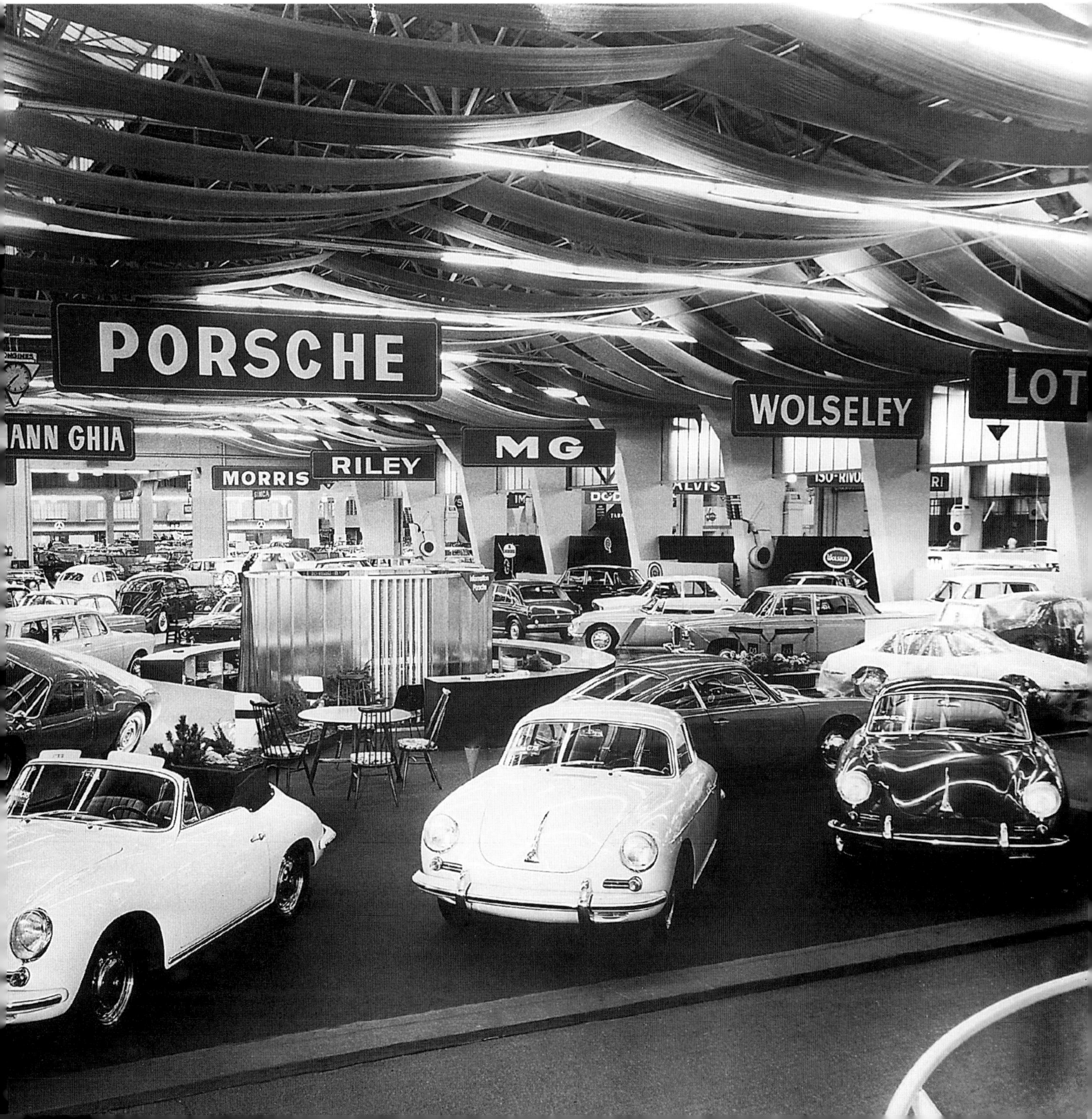
PORSCHE
ANN GHIA
MORRIS
RILEY
MG
WOLSELEY
LOT

the time was being updated, regularly gaining features tested in the field of motorsport.

Porsche thought that a white cabriolet – completed in September 1965 – was going to be the last 356, and indeed it was, officially, but then the Dutch Police placed a special order for ten vehicles in 1966 and these were initiated in March. The total number of 356s built came to 76,313.

Despite the demand for the 356, it was obvious that the model was not going to last forever, and Porsche began to prepare for its replacement in the late fifties. Ferry Porsche wanted the new car to be slightly bigger and a true 2+2. The Type 695 project began in 1959, but was later rejected in favour of a new coupé design from Butzi Porsche – the Type 901.

The Type 901

Born in 1935, Butzi (officially Ferdinand Alexander), was the eldest of Ferry Porsche's sons. He had joined Porsche's Styling Department in 1957, taking charge of it four years later. This was not a case of nepotism, however, as Butzi went on to become a very accomplished designer. Erwin Komenda, who had been with Porsche since its earliest days, took care of the engineering side of the bodywork.

With the flat-four nearing the end of development, it was also necessary to look at a new power unit. The flat-four was powerful enough in Carrera guise, but was expensive to build; in 1961, design work on a new engine began.

As time passed and the Type 901 project drew ever closer to reality, it was decided that the flat-eight Grand Prix engine would form the basis for the new unit. Shortened to a six-cylinder layout, and using just one overhead camshaft per bank instead of two, the 130bhp, two-litre engine was also given the Type 901 designation; it was developed by Hans Tomala and ready for testing in the early part of 1962.

The Porsche 901, whilst retaining many of the features of its predecessor, was a completely new car. Although the rear-mounted, air-cooled boxer engine layout was retained, along with the famous Porsche baulk-ring gearbox and all-round independent suspension, it was a larger car. The 901 was first seen at the Frankfurt Show in 1963, but production cars didn't roll off the line at

On the left is the Type 901 (which went into production as the 911), while in the centre of the picture is the mid-engined 904 competition car. Ferry Porsche is seen sitting over the front wheel of this fantastic machine, styled – like the 901/911 – by Butzi Porsche. The photograph was taken during a dealer visit from America in 1963.

Ferry Porsche (left) discussing the finer points of engineering with his eldest son, Ferdinand Alexander, better known as 'Butzi' Porsche.

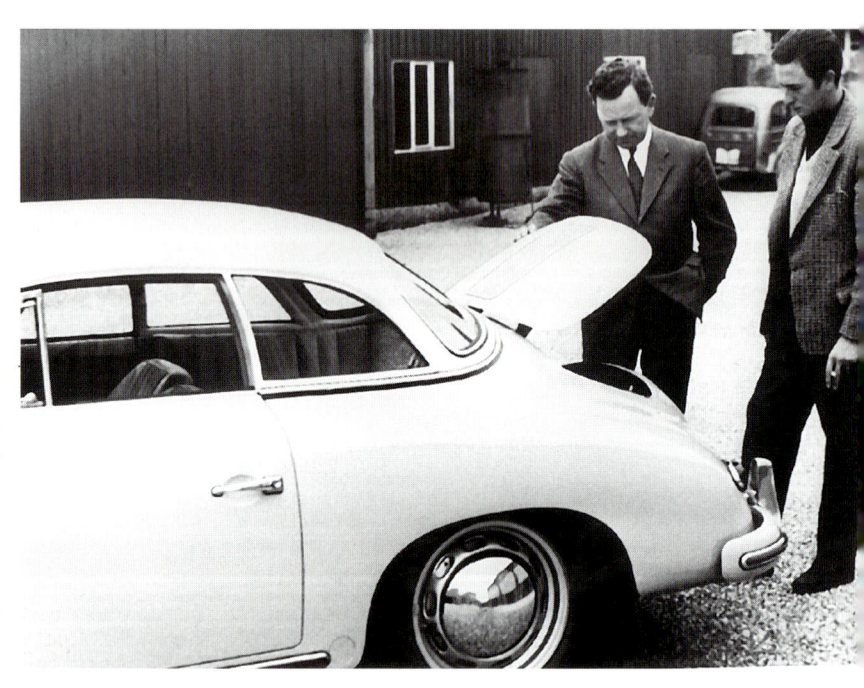

Herbert Linge and Peter Falk pictured after coming fifth overall and winning their Class on the 1965 Monte Carlo Rally (a 904 finished in second place). The 911 followed in its predecessor's footsteps by proving itself worthy in all forms of competition as well as on the road.

1965 Porsche 911 Targa prototype. The four-cylinder 912 looked virtually identical to the two-litre, six-cylinder 911, and could also be bought in coupé or Targa guise.

Zuffenhausen until the following year, by which time the 901 designation was changed to 911 after a complaint from Peugeot regarding the use of "their" numbering system.

Racing news

Meanwhile, Ferry Porsche gave the go-ahead for a new mid-engined competition car at the end of 1962. The lightweight glassfibre body (designed by Butzi Porsche) was bonded to the chassis for extra strength. Glassfibre was chosen for speed of production – four to five a day had to be built to qualify the car in time for the 1964 season. Records show that 120 were built: 104 vehicles were made and sold with four-cylinder Carrera engines and, of the 16 904s retained by the works, ten had six-cylinder engines and six had the eight-cylinder unit.

The new car's first major race was at Sebring in March 1964, where it ran as a prototype (it was homologated in April). Shortly after, the 904 driven by Colin Davis and Antonio Pucci won the 1964 Targa Florio, with Linge and Balzarini finishing second. The 904 dominated two-litre sports car racing throughout the 1964 and 1965 seasons.

Ferry Porsche had already approved the building of a further 100 cars for the 1966 season, but then Ferdinand Piech took over Research & Development and, therefore, the Competition Shop (Piech was actually the son of Ferry Porsche's sister, who had joined the Stuttgart firm in 1963). Piech had grander ideas and, from then on, Porsche's racing philosophy changed completely, with the marque's competition machinery moving further and further away from its road car roots. Piech set the company down the road of producing pure racers, culminating in the all-conquering 917.

911 update

The 911 was made available to the public at 21,900 DM from September 1964. Then, in May 1965, Porsche introduced the 912. The body, suspension and braking system were identical to the six-cylinder 911, but the 912 was far closer to the 356 in that they shared the same four-cylinder power unit (its origins could be traced back to the Super 90 lump), albeit in modified form. Most of the 356s built in 1965 had gone to the States, and the 911 was produced alongside the 356 in the latter's final years.

The most important change during the early life of the new car was availability of the Targa body (announced at the 1965 Frankfurt Show but not sold until the following year), listed for both the 911 and 912. Just over 30,000 Porsche 911s were produced from 1965 to 1969, although, during the latter years, a second generation model with a longer wheelbase had been launched. During this period, a total of 30,300 912s were built.

2
A joint project

Two of the Volkswagen Beetle prototypes designed by Ferdinand Porsche. No-one could have anticipated, when this picture was taken, that Beetle sales meant it became one of the most successful cars of all time.

As the Americans had proved with the Model T Ford and numerous other models that came after it, mass production was clearly the only way to make money with cheaper vehicles. Most large European concerns followed this lead at around the time of the First World War, although the only German car manufacturer that could rightfully claim to be a true volume producer was Opel. However, after the Second World War, it was not Opel but a company called Volkswagen that led the field.

The Volkswagen (or People's Car) had been designed by Porsche, of course, and was the dream of Adolf Hitler, leader of the Nazi party and Germany's Chancellor. Hitler was keen to promote German industry, but his boldest automotive plan by far was to equip every German in the Third Reich with a similar motor car, which later became known the world over as the Beetle.

As mentioned in the previous chapter, Professor Porsche had already made a name for himself, and was highly respected in automotive circles. The commission to design the Beetle came in mid-1934, and the first three prototypes were completed a couple of years later. By 1937, Daimler-Benz had produced another 30 cars for testing, and the following year the foundations were laid for a dedicated factory just east of Hannover.

It must be said that most other German manufacturers were unhappy about plans to produce the Volkswagen, for its proposed price was less than half that of its nearest competitor in the same class. Nonetheless, the VW was given state backing and Porsche was even told to visit America to study mass production methods. After 210 Beetles had been built, the events of 1939 intervened and soon put an end to the Volkswagen, albeit temporarily, as it happened.

Fortunately, the British (as an occupying force) helped get the project back on track following the end of hostilities: by 1948, control of the Wolfsburg factory had been handed back to the Germans. An ex-Opel and BMW worker, Heinz Nordhoff, was appointed General Manager, and under him the company thrived. The VW Beetle success story had begun.

At the same time, several hundred miles away in Austria, Ferry Porsche, son of the Beetle's designer, was starting another fledgling concern that would become equally famous, manufacturing sports cars based on VW components ...

Meanwhile, the Karmann four-seater cabriolet version of the Volkswagen was introduced in July 1949, by which time Beetle exports were becoming increasingly significant. By 1953, the factory at Wolfsburg was employing over 20,000 people to make an average of 670 cars a day, seeing off the competition (coming mainly from Auto Union in the shape of the DKW) by consistently cutting prices. On 5 August 1955, the one millionth Beetle was produced; within four years, the figure had already reached three million.

A pair of VW Beetles on the 1954 Carrera Panamericana. The car in front, a 1200 Super driven by De La Pena, finished 82nd, while the other came 85th overall. There were 149 starters.

The Karmann Ghia

The Karmann coachbuilding business was established in Osnabrück at the turn of the century, although its origins could be traced back to the 1870s. For many years Wilhelm Karmann's business grew slowly, until a large order for cabriolet bodies was placed by the Adler concern. From then on there was no looking back for Karmann, and large contracts were awarded one after the other.

During 1949, Karmann began producing cabriolet bodies for the Volkswagen Beetle, resulting in a large order from DKW for four-seater convertibles the following year. Wilhelm Karmann died in 1952 and was succeeded as head of the company by his son, Dr Wilhelm Karmann Jr.

The Karmann Ghia concept was first discussed in 1950. The management at Karmann wanted to produce a sporty convertible and, as they were building bodies for VW at the time, the Volkswagen Beetle platform seemed the obvious starting point. Negotiations between Karmann Jr and Nordhoff were somewhat protracted, with the Wolfsburg directors continually turning down proposals. Eventually, Karmann asked Luigi Segre at Carrozzeria Ghia to draw up some designs that VW might find more appealing. Unbeknown to Karmann, Ghia was already working on a similar project, but the only way it could get a chassis was through the Paris VW distributor.

The Karmann Ghia provided cheap and reliable sports car motoring. Launched in mid-1955, well over 1000 examples had been sold by the end of the year. A cabriolet version was offered in 1957.

22

One of the many projects Volkswagen commissioned Porsche to execute: this is the Type 555 styling exercise, begun in 1953.

Links with Porsche

After signing the agreement in 1948, as well as allowing Porsche access to components, and use of the Volkswagen sales and service network, Nordhoff provided the Stuttgart firm with a constant stream of commissions. Indeed, before the 914 model was instigated, Porsche had dealt with around 60 projects for VW, ranging from complete cars for the marque, to engines and transmissions, and a multitude of more mundane items such as heating systems.

Early projects – some actually started in Gmünd – included designs for a complete car that was slightly smaller than the Beetle (the Type 402), and even an electrically-driven machine. In 1952, the Type 534 coupé was developed for Volkswagen. The one litre car was presented to Nordhoff in the autumn of 1953 but failed to make it to production. In the meantime, VW decided to build a new bodyshell, which Porsche also had a hand in. However, the Beetle remained as popular as ever and the project was shelved.

One of the most interesting design proposals to come from Porsche was the Type 672 of 1955. This was to be a small car with a rear-mounted, underfloor engine. Tests were carried out with V6 engines of 1.2 and 1.5 litre capacities but, eventually, an air-cooled flat-six was chosen (the Type 673); the 1.5 litre version produced 54bhp and was, without doubt, a glimpse of the future. Further machines were developed from these projects but unfortunately all came to nothing.

Another noteworthy Porsche design for VW was the Type 700, an early form of people carrier. Various scale models were built during 1956 and 1957, but the Type 700 never got beyond this stage and Volkswagen retained the Type 2 instead.

In March 1958, Porsche was commissioned – alongside VW's own styling department and Ghia of Italy – to design a new bodyshell for a medium-sized car. Porsche came up with several variations powered by an underfloor flat-four engine. The Type 728 (or EA-53) eventually resulted in the VW Type 3 which, as will be seen, went into production in 1961.

Late in 1953, Karmann was called to meet Segre in Paris to see the results; not just a clay model, but a fully working prototype coupé. In many respects it was remarkably like the 1953 D'Elegance show car – a Virgil Exner design exercise for Chrysler in America, but built by Ghia in Italy. In fact, Exner insisted that the Karmann Ghia was merely a scaled down D'Elegance.

Whatever, the Volkswagen-engined machine was bought by Dr Karmann and, in November 1953, a contingent from Wolfsburg went to the Karmann works in Osnabrück to view it. Nordhoff was impressed enough to give the go-ahead for five test cars to be built; within 18 months, it was ready to go into production.

Launched on 14 July 1955, the Karmann Ghia was powered by an almost standard VW 1.2 litre Beetle engine. After the 1955 Frankfurt Show, the new model gained a loyal following and no fewer than 1282 had been sold by the end of the first year.

All of the modifications and improvements made to the Beetle were carried over to the Karmann Ghia, and a cabriolet version was launched in August 1957. By the end of 1957, around 15,000 Karmann Ghias had been built in the ever-expanding Osnabrück factory, with almost half of them going to the United States.

Over 23,000 Karmann Ghias had been produced by the end of 1962, by which time the 'Type 3' Karmann Ghia had made its debut. The Type 3 version, with its unique coupé body, was powered by the larger 1.5 litre engine (later enlarged to 1.6 litre in line with the Beetle saloon), but it was shortlived by Volkswagen standards, used only until mid-1969. However, the original style models continued to sell strongly. In actual fact, apart from the running changes brought about by improvements in the Beetle, the Karmann Ghia changed very little in its long history.

In the meantime, Porsche had developed a number of improvements for the Beetle, including the synchromesh gearbox which was adopted on this most famous of Volkswagens from 1951.

Building on success

During the 1950s, Volkswagen established a number of sales companies all over the world, including a special arrangement with the Porsche family in Austria, and had even begun to set up the first of many overseas production plants. On 22 August 1960, Volkswagenwerk GmbH was formed with a capital of DM 600 million. The federal government held 20 per cent of the shares, as did the local administration of Lower Saxony; the rest went to private investors.

However, in light of increasing competition, Nordhoff needed some new products, as it was obvious that VW couldn't rely solely on the Beetle forever. The all-new Type 3, or VW 1500, came in May 1961; like the Variant that followed in 1963, it was available as either a saloon or estate car.

Competition came mainly from Ford in Cologne and Opel. Launched in September 1962, the 1.2 litre Taunus 12 M was a worthy adversary with a list price of DM 5330, and then there was the new Opel Kadett, with prices starting at just DM 5075. The one millionth Kadett was built in 1966, but by this time VW was easily producing a million cars a year.

Auto Union had been bought by Daimler-Benz during 1958/59, but executive control shifted to

The Beetle was still popular, but there was no doubt that sales were slowing. Total production overtook the Model T Ford early in 1972, making the little VW the world's best-selling vehicle.

24

Wolfsburg in 1964 and Audi AG was formed. At the end of the decade, Volkswagen bought the ailing NSU concern and merged it with Audi in August 1969.

By 1967, Volkswagen had quite an extensive range on offer, and, in the background, Porsche was developing a replacement for the Beetle. However, despite this, the German company was replaced by Fiat as the largest car producer in Europe at that time.

Sharing resources

In view of the vast history shared by Porsche and Volkswagen, it was, perhaps, inevitable that the two companies should at some stage collaborate on a joint project. That time came in the mid-1960s when both concerns each faced a dilemma.

Although the Beetle, in February 1972, went on to replace the Model T Ford as the most successful automobile ever made (production easily passed the 15 million mark), sales had been declining for several years beforehand as competition increased from a new breed of economy cars. VW, with a distinct lack of new models to augment the line-up, came in for a great deal of criticism from several quarters. It's true that new machines were in hand to cover the compact sedan sector of the market, but as the Karmann Ghia was deemed out of date as well, a new affordable two-seater sports car was also needed.

Porsche, too, was in need of something new. The price of the 911 had escalated far more than the Stuttgart firm had anticipated, and the cheaper 912 was not selling anywhere near quickly enough to keep the dealers happy, mainly because less expensive but equally competent sports cars were available from a number of other manufacturers.

Following the demise of the 356 range, the 912 had been introduced to offer customers the choice of a less complicated and lower powered version of the 911. Announced in May 1965 (nine months after the 911 launch but well before the last of the 356s were produced), it used a slightly modified four-cylinder engine from the outgoing model (designated 616/36), although, except for the equipment level, the rest of the 912 was identical to the 911.

On introduction, the four-speed 912 was listed at $4690; put another way, it was around 72 per cent of the price of a 911. The body/chassis modifications applied to the 911 series were carried over to the 912, but, by 1968, the price of the four-cylinder car was within just 12 per cent of that of the basic six-cylinder model – it simply wasn't worth Porsche selling it any cheaper. With substantially less power on tap but only

Despite the high price, 911 sales consistently grew, due, not least, to the success of the model in competition. These were the works machines entered for the 1969 Monte Carlo Rally; Bjorn Waldegaard (third from the left) won the event outright.

a marginal difference in price, naturally enough most buyers opted for the 911 and sales of the 912 were very slow in later years.

Porsche needed an entry level machine that would sell in volume, preferably using a six-cylinder engine in the interest of standardization. But developing a new model from scratch was a costly exercise and, besides, Porsche had neither the finance or production capacity; a joint project with VW was the obvious answer. Ferry Porsche went on record stating that it came about "... from the realization that we needed to broaden our programme at a less costly level and that we couldn't do it alone."

At this early stage, whilst talking over the arrangements, Nordhoff agreed that if Porsche designed and helped develop the new sports car, the Stuttgart company could use the bodies in order to ultimately make two versions: one with a VW engine and badge; the other a more powerful model with a Porsche crest on the bonnet and six-cylinder unit. Of course, the cost to Porsche would be significantly cheaper than a body of its own, as VW would be ordering the car in large quantities.

It was the perfect solution for both parties, as Volkswagen (apart from benefiting from Porsche's expert knowledge in an area in which it had little experience) would have a replacement for the Karmann Ghia, and, for its part, Porsche gained access to a much needed, high volume seller without having to invest in expensive tooling and development costs.

Left: For 1969, the 912 coupé cost $5095 in America (the Targa version was just $520 more), compared to $5795 for the cheapest 911. Given the performance difference, the margin was not great enough to achieve big sales of the smaller engined 912 model.

The interior of the 912 – the car the 914 would go on to replace.

Left: The Targa version of the 912. From the outside, there was little to differentiate the four-cylinder car from the six-cylinder 911.

The 914 is born

The age of the mid-engined coupé had arrived. As Denis Jenkinson related in 1971: "I cannot really recall which was the first mid-engined coupé I saw, but the fibreglass Porsche 904 was probably the first I drove and about which I became convinced that this was the best layout for a sports car. Back in 1954 Porsche had built the RS Spyder with its four-cam engine mounted just ahead of the rear axle and the whole layout had looked right, but one felt that Porsche were fortunate in having a transverse flat-four engine that would fit into the scheme of things. It was some years later, in the sixties, that thoughts of mid-engined sports cars with large engines began to emerge, and Ferrari built the 250LM coupé, with the three-litre V12 engine between the cockpit and the rear axle; Eric Broadley's prototype Lola coupé, with a Ford V8 in the right place, convinced everyone that this was the layout for sports/racing cars, and eventually, one hoped, for race-bred roadgoing sports cars."

A whole string of mid-engined sports cars appeared in the mid-1960s. The Lamborghini Miura had made its debut in 1966, and in the following year appeared the Ferrari Dino, Lotus Europa, Matra M530, and the DeTomaso Mangusta.

It was also quite interesting to note that a number of specialist manufacturers were turning to larger concerns for their engines. Of the serious competitors to the proposed new sports car the Pininfarina-bodied Ferrari Dino had its V6 engine produced by Fiat; the Lotus engine was sourced from Renault, and Matra used the Ford Taunus V4 engine and transmission.

Porsche, as already mentioned, had appreciated for several decades that the mid-engined concept was ideal for sports cars. As *Road Test* magazine pointed out in January 1970: "Although the 356 and 911 series production Porsches have always had the engine behind the rear wheels, Porsche is by no means a stranger to the mid-engine concept. Porsche competition cars have always utilized the mid-engine layout, stemming from the Porsche-designed Auto Union Grand Prix car which dominated European racing during the mid-1930s. The first competition Porsche not derived from the rear-engined 356 series was the mid-engine 550 Spyder which was produced in several versions for a number of years, enjoying a fantastic competition record. Later mid-engined Porsche competition cars include the 904, 906, 907, 908 and the current 917, all of which have posted enviable records."

The basic layout of the 914 series borrowed from Porsche's racing experience, and followed the fashion of a new breed of mid-engined sports cars.

It was fairly inevitable that Porsche should opt for this layout for a road car, and VW was more than happy to back the proposal. The possibilities of adapting the 904 for road use had been looked into in the past but, sadly, the notion was rejected: in any case, the design for the new sports car had to be far more practical and, as part of the brief, had to look neither too much like a Porsche nor too much like a Volkswagen, whilst at the same time being agreeable and appropriate to both parties.

As it happened, Porsche already knew of a suitable styling proposal produced by Gugelot Design GmbH. Based in Neu-Ulm, Gugelot was actually a highly respected industrial design house during the 1950s and 1960s, named after its founder, Hans Gugelot. Although hardly a household name, at least outside German creative circles, the company's list of customers at this time was very impressive.

Anyway, during the early 1960s, Gugelot decided to produce a proposal for an automobile. Once the shape had been finalized, the next problem was, of course, choosing the materials from which to build the car. Gugelot enlisted the help of the Bayer-Werke chemical company, and between them they came up with an ingenious system of using glassfibre sheets bonded each side of a foam plastic core. From 1966, BMW-powered test cars were presented to a number of big German car companies, Porsche included.

Ultimately, the running prototypes were nothing like the forthcoming Porsche/VW. They were front-engined machines made of advanced composite materials and, in fact, they looked more like a Lamborghini Jarama in profile (albeit with a heavier B-post and minus the distinctive headlight covers), or the Jaguar-based Bertone Pirana than a 914. Butzi Porsche has gone on record stating: "Gugelot has not done anything on this car. There was once a car that resembled the 914 – but nothing more. There is no connection between Gugelot and the 914."

Indeed, it is fair and correct to say that the Neu-Ulm company was not involved with the production car in any way, but an alternative one-fifth scale wind tunnel model put forward by Gugelot was very similar indeed to the new Porsche. If nothing else, it certainly provided a great deal of inspiration, although the same could be said of several other designs, such as the 1963 Pininfarina study based on the Fiat 2300 chassis.

When the joint sports car project was first mooted, the Gugelot design seemed like an ideal starting point. Naturally, the composite materials were dropped in favour of more conventional steel panels over a welded pressed steel structure, and it was quickly converted to mid-engined configuration to accept either a VW or Porsche power unit. Given the Type 914 designation, it was developed over the autumn of 1966.

The vehicle was remarkably strong for a targa-topped car, thanks to deep boxed sills below the doors and a tunnel carrying the torsional strength of the body through the centre of the cockpit area; the integral roll-over bar at the rear (like that used on the

A rather fuzzy still from a film showing the statutory crash test. It was passed without a hitch: the 914 structure was very strong.

Extensive testing was carried out at the Research & Development facility at Weissach. Handling was said to be equally predictable in wet and dry conditions.

911/912 Targas) had the advantage not only of being a safety feature, but also of maintaining bodyshell rigidity, despite the lack of a roof. The structure allowed for progressive crumple zones at both front and rear, separated by bulkheads protecting the cockpit at each end – when the time came, the 914 passed its mandatory crash test with ease.

Because the car was so low at the front (in fact, the final vehicle sat some 100mm, or four inches, lower than a 911), Gugelot decided to use pop-up headlights on its alternative design in order to comply with strict minimum height requirements in the USA; after all, it was almost taken for granted that America would provide any sports car with its largest market. This feature was retained by Porsche stylists, led by Heinrich Klie and Butzi Porsche. It is interesting to note that, aerodynamically, the 914 displayed 20 per cent less drag than the contemporary 911.

The final designs were passed by Volkswagen in 1967. As Karmann was producing the Karmann Ghia at the time, and had been heavily involved with both companies in the past, it was a natural choice to build the bodies for the new car. It was agreed that the VW model would be completely built, assembled and trimmed in Osnabrück, whilst the six-cylinder version would be shipped as a plain bodyshell to Zuffenhausen so that Porsche could assemble and finish the machine on the same line as the 911.

A death in the family

Ferry Porsche and Heinz Nordhoff had enjoyed a splendid working relationship for many years, a bond which was strengthed by the marriage of one of Porsche's nephews to the VW boss' daughter, but Nordhoff was due to retire in 1970. In preparation, Kurt Lotz was brought in in June 1967 (from an industrial company in Switzerland) as Nordhoff's deputy, to gradually take over the reins. However, Nordhoff became seriously ill only one month after Lotz arrived, giving the newcomer no time at all to learn of Nordhoff's personal arrangements with associates.

On 1 March 1968, the first prototype 914 (a four-cylinder model) was driven, but then, on 12 April, Professor Heinz Nordhoff died. Not only was this a great blow to Volkswagen and all those who knew him, it also caused immense problems for Ferry Porsche with regard to the 914 project. The problem was that Nordhoff and Porsche had only a 'gentleman's agreement' on the supply of 914 bodies from Karmann. This was nothing unusual, as the two men often worked

Porsche's mid-engined heritage

Porsche Number One dating from 1948.

The successful 550 and 550A Spyders.

The 718 series of cars; this is the 718 RSK.

The elegant Porsche 904, seen here at Le Mans in 1964.

The predecessor of the 917; this is the 910 pictured in 1966.

Professor Heinz Nordhoff, 1899-1968.

For a number of years, Porsche used the Volkswagen dealer network. Occasionally, Porsche would have a special exhibition, such as this one in Hamburg. This picture, dating from 1954 (note the new position of the bumpers, away from the body) shows three Porsche 356s and one of the 550 Spyders, in this case, the 'humpback' prototype made to look like the 1954 Mille Miglia car.

on a verbal deal, but the new man at Wolfsburg, quite naturally, wanted to see something in writing.

Lotz considered that VW had exclusive rights to the 914 design. Porsche was told that if he wanted 914 bodies, he would have to buy them at a price that accounted for a percentage of the tooling costs, naturally making them much more expensive. The whole episode could so easily have ended in deadlock, but fortunately a deal was struck that ultimately suited both parties. After much negotiation, an agreement was reached which entailed Porsche and Volkswagen forming a separate company, in which both partners had a 50 per cent holding. The plan was announced in January 1969, and the following April, VW-Porsche Vertriebsgesellschaft GmbH (or VG, for short) was established in Stuttgart with a working capital of DM 5 million. This new concern was to be responsible for marketing and distribution of the VW-Porsche 914 series and the 911 in most markets, with the notable exception of America, which would have a completely separate sales organisation. One Managing Director was appointed from VW, in this case, Klaus Schneider, while the other came from Porsche – Otto Filius. Huschke von Hanstein was given the job of handling publicity. Although, on the face of it, this seemed a rather dramatic move, it was, in effect, simply making a previous arrangement official; everywhere, except in Britain and France, Porsche cars were distributed through VW outlets, anyway. Nonetheless, the announcement sent rumours around the globe about a possible merger until they were quashed by a matter-of-fact Stuttgart press release.

The firm soon found the temporary premises in Stuttgart too small, and a new site was purchased by Porsche in Ludwigsburg, close to the Zuffenhausen plant. This was then leased to VW-Porsche VG and the operation gradually moved there over the ensuing months. In the meantime, Lotz had brought in Werner Holste as Director of VW's Research & Development department, but nonetheless Porsche was still asked to develop the successor to the Beetle (EA-266, or Type 1966 within Porsche), along with Audi and NSU. The latter soon fell by the wayside, leaving just Porsche and Audi working on the project.

Porsche came up with a number of mid-engined designs, including a four-seater saloon, a two-seater version, and a 2+2 coupé. The powerplant was to be a four-cylinder, water-cooled unit of between 800cc and 1.8 litres, developing up to 105bhp for the larger capacity engine. However, after much development work under the supervision of Ferdinand Piech (said to have cost up to DM 250 million), the whole programme was eventually cancelled in the early 1970s as the vehicles would simply have been too costly to produce.

Final details of the 914

There were to be two different models of the 914 – one Porsche and one VW. The Volkswagen version, the 914/4, would be powered by the 1.7 litre, air-cooled flat-four engine from the 411E model, using VW's new electronic injection system, allowing it to meet all American emission requirements (including those for California).

It was expected that around three-quarters of the 914s produced would be fitted with the four-cylinder Volkswagen engine. Many Porsche fans were enraged by this, but, as *Road Test* magazine pointed out: "Although the concept of a VW engine in what is obviously intended to be a spirited performing GT machine might raise a few eyebrows, the current 411 engine is nearly on a performance par with the Super 90 or 912 engine, which was at the top of the four-cylinder Porsche engine line."

The VW 411 had been introduced in August 1968. Of the new model, *MotorSport* said in a preview: "I am delighted that the 411 retains the famous rear-placed VW flat-four air-cooled engine with all the ingenious but deeply-hidden technical features and magnesium alloys that place it deservedly amongst the world's great internal combustion powerplants. It has increased in size to 1679cc and 68 (net) bhp, still runs at modest crankshaft speeds, on a modest c.r., and, they tell me, is good enough for 90mph and 25mpg of inexpensive fuel in the spacious new saloon."

In a later article by the same magazine following a road test of an automatic 411L, it was noted: "It is splendid to find that the engine, having a compression ratio of only 7.8:1, will burn the least expensive 90-octane fuel. It gave a consumption of 25.0mpg, inclusive of using the petrol heater. The engine is a fine piece of engineering …"

The fuel-injected 411E followed in August 1969 and there was little doubt that, within the industry, the VW engine was a highly respected unit. In addition, the mid-mounted position of the engine endowed the 914 with excellent weight distribution, said to be some 10 per cent better than that of the contemporary 911.

In theory, mid-engined cars handle better due to superior weight distribution: there is no heavy front end to steer as in a conventional vehicle, or a heavy back end to slide out on rear-engined machines when approaching the limits. Weight distribution on a 914 was approximately 45 per cent front, 55 per cent rear, although, once the car had a full petrol tank and the spare wheel in place, this became almost 50/50.

Naturally, this helps the balance of the car, and later road test reports praised the handling and roadholding of the 914 range, despite the use of narrow wheels

Pop-up headlights were used to conform to US regulations, whilst keeping a low frontal area. Note the lack of headlight surrounds on this 914/6 prototype.

Another view of the 914/6 prototype. Note the awful panel fit compared to the production models, and the Porsche crest not only on the hubcaps but also on the front compartment lid. The Porsche badge was destined to appear on only a few pre-production six-cylinder cars.

A pre-production version of the 914/4, registered in Wolfsburg.

The new design certainly attracted a lot of attention in Stuttgart, but, judging by the faces, initial public reaction was fairly mixed ...

This pre-production, four-cylinder car tried some Fuchs-style hubcaps. Unfortunately, the idea was not carried over to the production vehicles, presumably on the grounds of additional expense.

and rubber (the rims were just 4.5J or 5.5J wide, shod with radial tyres). However, as an ex-development engineer once told the author, the original equipment is very often the best compromise for a road car, as the manufacturer will have tried hundreds of options long before the customer even gets to hear of a new machine.

An added bonus was that, being a pure two-seater machine, the layout allowed for luggage space at both front and rear. The rear luggage compartment had seven cubic feet of usable space, while the front had nine. This gave a total of 16 cubic feet (4.53 cubic metres) of storage space; a contemporary Alfa Romeo Spider, for instance, was blessed with just 6.9 cubic feet (1.95 cubic metres) of boot space, although, if the owner wasn't too worried about it being seen, more luggage could be stowed behind the seats.

The mid-engined layout also allowed a great deal of space for the driver and passenger, with no bulky transmission tunnel encroaching on the footwell area; as it was a pure two-seater design, the seats could be pushed well back to give even more room.

The Porsche model, known as the 914/6, was equipped with the classic six-cylinder, air-cooled engine from the 1969 model year 911T, rated at 110bhp – 30bhp more than the VW unit installed in the 914/4. As a matter of interest, three 911 engine options were available at that time: the 911T; the 140bhp 911E, and the top-of-the-range 170bhp 911S.

The definitive flat-six Porsche engine appeared in the autumn of 1963. Overseen by Hans Tomala and known as the Type 901, it was a two-litre, air-cooled unit with a chain-driven single overhead camshaft per bank. To overcome oil surge during hard cornering, it was given dry sump lubrication.

With a bore and stroke of 80 x 66mm, cubic capacity was 1991cc; this produced 130bhp at 6100rpm, giving a specific output of 65bhp per litre. All early production engines had aluminium alloy castings and a two-part crankcase. The cylinders used Biral construction (cast iron barrels surrounded by finned aluminium castings for cooling), and the cylinder heads were of light alloy. Originally three single-choke downdraught Solex carburettors were used on each bank, but these were later replaced, from the beginning of 1966, by triple-choke Webers.

Incidentally, the 1969 model year engine was chosen for the 914/6 as this kept the new model at two-litres; the 911 range had been given 2.2 litre engines (available in three states of tune) for the 1970 season, introduced alongside the new 914/4 and 914/6 in September 1969.

A five-speed gearbox was offered in both versions to give effortless high speed cruising, although the ratios were altered to suit the torque of the different engines (the 914/11 was used for the VW-powered car, with the 914/01 specified for the six-cylinder model). Both variants shared the same 4.428:1 final-drive ratio, and a Sportomatic four-speed semi-automatic transmission option was also planned.

Introduced for the 1968 model year 911 series:

Lighting arrangements on the new series. A plastic surround tidied the appearance of the pop-up headlights, and there was the option of fog or driving lights in the bumper.

The rear compartment was quite shallow as the transmission was underneath it, but with the additional space up front, there was plenty of room for luggage. Until 1972, the exhaust pipe exited through a hole in the longer rear valance. Also note the early style of number plate area with sharper, squared-off outer edges. The badge on the six-cylinder model read '914-6 VW Porsche' on non-US cars.

"The automatische Getriebe is a combination of a torque converter, automatic clutch and the usual four-speed Porsche manual gearbox," said *Road & Track*. "Called Sportomatic, it dispenses with the clutch pedal and has P/R/L/D/D3/D4 marked on the gearshift knob. The P is for park, naturally, and a parking pawl is added to the gearbox for the purpose. L is first gear, recommended for steep hills only; D is second, for city traffic; D3 and D4 are third and fourth and it should be possible to do some leisurely driving in D4 with the 911T. A touch on the gearshift lever signals the automatic clutch to disengage via a vacuum servo unit."

Suspension was by MacPherson struts, lower wishbones and longitudinal torsion bars at the front, with semi-trailing arms and coil springs to the rear in order to make room for the engine. The spring rates were very hard, eliminating the need for anti-roll bars on the standard road cars – despite this, Porsche tests recorded higher cornering powers for the 914 than posted by the contemporary 911.

Disc brakes were employed on all four wheels and, like the steering components, came from

The interior of the 914/6. There were a few small differences on the 914/4, but they were indeed subtle.

either the Porsche or VW parts bin, depending on the powerplant. The 914/4 had hubs, brake discs and wheels sourced from the VW 411 (although a special rear disc incorporating the handbrake mechanism was needed), whilst the 914/6 had the same hubs and brake discs as the 911. Both models had the handbrake situated between the driver's seat and sill to allow for the optional third 'seat'.

The results from extensive endurance testing in all weather conditions satisfied the partners that the 914 series was at last ready for sale.

The wheelbase was listed at 2450mm (96.5in), length was 3990mm (157.0in), width 1650mm (65.0in), and height 1230mm, or 48.4in (at least on the 914/4; the six-cylinder model sat a fraction higher due to an increase in ground clearance, up from 120mm to 130mm – 4.7 and 5.1in respectively). Track measurements were also slightly different, the front being 1340mm (52.8in) on the four-cylinder car, and 1360mm (53.6in) on the 914/6; the latter was a little wider at the back, too, listed at 1385mm (54.5in) instead of 1380mm (54.3in).

Launch of the new model

The launch was all set for the Frankfurt Motor Show in September of 1969. The Frankfurt Show was a bi-annual affair, and the star of the event that year was, undoubtedly, the gullwinged Mercedes-Benz C111 with its Wankel engine. Not to be outdone, the 914 was displayed on the stands of both Volkswagen-Porsche VG and Karmann.

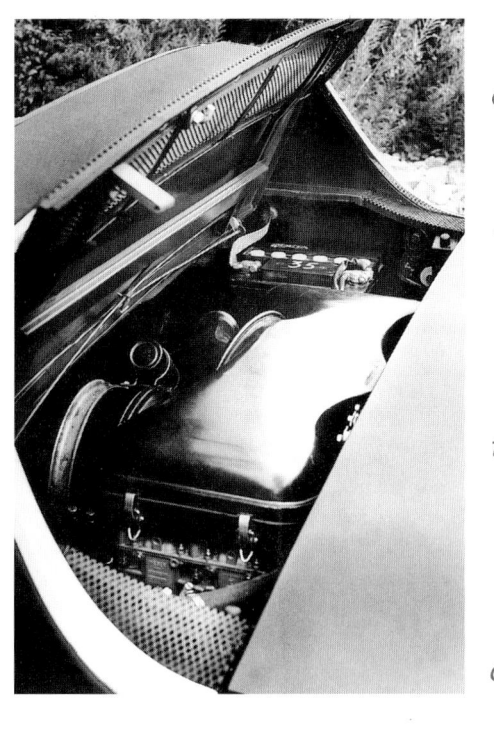

Engine installation on the 914/6 model. The engine ran slightly hotter in the 914 series than in the 911, but it was well within limits. A special oil temperature gauge had to be ordered with the red segment adjusted to compensate for this.

The four-cylinder model was available almost immediately, whilst its six-cylinder stablemate became available from the following February. Initial production schedules called for a total of 30,000 cars a year, production of the 1.7 litre four-cylinder car commencing in October 1969, with 914/6 production due to start at the end of the year, replacing the 912 in the Porsche range.

Part of the agreement with Volkswagen stipulated that the 914 range would be badged as a VW-Porsche, naturally adding kudos to the four-cylinder model. The only exception to this rule was in America, where all models would be given the Porsche moniker regardless of power unit. Of course, the United States was going to be the most important market, and this ploy tied in perfectly with the newly formed Porsche+Audi sales organisation, headed by John Reilly, and based in Englewood Cliffs, New Jersey.

In the October 1969 issue of *Motor Trend*, the situation in the USA was explained as follows: "Unlike the old days, when you knew exactly what a VW stood for and Porsche stood for, there is already some clarification needed to understand the Volkswagen Porsche amalgam. First, with the combining of VW and Porsche and then the acquisition of Audi, the Auto Union car, the long standing practice of having VW dealers also handle Porsche is no more. Henceforth,

Final testing of the 914/6 at Weissach gave more than satisfactory results, and the car was duly launched at the Frankfurt Show in September 1969. Note the registration number.

Ferry Porsche (right) and VW boss, Kurt Lotz, talking to Chancellor Kurt Kiesinger at the 1969 Frankfurt Show. Kiesinger replaced Ludwig Erhard as Chancellor in October 1966, but was ousted by Willy Brandt within days of this picture being taken. Brandt won the Nobel Peace Prize, but was later forced to resign over a spy scandal. It was an eventful era in Germany!

Volkswagen will be an entity unto itself and Porsche-Audi will go together."

The same magazine carried this in-depth profile of the marketing situation for America in its June 1970 edition: "Last year Porsche entered into a marketing/engineering agreement with Volkswagen who had just bought control of Audi-NSU. Porsche would enjoy VW's worldwide organization to disburse their finely crafted sports cars and VW would have access to Porsche's super engineering staff for development/prototype work. More than that, Porsche would equip its 914s mostly with VW engines – the powerplant Wolfsburg created for their 411 model.

"In the US, Volkswagen of America, which is still the funnel through which all VW-Porsche products flow, decided that it was best to now separate the familiar old VW-Porsche dealer. The VW is an economy car and they want it left that way. The Porsche is an expensive (in comparison) sports car and should rightly have its own place in the sun. So VW of America went to their VW-Porsche dealers and said they would have to decide between VW or Porsche or split their dealership in two and have one location for VW, one for Porsche. No more of this under-the-same-roof-stuff. To make life easier for the Porsche man, he was given the Audi, making him a Porsche-Audi man.

"Last October 1, Porsche-Audi made the paper switch from VW and on November 1 (I keep wondering what they did for that month), began establishing new dealers, worrying about delivery routes and dates, wondering where they would keep all those spare parts. A monumental task to begin with, until you remember they still have VW of America behind them, a firm whose organizational powers have been so successful its story will bore first year marketing students to death for years to come.

"In late January, a few 914s trickled in to let the dealers know the car actually existed, remembering all this time all they had to live on were $6500 and up 911s and you don't sell enough of those to eat unless you live in Southern California (40% of all Porsches sold last year and 80% of all Porsches registered are in Southern California). February, and more cars arrive, ready to go to purchasers who put down deposits sight unseen months earlier. March and still more arrive with a very light sprinkling of 914/6s. April and things appear as though they might someday become normal. Porsche-Audi lives.

"On the showroom floor there's no hard sell. There doesn't have to be. There can't be when you're in a position to sell more cars than you can get. A customer's car comes in, the wrong colour. Call the guy and tell the sad news, but he doesn't care, to heck with the colour, he wants his new 914. When can he pick it up? Now.

"A customer has two choices: order or buy from stock (or what will be stock). If he orders his car specially, waiting time is around three months. If he orders from stock, chances are good he can get just what he wants. The option list isn't that long. The dealer, in turn, gets his cars from the regional distributor who already has a pretty good idea of what the customers' desires are

continued page 43

Pages 39-41: The first 914 catalogue. It features one of the prototypes (the orange car) and an early pre-production model, seen with all the wheel combinations. The S-M 2383 number plate would become very famous over the next few months, appearing in a variety of publicity material and a number of magazine reports.

Der VW-Porsche 914.

VW und Porsche entwickelten einen Sportwagen, zu dem es in Leistung, Qualität und Preis kaum eine Alternative gibt.

Gewiß gibt es Sportwagen, die in ihrer Leistung vergleichbar sind mit dem VW-Porsche 914. Und ebenso gibt es Sportwagen, die gleich viel kosten. Aber Sie werden wohl kaum einen finden, der ihnen zusammengenommen so viel bietet wie dieser neue Sportwagen.

Denn VW und Porsche entwickelten diesen Wagen in der Absicht, einen echten Sportwagen anzubieten, den Sie schon für 12000 DM haben können. Er sollte einerseits ein optimales Fahrverhalten wie ein Rennsportwagen haben. Andererseits sollte er aber auch alle guten Eigenschaften einer Alltagslimousine bieten.

Deshalb hat der VW-Porsche einen geräumigen und komfortablen Innenraum, der den letzten Erkenntnissen passiver Sicherheit entspricht. Deshalb hat er auch zwei Kofferräume von zusammen 460 Litern.

Und deshalb ist auch alles an ihm so verarbeitet, wie man es von VW und Porsche gewohnt ist.

Aus Rennsporterfahrung weiß man,
daß ein Fahrzeug ein optimales Fahrverhalten hat,
wenn der Motor in der Mitte liegt.
Deshalb hat der VW-Porsche 914 einen Mittelmotor.

Es gibt heute kaum noch einen Rennwagen mit Front- oder Heckmotor. Das liegt wohl daran, daß er kaum noch eine Chance gegen einen Wagen mit Mittelmotor hätte.
Wie kommt das?
Ein Mittelmotor gibt dem Fahrzeug eine äußerst günstige Schwerpunktlage und ideale Gewichtsverteilung. Und deshalb ein optimales Fahrverhalten. Er ermöglicht ihm eine kleinere Stirnfläche und damit eine aerodynamischere Karosserie. Er sorgt für eine günstige Bremskraftverteilung, weil das Gewicht des Wagens gleichmäßig auf allen vier Rädern lastet. Und durch die Mittellage des Motors konnte man auf Karosserieüberhänge verzichten.
Das Fahrverhalten des VW-Porsche ist neutral. Deshalb hat er auch die für einen Sportwagen optimalen Querbeschleunigungsreserven.
Woran liegt es dann, daß Mittelmotoren trotzdem meist nur in Rennwagen zu finden sind? Und nicht in jedem Wagen?
Ganz einfach: Am Platz. Ein Mittelmotor würde genau den Platz einnehmen, den die hinteren Fahrgäste einnehmen.
Deshalb hat der VW-Porsche hinten keine Notsitze. Aber einen Innenraum, der breit genug ist, daß sogar drei Personen Platz finden können.

Kompromißlos ist auch sein Karosseriekonzept.
Er ist gleichzeitig Coupé und Cabriolet und
hat zwei ungewöhnlich große Kofferräume.

Den VW-Porsche brauchen Sie nicht als Coupé oder Cabriolet zu bestellen.
Er ist beides in einem.
Er hat serienmäßig einen Sicherheitsbügel und ein abnehmbares Dach, das Sie mühelos im hinteren Kofferraum unterbringen können, ohne daß es viel Platz wegnimmt.
Das Geld für ein Hardtop können Sie sich also sparen.
Was der VW-Porsche indes an Kofferraum mitbringt, ist nicht nur für einen Sportwagen ungewöhnlich. Sondern selbst für manche Limousine: 210 Liter vorn. 250 Liter hinten.
Und durch die zwei großen Kofferräume hat der Wagen zwangsläufig auch zwei große Knautschzonen, die Ihnen in Verbindung mit der steifen Passagierzelle größtmöglichen Schutz bieten.

Der Mittelmotor gibt dem VW-Porsche also nicht nur ein Fahrverhalten wie im Rennsport. Sondern auch noch eine Menge Vorteile für den Alltag.

Den VW-Porsche 914 gibt es in zwei leistungsstarken Versionen.

Den 914 mit einem 1,7 Liter-80 PS-elektronisch gesteuerten Einspritzmotor mit 4 Zylindern.
Er fährt 177 km/h, beschleunigt von 0 auf 100 in 13,0 Sekunden und verbraucht 9,0 Liter (DIN).

Den 914-6 mit einem 2 Liter-110 PS Vergasermotor mit 6 Zylindern.
Er fährt 201 km/h, beschleunigt von 0 auf 100 in 10,0 Sekunden und verbraucht 9,0 Liter (DIN).

VW-PORSCHE VERTRIEBSGESELLSCHAFT MBH · 7 STUTTGART · HEILBRONNER STRASSE 67

Printed in Germany · Änderungen vorbehalten
W 6 - 500 - 0969 - 0404

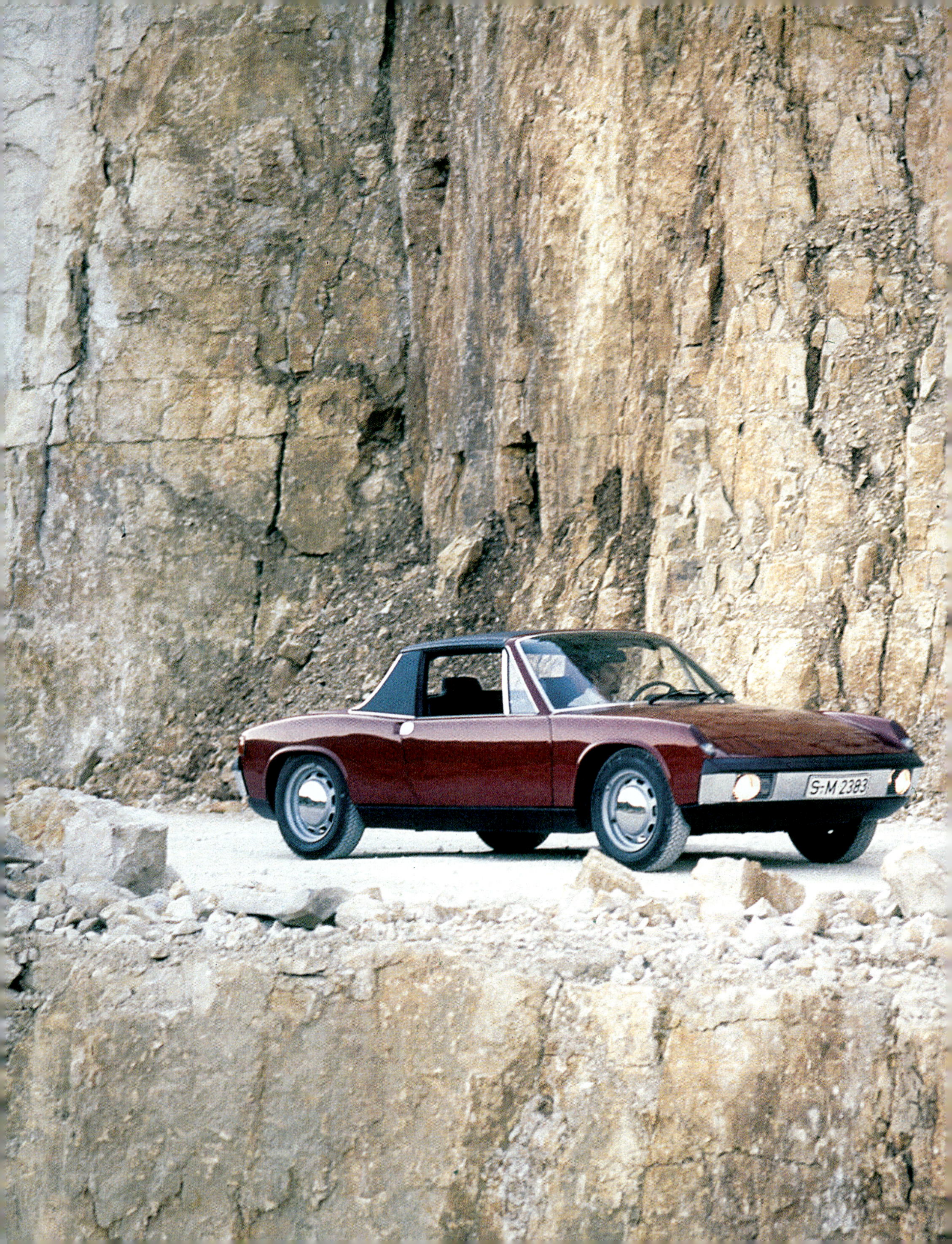
S-M 2383

A stunning shot of the early 914/6 that appeared in the first catalogue.

and has ordered cars accordingly and along guidelines established by VW of America.

"Then it's a matter of getting the cars. Before the VW-Porsche tie-in, Porsches weren't shipped with VWs, often leaving the Porsches in something less than concours condition. Now they're all shipped together to various unloading points around the country and shipped inland by car carrier. Then it's on to the dealer.

"You're not going to be seeing a lot of 914 advertising in the next six to eight months, mainly because, as we said, the car is already virtually sold and the division has that other car, the very fine Audi, to tell the public about ...

"You really have to admire Porsche and VW, not just for their cars, but their thinking. In the early 1960s the cost of a Porsche, be it the Normal or Super 90 model, ranged in the area of $4000 to $5000. Up until the 914s, the only Porsches available were the $6000 and dearer 911 series. Now they've taken us back to the early 60s, cost-wise, and have not only saved us money, but offered a faster, better handling car that's just as revolutionary as the Porsche Normal of the early 60s. Guess Porsche just never heard of inflation."

However, behind the scenes, there were naturally problems with the new system. Before the 914 went on sale in America, the number of authorised Porsche retail outlets fell by one-third, the reason being that any dealer wishing to retain the Porsche franchise had to invest around $250,000 on a separate facility to sell the 914. It was hardly surprising, therefore, that many dealers decided the outlay simply couldn't be justified.

For Porsche the situation was not helped by the fact that, as part of the agreement regarding the 914, bodies were only supplied by Karmann fully painted and trimmed, adding to their cost. Furthermore, as mentioned earlier, the bodies were already costing Porsche far more than was first anticipated – in actual fact, they were now dearer to buy than the more complicated 911 bodyshells. As a result, the sticker price of the six-cylinder 914 was very similar to that of the 911, which reduced its worth somewhat in the Porsche line-up.

In the meantime, some fresh competition had appeared from Opel which, in September 1968, presented the fibreglass-bodied Opel GT, a particularly attractive coupé powered by either a 1.1 or 1.9 litre engine. Porsche could only hope that this latest Opel – which was quite a quick machine on the road – performed less admirably in the showrooms ...

3

The early production models

The 914/6 came with the option of Mahle cast mag-alloy wheels. Of the same 5.5J x 15 size as the standard steel items, it was the lightest wheel ever to be fitted to a production Porsche.

This 914/6 was featured in a number of shots by a lake. Some of the pictures were later used in a 914 series catalogue.

"If there's one thing we've learnt from racing, it's where to put the engine.

"A sports car built just for racing doesn't need a back seat. So, unlike a Grand Touring car, its engine can be mounted in front of the rear axle, near the middle of the car.

"That distributes its weight more equally, front and rear. And gives it a whole bundle of advantages over ordinary cars.

"We think it's time you shared those advantages. So we've built a couple of mid-engine cars you can use on the street." – American advertising, 1970.

After the launch of the 914 series at the Frankfurt Show (which ran from 11 to 21 September), not unnaturally the public was keen to read the press reports about this futuristic-looking car. A 914/6 had been loaned to a number of influential journalists during the show but, sadly, it had not been checked beforehand; it was later found that several faults existed after the machine's drive to the Hockenheim circuit, causing it to handle badly. The damage had been done – the journalists, having been told to expect so much, were not impressed.

Knowing the reasons why the reports were poor in areas where the 914 should have excelled, it is probably historically correct to discount certain parts of these earliest tests. However, there were still some problems that could not be blamed on a lack of preparation. The

A 914/6 is seen wearing the standard 5.5J x 15 Porsche wheels as used on the 911s. Usually finished in silver paint, they could also be purchased chrome finished; in both cases a stainless steel hubcap was supplied. Used throughout the run of the 914/6, they are distinguished from the VW wheels by ten (instead of eight) ventilation holes.

914 was hardly affected by sidewinds, although brake fade (albeit after continued hard use) was mentioned in a number of magazines; the 914/6, with its ventilated Porsche brakes at the front, did not suffer from the same trouble. One magazine commented on the poor location of the fuel filler, it being both awkward to get at and ideally placed to spray valuable luggage with petrol. Porsche had actually wanted an outside filler on the right-hand side of the scuttle but it was ultimately located under the bonnet simply because this was cheaper.

The fixed passenger seat was considered strange, but it was lighter as it did not require adjusting mechanisms and, once again, reduced production costs. In fairness, it also allowed the back of the seat to extend sideways toward the driver's seat, thus acting as extra noise insulation. *Popular Imported Cars* seemed to like this arrangement anyway: "Seating in the 914 is excellent, even surprising when you consider the engine placement and the amount of space in the forward trunk compartment. Only the driver's seat can be adjusted but the passenger has loads of room to stretch her legs. Support for the thighs is excellent, making high-speed touring for long periods of time a real snap."

The window winders also came in for criticism as testers continually damaged their knuckles. A number of testers also experienced scuttle shake with the 914s – something previously unheard of in a Porsche, even in the drophead versions.

Hubert Davis reporting for *World Car Guide* in May 1970 said: "The shift, in short, is good by VW standards, but miserable by Porsche's ..." Davis was far from alone in picking up on the vague feeling in the long and complicated gear selector arrangement, made necessary because the gearbox was mounted behind the engine. In fact, most magazines mentioned it.

A pair of 914/4s bought by Radio Luxembourg. The car in the foreground is to 914S specification, while the other is in standard four-cylinder trim. The popular S-pack option brought a number of extras, taking the car nearer to the six-cylinder model in appearance.

Although this was hardly the start Porsche had hoped for, fortunately, not all of the news was bad. Later in Davis's report, he wrote: "Handling is something else again ... You couldn't tip it over unless you hit a curb."

The glassfibre Targa top went down well with most testers. It occupied only the upper 75mm (three inches) of the rear luggage compartment and, due to its lightness, could be singlehandedly removed and fitted by a woman. Luggage space was also singled out as a plus point for a sports car.

Summing up, *Wheels* magazine noted in March 1970: "This new departure in sports cars is billed as a joint project of Germany's largest and smallest automobile producers. Drivers among us will be glad to know that the smaller partner had the biggest clout when it came to settling the 914 design."

Standard colour schemes 1970 MY

Standard coachwork colours

Adriatic Blue, Canary Yellow, Light Ivory, Signal Orange, Irish Green, and Tangerine

Special coachwork colours

Metallic Red, Metallic Green, Metallic Blue, Silver Metallic, and Gemini Blue

Seats

Black, Beige or Brown leatherette or genuine leather. Inlays in Black, Beige or Brown leatherette basketweave, genuine leather basketweave or corduroy; alternatively, dogtooth check fabric in Black or Brown

Carpet

Black or Brown needle loom or pile-type carpet

Notes: The brown listed on interior colours for 1970 was a light brown. Door panels were trimmed to match the colour of the seats for all years. Leather trim was available on the six-cylinder model only.

The 914/4 in Europe

The guide to the 1969 Earls Court Show stated: "History comes full circle with the introduction of cars combining elements of the exotic Porsche and the homely Volkswagen. In one respect the new 914 and 914/6 are a more advanced design concept than

The four-cylinder Volkswagen engine of the 914/4. Producing 80bhp and 100lbft of torque from its 1.7 litres, it weighed around 127kg (280lb) – over 45kg (100lb) lighter than the Porsche engine.

the Porsche itself, for both types have their engine amidships, Grand Prix car fashion, rather than at the rear. Engines are, respectively, a fuel-injected VW flat-four developing 85bhp (SAE) and a Porsche flat-six with two three-choke Weber carbs giving 125bhp. Bodies are identical and distinguished by a detachable glassfibre top. Made with lhd only."

Writing in March 1970, *MotorSport* reported: "Porsche Cars Great Britain Ltd had the first Porsche 914S to arrive in the UK delivered to them in January and customer deliveries commenced last month. 914 four-cylinder roadster £2163; with Sportomatic transmission £2333; six-cylinder roadster £3475; with Sportomatic £3645. This is to the nearest round figure, ignoring shillings and pence, with purchase tax." It should be noted that the UK had the 914S specification four-cylinder cars only.

Later, in the May 1970 issue of *MotorSport*, Bill Boddy gave his first impressions of the VW-Porsche 914. As usual, he gave an honest and in-depth point of view which, for the author, always makes a Boddy report one of the most historically significant. He wrote: "Through the courtesy of AFN Ltd of Isleworth I was able to borrow a mid-engined VW-Porsche 914 for an enthralling weekend. As *MotorSport* has frequently emphasized, the mid-engined concept is bound to develop, because anyone who has handled a car with this weight distribution will not wish to accept any lower standards of roadholding. Road-clinging, coupled with a splendidly level and well-damped ride, are the outstanding attributes of the 914. Volkswagen were well placed to introduce a mid-engined car, having such a compact power pack which they are well accustomed to burying beneath the floor of their estate cars. With Porsche to mix-in the necessary suspension set-up and other requirements of fast motoring, something really notable could hardly fail to materialize.

"Driving the 914 on dry roads, I was quite unable to reach optimum breakaway; you corner faster and faster, in unbelief that the little car will get round. But it always did, so that, once convinced, cruising speed became also the pace at which open bends and corners were negotiated. It is handling to competition-car standards. Here it is opportune to say that the red 914 I tried was on Michelin ZX tyres, which are popular wear on many fast cars these days. In view of what has been written about the shortcomings of central-engined cars, let me report right away that the VW-Porsche conception is free from them. The seat squabs are vertically upright without adjustment, but the seats are nevertheless amongst the most comfortable I have experienced. The sales literature tries to kid one that this is a three-seater, sitting abreast, and there is an 'extra' in the form of

The 914/4 on test. This model was running on the optional wider 5.5J wheels, which looked almost the same as the standard 4.5J items except for the depth of the rim. VW hubcaps were used in both cases, although American cars did not have the VW emblem.

Right: The 914/4 received some favourable road test reports, and proved itself comparatively reliable mechanically. As expected, sales of the smaller-engined car were far higher.

48

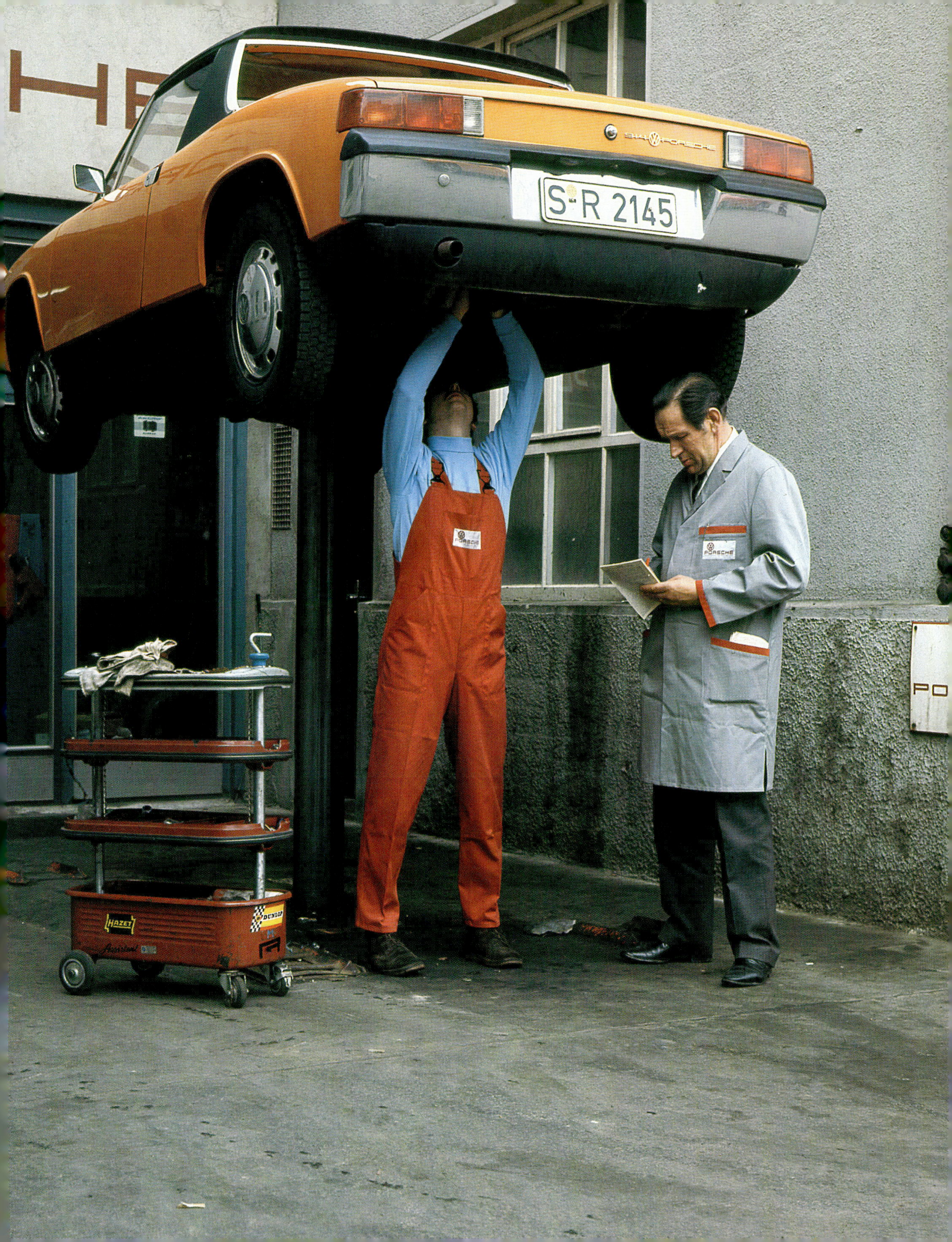
S-R 2145
HAZET
DUNLOP

After its check over, S-R 2145 was ready for action ...

a little pad to put in the well between the two main seats. This would accommodate a child but for all practical purposes this is a two-seater motor car – and why not? There is no undue noise, no heat transfer from the central power pack, perhaps because it is set so compactly low down in the car. As for driver vision, forward it is excellent, the thick screen pillars scarcely intruding; the non-dazzle rearview mirror is rather cut off by the shallow screen, but I found I had an excellent rearwards view in the external mirror of this lhd car. AFN are experimenting with a Delodur heated rear window, which worked well. An occasional glance over the right shoulder and in the aforesaid mirror was all that was needed, and reversing wasn't difficult, but the hooded rear window reflected the body colour, and the instruments acted as facial mirrors. The mid-engined layout as conceived by VW incurs no obvious snags and normal doors with VW-Porsche-type releases-cum-locks permit conventional entry.

"The interior of the car is austere, in black trim, with knobs and a left-hand stalk as controls, but all is well contrived, except that the small steering wheel tends to blank the more interesting sector of the speedometer. There is also the luxury of two luggage boots, with a combined capacity of 16.1 cubic feet; one in the nose, one behind the 'engine room', although rather shallow luggage is advisable.

"On the road, as I have said, the outstanding enjoyment is that of an impeccable ride and astonishingly safe cornering powers, conferred by the weight distribution, low build, and a 'wheel at each corner'. The suspension, torsion bar in front, coil-spring at the back, is so well damped that the wheels follow surface irregularities faithfully and humpback bridges cause no discomfort. So unyielding is the springing that some mild rattle is conveyed to the obviously rigid body, but the clean undertray treats rough lanes with disdain. The central gearlever controls a five-speed 'box but whereas it can be said that an Alfa Romeo has a ratio for every purpose, it is kindest to remark that the modern Porsche gearchange is an acquired taste. Once one of the best gearchanges in the world, initiates are now never really sure which cog they are in, or are going to select, and even neutral is a trifle vague. As to performance, I saw the speedometer register 100mph on occasions but the VW 411 1.7 litre, electronic fuel-injection power unit, poking out only 80bhp, does far less than justice to this remarkable car. Moreover, there is unlikely to be a rhd version and as the high cost of the Karmann body, allied to import duty, etc, has inflated the GB price to £2261, sales are not likely to be exactly brisk in England. Even in Germany the prospect of the 914 being the poor sportsman's Porsche, at around £1500, has, I gather, tarnished. The VW engine peaks at about 4900rpm but can be taken in short bursts towards the warning mark on the tachometer at 5600rpm. However, this futuristic car in £3475 914/6 form with Porsche flat-six engine must be a very exciting proposition indeed; a sort of landbound light 'plane from the A to B average speed aspect, with the 'dodgeability' of a good motorcycle (just over three turns of the steering wheel, lock-to-lock) ... AFN Ltd are concessionaires for both models – VW Motors do not sell the 914.

"Whether you have it in four- or six-cylinder guise, the VW-Porsche has some unusual features. The right-hand handbrake, for instance, pulls on in the normal fashion but then drops to the floor. This is to give

This early four-cylinder 914 has been given a colour-keyed bumper and roll-over bar.

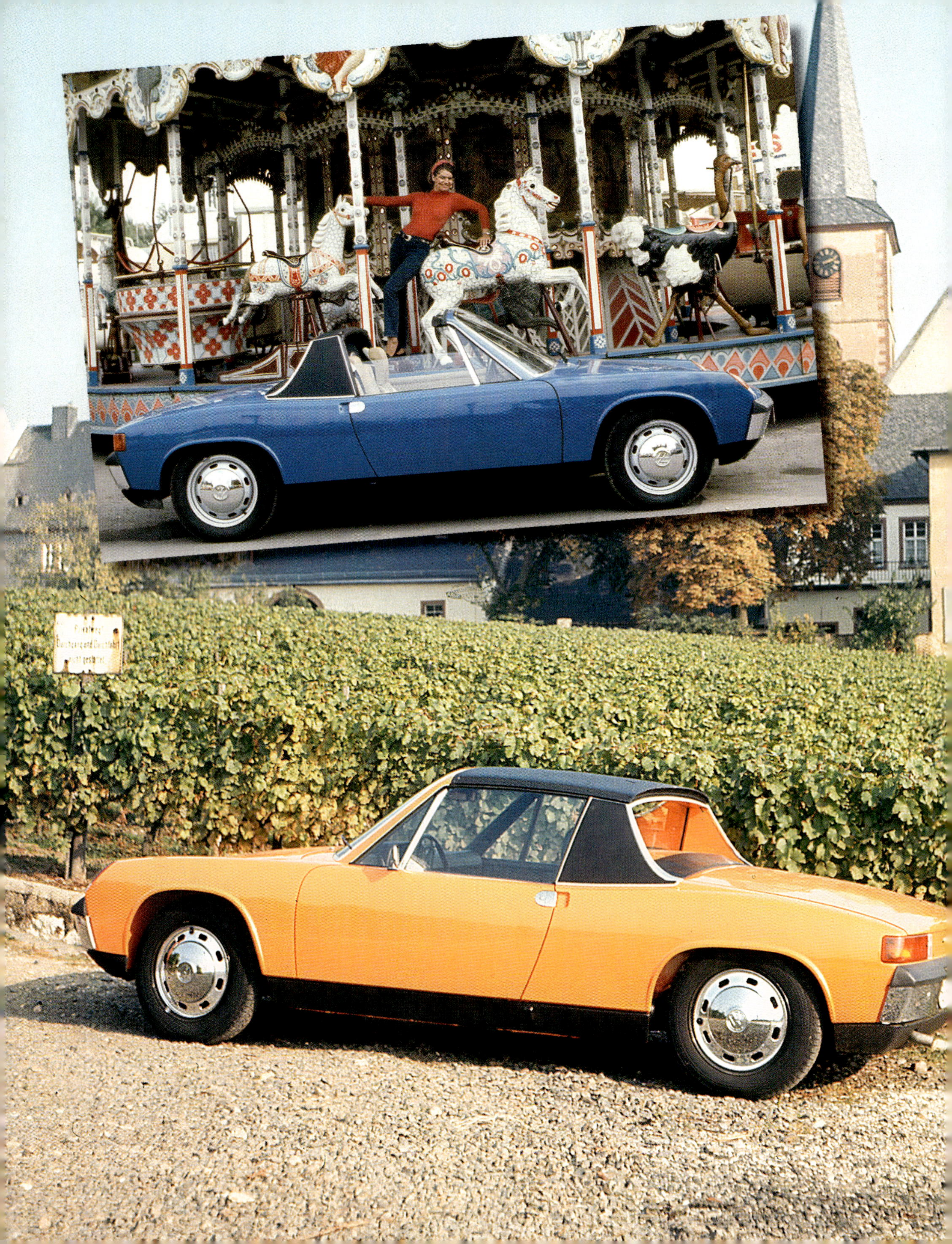

Left: A couple of beautiful publicity shots of the 1.7 litre 914.

The 914 was extremely practical for a mid-engined sports car, as this shot clearly shows.

unimpeded exit to the driver. To release the brake the lever is again pulled up until resistance is felt, its button depressed, and the lever moved down. The need for a brake warning light, provided as a segment of the warning light cluster, is even more essential with such a system than with less elaborate handbrakes. Another peculiarity is that to comply with German requirements, the normally concealed Hella headlamps become erect if the sidelamps are switched on. As there is growing use of dipped headlamps even in built-up areas this is no great disadvantage, but AFN talk of introducing a diode in the circuit for neater use of sidelamps in this country. Incidentally, the dipped beam is poor, but there are in-built Hella spotlamps. A further unique item is that the hardtop detaches and will go in the rear boot, so that the VW-Porsche is a true convertible, without the need for a flexible hood – it is, indeed, a sort of coupe de ville. An unintended peculiarity is that the turn flashers reflect in the headlamp backs; nor was I enamoured of the turn indicator warning lights on the fascia winking in my line of vision. The passenger gets a door grab-handle and a felt-covered footrest, the latter anchored with a short strap to prevent it intruding on the driver. As well as a tool roll, a big screw-in tow-hook is provided.

"The fuel tank in the front boot has a catchment well and is also fully vented to US and Canadian requirements. It takes its fuel slowly but when full gave a range of 328 miles before the low-level warning light came on fixedly, after which there is about 1.3 gallons remaining, so the former VW attribute of infrequent refuelling has been achieved. A rough check

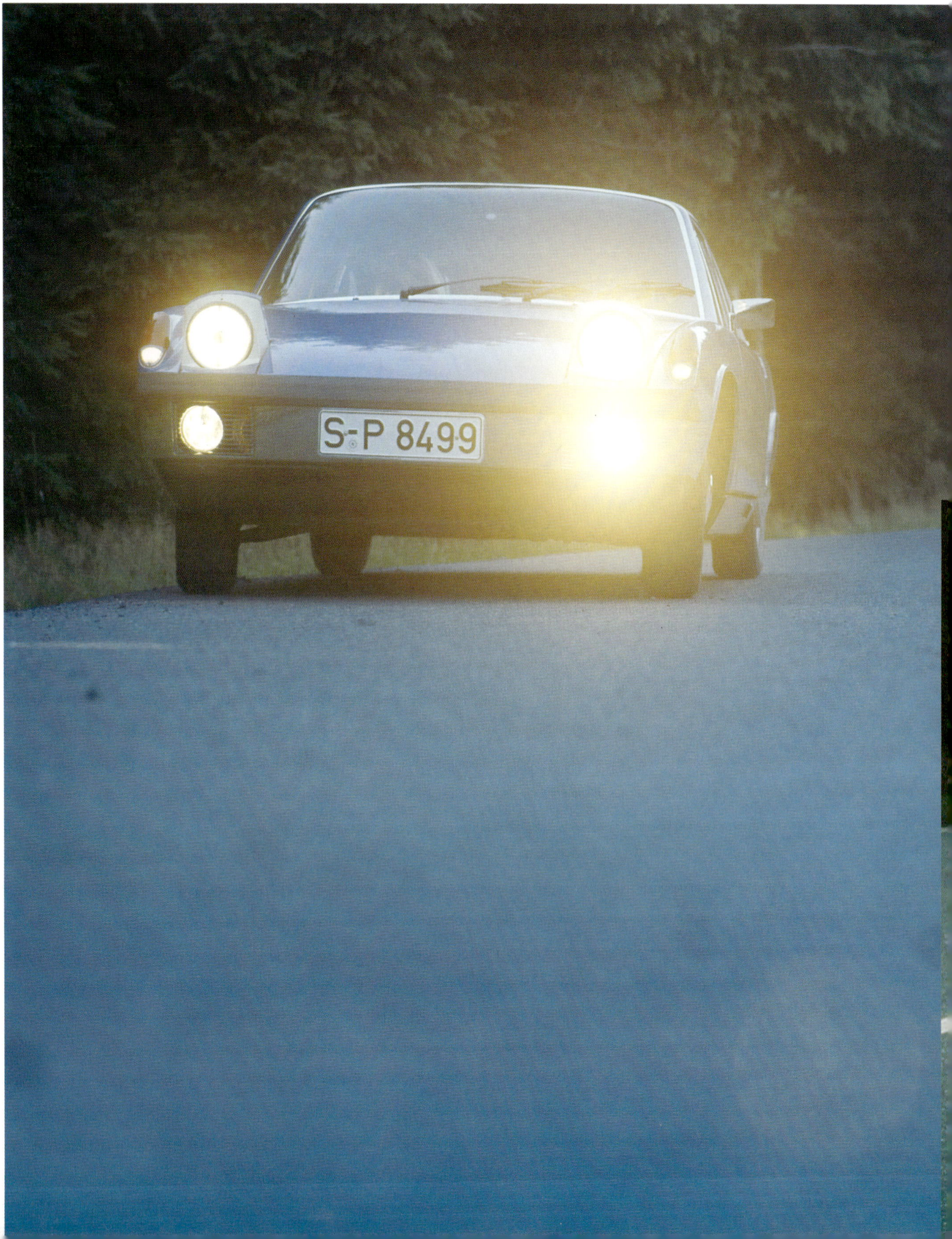
S-P 8499

of consumption showed approximately 26.5mpg of four-star.

"So much, then, for preliminary impressions of one of the great new cars of the 1970s. The VW-Porsche, officially, I believe, the Type 47, is a motor car which the connoisseurs will soon be discussing with enthusiasm."

Autocar tested the model in July 1970. At a basic price of £1730, purchase tax and seatbelts took it to £2270 on the forecourt. Options included a leather-rimmed steering wheel at £16, a centre seat cushion at £6, heated rear window at £13, and a radio/cassette player at £90. *Autocar* said: "On top speed the 914 achieved a lap time at MIRA equivalent to 102mph, and would probably go even faster in a straight line. In the high overdrive fifth the most we saw on the rev counter was 4650rpm, which is below the power peak at 4900rpm. The manufacturers claim 110mph which is equivalent to the peak. In fourth the 914 ran easily up to the red mark on the rev counter at 5600, equivalent to 97mph."

The magazine recorded 19.9 seconds for the standing-quarter, and some reasonable times from standstill until the magic mile-a-minute was reached; 0-60 was covered in 14.8 seconds, but to reach 70mph (112kph) took 20.2 seconds, and 90mph (144kph) 41.4 seconds. However, average fuel consumption was very respectable at 25mpg.

The 914/4 in America

By 1970, Porsche was producing around 70 cars a day, taking the annual total to 16,757. Now capitalized at DM 20 million, the factory employed around 4000 people. By far the most important market for the Stuttgart firm was the United States.

As noted in the previous chapter, sales in America began after 1 January 1970. Estimates, based on the fact that 46 per cent of Porsche production went to the

Two views of a 1970 model year 914/4 with Stuttgart registration plates.

USA in 1969, predicted that around 14,000 914s (split 11,000 914/4s and 3000 914/6s) would be sold in the States during 1970, in addition to approximately 6000 911 models. However, in very atypical Porsche fashion, an owner's manual was not available in the English language until well after the launch: was this somewhat rocky start a sign of the what was to come?

Car & Driver noted: "What we've said up to now is that the 914 is a compact but spacious mid-engined sports car – a well-conceived machine. Brace yourselves, Porsche fanatics. That is the outer boundary of its excellence. The name Porsche is automatically associated with performance, mechanical refinement and quality workmanship – all assets of which the 914 is conspicuously bankrupt. It's being touted as a budget Porsche, and with an as-tested price of $3935, it is that. It's about half the cost of a 911S – and about half as good as a 911S – but that isn't good enough. Not when there are Datsuns, Opels and Fiats, each with strong points and all for less money. The 914 just can't compete. Sadly, it has been miscast."

The writer went on to say: "As a second generation replacement for the Karmann Ghia it would bring the house down. It even has the credentials for the job. The body is made by Karmann for starters. And don't forget the VW engine ... Considering that price, the Porsche 914 is an altogether underwhelming car."

It is probably fair to say that *Car & Driver* was not overly impressed by the four-cylinder car. Its test did, however, record a 0-60 time of 11.3 seconds, and an estimated top speed of 105mph (168kph). These figures were more or less confirmed in a *Road & Track* test published two months earlier which recorded the following results –

```
0-50mph .............. (80kph)............ 10.0 secs
0-60mph .............. (96kph)............ 13.9 secs
0-70mph ............ (112kph)............ 19.1 secs
0-90mph ............ (144kph)............ 37.8 secs
```

Speed in gears:
```
1st........................ 28mph (45kph) at 5600rpm
2nd....................... 48mph (77kph) at 5600rpm
3rd ...................... 72mph (115kph) at 5600rpm
4th....................... 97mph (155kph) at 5600rpm
5th..................... 109mph (174kph) at 4850rpm
```

On the other hand, *Motor Trend* voted the 914 range as its 1970 'Import Car of the Year', stating: "Some think it ugly, underpowered, overpriced. Critics have even accused it of not being a real Porsche ... whatever the car is or is not, there is a consensus on one point: the 914 is a thoroughly modern automobile."

The May 1970 edition of *Road Test* magazine, following its test of a $3695 914, noted: "By now it might have become apparent that we feel the Porsche 914/4 to be a heck of a car. Not without reservations, to be sure. But on an overall basis we'll just about stake the deeds to the plantation that this model will be the hottest selling item to ever carry the Porsche nameplate."

Incidentally, the $3695 tag mentioned is the American West Coast price, which was $100 more than the East Coast port of entry (POE) price. On the West Coast the 914/6 would have cost $6099 and the 911T Targa $7205 during the same period (the latter was only $6235 in the previous year).

The standard four-cylinder car was quite basic – probably too basic – but it could be dramatically improved with the addition of the $200 Appearance Group Option Package (basically the European S-pack). It included a vinyl-covered roll bar, chrome bumpers, wider 5.5J x 15 steel wheels with 165 SR-rated tyres, dual horns, foglights (driving lights were not allowed in the States at the time), a leather-covered steering wheel and pile-type carpet.

All US models (both four- and six-cylinder) had combined side indicators/reflectors on the front wing which also acted as running lights; these were not seen in any other market. However, cars destined for Japan, Italy and Denmark did have a similar light, also mounted just behind the original front indicator lens, but these were purely extra turn indicators.

Other unique features on American cars included front indicators that were fully amber to allow them to be used as combination running lights. In all other markets they were amber over clear (the latter being a sidelight); except Italy, that is, where the front indicator was completely clear.

Indicators were fully red instead of amber and red on the back (ie featuring a combined turn indicator and running light), and incorporated two reflectors: one at the rear and one where the lens wrapped around the side of the car, doing away with the need for an unsightly additional reflector. Reversing lights were on the innermost part of the rear lenses on both sides, and were clear in all markets except for France, where yellow was used.

Badging was different in America due to the 914 being sold purely as a Porsche. There was gold-coloured 'PORSCHE' script on the engine cover, with no sign of a VW-Porsche nameplate on the rear end.

A 1970 914/6 with Fuchs alloy wheels.

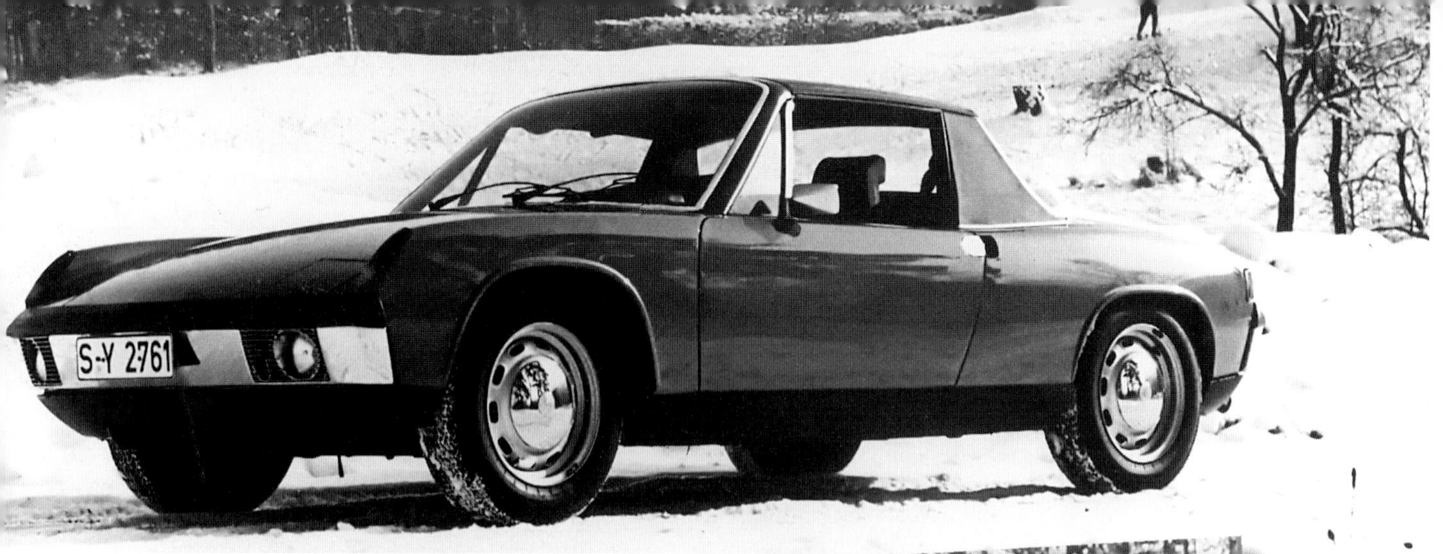
S-Y 2761

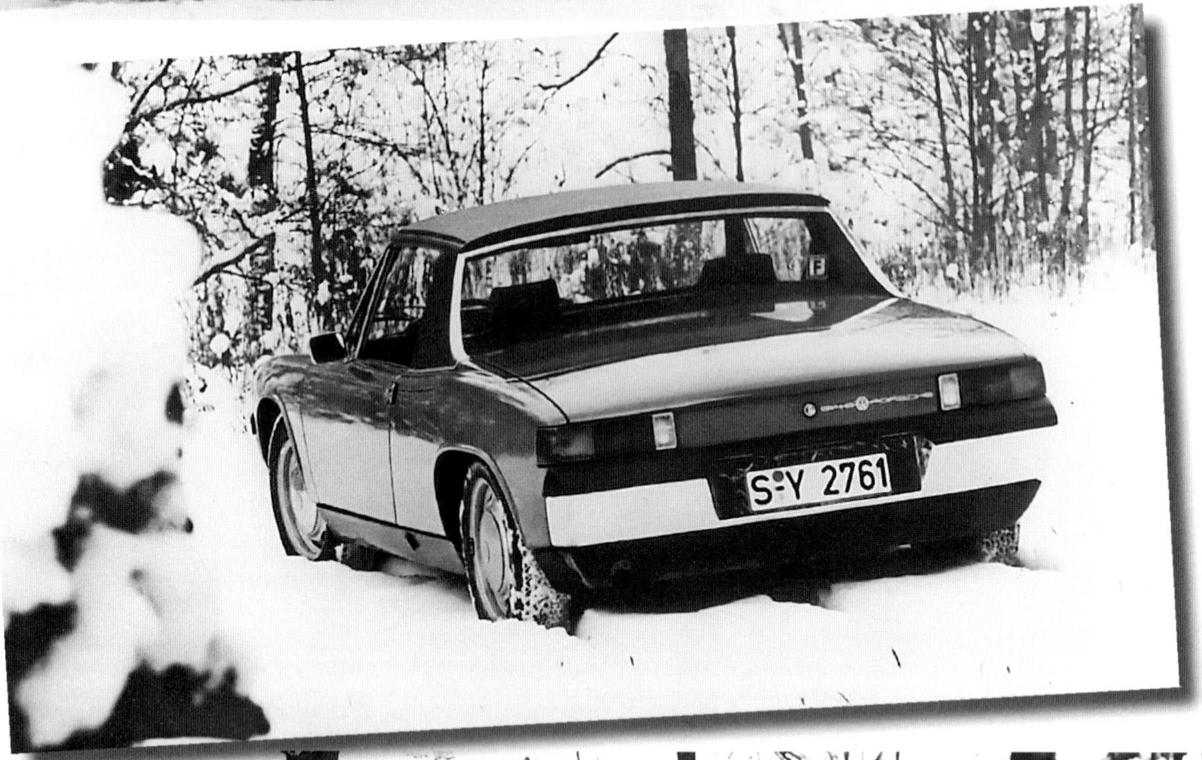
S-Y 2761

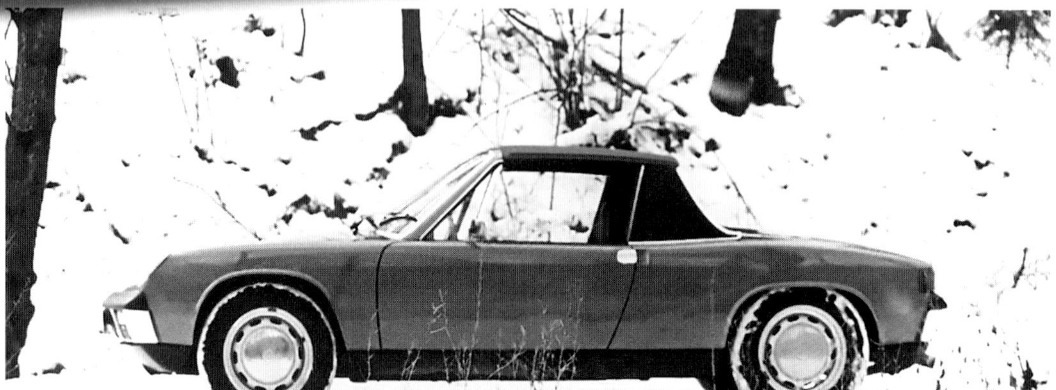

Opposite, top: A very early 914/6. Apparently, following testing by the works, the 911s were found to be better on snow because of the extra weight over the driving wheels. Nevertheless, the 914 was far better than a vehicle with a conventional FR layout in conditions like these.

Opposite, middle: The same 914/6. Note the badge of the six-cylinder car, and also the sharp shapes of the rear bumper in the area around the number plate, which was changed to a smoother design for the 1971 model year.

Opposite, bottom: Viewed from the side, the shape of the 914 series is seen in its best light.

The Porsche six-cylinder engine was basically the same unit as that used in the 1969 model year 911T. Producing a modest 110bhp from a two-litre capacity, it weighed around 177kg (390lb).

Instead, there was just a simple gold-coloured '914' or '914-6' badge, depending on the engine.

To make the marketing ploy a little more convincing, for the American market the hubcaps on the 914/4 were shipped minus their VW emblem, completely plain. In addition, where the 914/4 steering wheel would have a Wolfsburg badge in the centre, this was replaced by a Porsche crest for America.

The 914/6

Road & Track ran an interesting article in its December 1969 issue. It said: "The engine and drivetrain of the 914/6 is taken directly from the 1969 911T (the 1970 911T is increased to 2.2 litres) and turned around – the only modification necessary was changing the differential ring gear around to the other side of the differential.

"I was aghast at the small access panel above the engine when I first saw the 914. But Porsche engineers [Helmuth] Bott and [Ferdinand] Piech, whom I interviewed at the Frankfurt Show, assured me that the following service operations can be performed from above with relative ease: belt changing, all tune-up work, sparkplug change and valve adjustment. The basic service interval for both models is 12,000 miles – including plug changes. This is a new step toward less maintenance for Porsche, and a good one indeed.

"Cooling was a potential problem with the new engine location ... but Bott considers the cooling still satisfactory and made no changes in the fan of either engine."

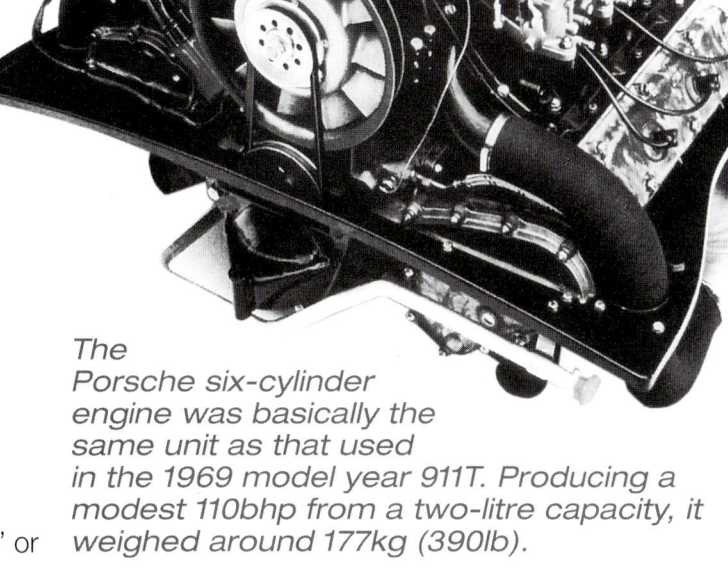

In actual fact, the six-cylinder engine did run slightly hotter in the 914 body, but was still well within its efficiency limits.

The article concluded: "It is the first mass-produced mid-engine sports car – there are a few limited production ones already, but none produced in quantities of 1000 a year – and it could revolutionize the world of two-seaters."

A big problem for the marketing people was that the outward appearance of the six-cylinder model was not all that different from the much cheaper four-cylinder version with the S-pack. Even the interior was very similar to that of the 1.7 litre model before options were added.

There were detail changes, of course, but it took a knowledgeable enthusiast with a keen eye to spot them. Most concerned the switchgear and instruments: on the 914/4, the rev counter read from 0-7000rpm and the speedometer was calibrated to 120mph (or 200kph), whilst on the six-cylinder model the same instruments read from 800-8000rpm and a maximum of 150mph (or 250kph) respectively. The large dial on

Right: The interior of the 914/6 with optional leather trim and corduroy seat inserts. The fixed passenger seat can clearly be seen in this photograph, and all cars were built as left-hand drive only.

the left of the rev counter, which contained the fuel level gauge, also carried one monitoring oil temperature on the 914/6 model.

The 914/6 had three-speed wipers and electric windscreen washer controlled by a stalk on the steering column, whereas the 914/4 had a two-speed motor with a switch on the fascia and a manual screen washer. The six had its ignition switch on the left-hand side of the fascia, and was located on the right-hand side of the steering column in the smaller-engined car.

The 914/6 had a hand throttle located on the centre tunnel, but the 914/4 didn't have one at all. Other subtle differences included lack of a headliner on the basic four-cylinder car and, on the six-cylinder model, no centre air vent on the fascia top roll.

Outside, the 914/4 bumper was painted in body colour (chrome was optional on 914/4s and fitted as standard on the 914/6). The 914/4 roll bar was also in body colour with the option of being trimmed in black vinyl, as was standard on the 914/6.

The driver's side door panel. Note the lack of a grab handle – a small cut-out was provided in the lid of the storage box instead. The majority of aftermarket right-hand drive conversions did not make this change.

The dashboard of the 914/6. The main gauges (from left to right) informed the driver of oil temperature/fuel, engine speed, and road speed. Minor switches along the fascia (again from the left) controlled the headlights, fog/driving lights (if fitted), hazard warning lights, and the ignition. On the steering column, the indicators and main beam were on the left-hand stalk, whilst the other one was for the windscreen washer and wipers. To the right of the steering wheel was a switch for the optional rear window heater, and a cigarette lighter.

An attractive shot of the 1970 914/6.

Wheels were also different. The 914/4 had four-stud VW steel rim wheels of 4.5J width (or optionally 5.5J of a similar design), with VW hubcaps. The 914/6 had five-stud Porsche 911 steel rim wheels (usually painted silver with a chromed finish as an option) and stainless steel hubcaps, with the option of the familiar forged five-spoke Fuchs alloys fitted to the 911s, or ten-spoke Mahle alloys. The Mahle wheels, cast in a magnesium alloy, were half the weight of the standard 5.5J steel items.

Adding extra kudos to the six-cylinder model was the fact that a competition version was available: the 914/6 GT, homologated in March 1970. Further details on this special machine and its racing history can be found in chapter five.

The 914/6 in Britain

The first 914/6 to arrive in Britain was AFN's road test car (chassis number 9140430059 and registered DGU 914H in May 1970). Tested by *Motor*, *Autocar* and *Cars & Car Conversions*, the car has survived to this day, owned for some time by enthusiast Dave Fagan.

Following its road test in August 1970, *Motor* said: "Visibility is excellent, especially in the critical three-quarter rear direction where it is generally so poor in other cars with the same layout.

"We ... consider that some further aerodynamic study is needed to reduce buffeting when the Targa roof is removed to bring open-top comfort into line with the advanced nature of the concept.

"The cockpit is exceptionally roomy and airy for a sports car ... The Targa roof is retained by four over-centre catches and is easily removed by one person. It stows neatly in the rear boot.

"The minor controls are splendidly laid out with a stalk controlling the headlamps and indicators, another for washing and wiping the screen, and a horn ring on the steering wheel. But it is a long stretch to the radio, especially when belted in.

"We find the absence of separate fresh air vents a rather strange omission in such a recently developed car, but a reasonable flow of cool air can be obtained through the windscreen vents.

"Although the standard of finish and trim is good, a few poorly executed details brought it below the

The same 914/6 was featured in a series of shots involving girls and blossom. The Mahle mag-alloy wheels can be seen in detail in this picture.

Either fog or driving lights could be fitted in the front bumpers. Various bulb arrangements were needed to cope with different markets: H-3 white bulbs for the vast majority, with H-3 bulbs in yellow for France. Italy specified the H-1 type in white, whilst America was different again: driving lights were not allowed at the time, and foglights had to be non-Halogen.

A final shot from the 'girls and blossom' series.

standard of a 911. Nevertheless, the general level of the fittings and equipment is much more to Porsche than to Volkswagen standards."

A standing-quarter time of 16.1 seconds was recorded, with a top speed of 120mph (192kph). From standstill, 50mph (80kph) was indicated at 6.3 seconds, while 0-60 took 8.8; 70mph (112kph) came up in 11.4 seconds, and 90mph (144kph) was achieved in 19.5.

Autocar's test of a VW-Porsche 914/6 in January 1971 listed the car at £2660 basic, or £3484.57 including purchase tax and seatbelts; about £10 more than when *Motor* did its report. Maximum speed was put at 125mph (200kph), with 0-60 coming up in 8.3 seconds.

Interestingly, after a great deal of hard driving, 23mpg was given as the typical fuel consumption. At a constant 30mph (48kph), 36.0mpg was achieved, while at 50mph (80kph) it was quoted at 37.7mpg – an exceptional figure for the time. As speed increased to 70mph (112kph), so too did fuel consumption (30.7mpg); by 90mph (144kph) the figure was just 23.8mpg.

Options quoted by the magazine included Sportomatic transmission at £169.72, alloy wheels with 185HR tyres at £175, a heated rear window at £13, centre seat cushion at £6, tinted glass at £30, listed special paint at £50 (or unlisted at £75), and various items of stereo equipment.

It should be noted that just four 914/6s were equipped with the four-speed Sportomatic transmission – and that's all. There were probably even fewer four-cylinder cars with it, but although it wasn't available as such, it continued to be listed as an option.

In summary, the *Autocar* thought the 914/6 to be an "... expensive but practical mid-engined coupé." The Targa top was a good compromise for the English weather; performance was excellent, and fuel economy quite good. The engine was "... rather noisy at town speeds ..." and the gearchange "... tricky." However, the car's stability and handling characteristics were singled out as outstanding.

News from the USA

The gearchange on early cars came in for criticism from almost every magazine. *Road & Track* was perhaps the most historically useful in its comments, pinpointing the main concern: "There was still a minor shift problem on the 914/6, though; sometimes first gear was reluctant to disengage, making the one-two shift dodgy. Using sufficient force to get out of first was worrisome with reverse directly above."

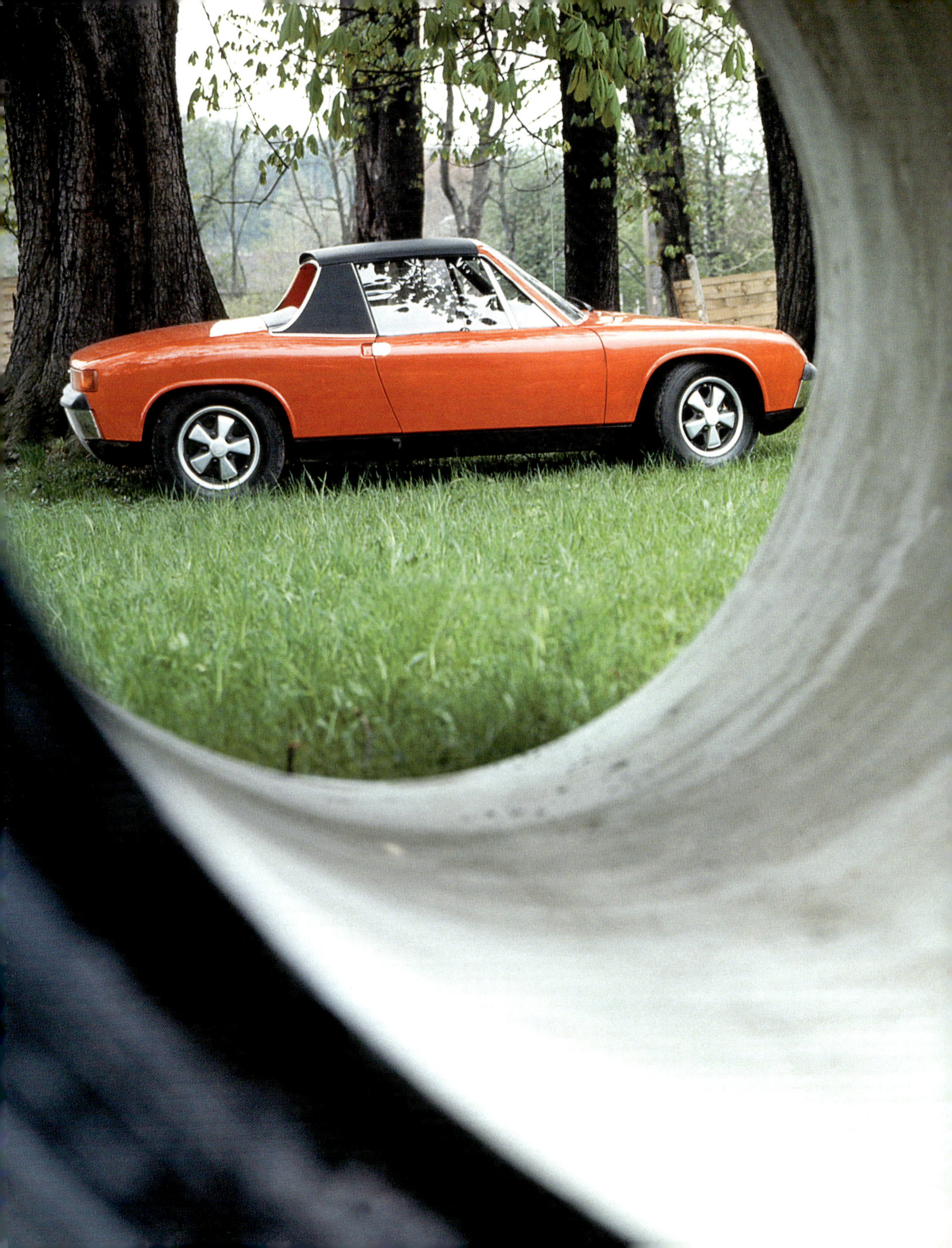

An early 914/6 with Fuchs alloys.

The same journal noted an average fuel consumption for the 914/6 of 21.3 miles to the gallon. Speeds through the gears (all recorded at 6200rpm, except for top speed, taken at 6000rpm) were as follows: 33mph (53kph) in first; 57mph (91kph) in second; 82mph (131kph) in third; 105mph (168kph) in fourth, and 123mph (197kph) in fifth.

Another American test drew up a comparison between the two 914 models. The four-cylinder car covered 0-30mph (48kph) in 4.0 seconds; 0-45mph (72kph) in 7.5 seconds; 0-60mph (96kph) in 12.4 seconds, and 0-75mph (120kph) in 18.2 seconds. The same increments were covered in 3.3, 5.3, 8.4 and 12.5 seconds respectively in the 914/6. The latter was quicker over the standing-quarter, too, covering the distance in 16.0 seconds (terminal speed 85.5mph, or 136.8kph), while the VW-powered machine took 18.3 seconds for the same exercise, passing the marker at 75.2mph (120.3kph).

The 1971 model year

The German price list from November 1970 had the standard 914/4 at DM 11,955, whilst the same model with the popular S-pack option was just DM 745 more. The standard six-cylinder 914/6 was quoted at a rather hefty DM 19,980.

However, the stronger economy in Germany led in turn to a weaker dollar, making cars like Porsches very expensive. The value of the deutschmark had risen steadily against the dollar after the 914 was launched, which not only made imported cars more expensive, but if a price was retained in America, also gave the manufacturer less return in dollar sales. Whichever your viewpoint, it was not a good situation for the German marque; in fact, by the close of 1970, VW-Porsche's financial results were so bad that it seriously considered abandoning the entire 914 project. After all, a loss of DM 200 million is not something to be taken lightly!

Despite reservations, the 914 was continued and, for the 1971 model year, a number of minor changes were introduced, and for the four-cylinder car, there was also the option of a Pedrini alloy wheel of 5.5J x 15. The oil sump was modified on the W80 four-cylinder engine, and the 914/4 was also given a power screen washer via air in the spare tyre. Changes affecting the whole range included modification to the rear number plate area – which now had rounded corners and a smaller space for the plate itself – and the addition of a coat hook on the passenger side to go with the existing one on the driver's side. Slightly later, but still

The cheapest 911. The 911T coupe, as seen here, had stolen a large chunk of sales that the 914/6 was supposed to be taking. The future of the 914 series was thrown into doubt ...

However, it did continue and, for the 1971 model year, there were a number of changes. This test driver, carrying out tyre wear research, is taking advantage of one of them – a passenger-side coat hook.

Standard colour schemes, 1971 MY

Standard coachwork colours

Adriatic Blue, Canary Yellow, Light Ivory, Signal Orange, Irish Green, Tangerine, Bahia Red, and Willow Green

Special coachwork colours

Black, Gold Metallic, Silver Metallic, and Gemini Blue

Seats

Black, Beige or Brown leatherette or genuine leather. Inlays in Black, Beige or Brown leatherette (perforated) or corduroy

Carpet

Grey, Beige or Brown needle loom or pile-type carpet

Notes: Leather trim was only available on the six-cylinder model.

in the 1971 MY, the passenger gained a small vanity mirror in the sunvisor.

In May 1971, Porsche launched the M471 body/wheel package, which gave 914/6 owners the chance to own a GT lookalike; it was not offered for the 914/4. The option included steel wheelarch extentions to cover the 6J x 15 forged Fuchs alloy wheels (used with spacers at the rear), new fibreglass sills to blend in with the flared arches, and a front spoiler to match. According to Porsche, the rear valance was deleted with the M471 option.

No right-hand drive cars were produced by the factory (early reports said the rhd option may be available for the 1973 season) as the Volkswagen element of the partnership was anxious to recoup tooling costs as quickly as possible. However, during 1971, Crayford Auto Developments of Westerham began to offer rhd conversions for the 914 range. With the modification costing £631 in mid-1971, naturally enough, very few people chose to make an expensive car even more costly (at the time, a Triumph Spitfire cost just £1053, whilst the TR6 from the same stable was £1621); contemporary reports suggest that between 30 and 40 cars a year received the high quality conversion from the Kent-based firm.

Although the 914 was reported to be selling better in the USA than the 912 had in the previous year, it was still not living up to sales expectations, and price seemed to be the 914's biggest problem. Of the 914/4, the respected British magazine, *Car*, wrote in July 1971: "All its impeccable manners, its excellent finish, its comfort, and its individuality do not alter the very fact that this is a 1971 sports car that's in the MGB class, and not the E-Type/XJ6/BMW 2800 bracket that its price dictates. As a

Another change for 1971 was a different rear bumper with a more rounded area surrounding the number plate. If a rear foglight was fitted, it was located on the nearside next to the rear lamp cluster. Note also the location of the wheel jack, which moved to the back of the rear compartment in mid-1972.

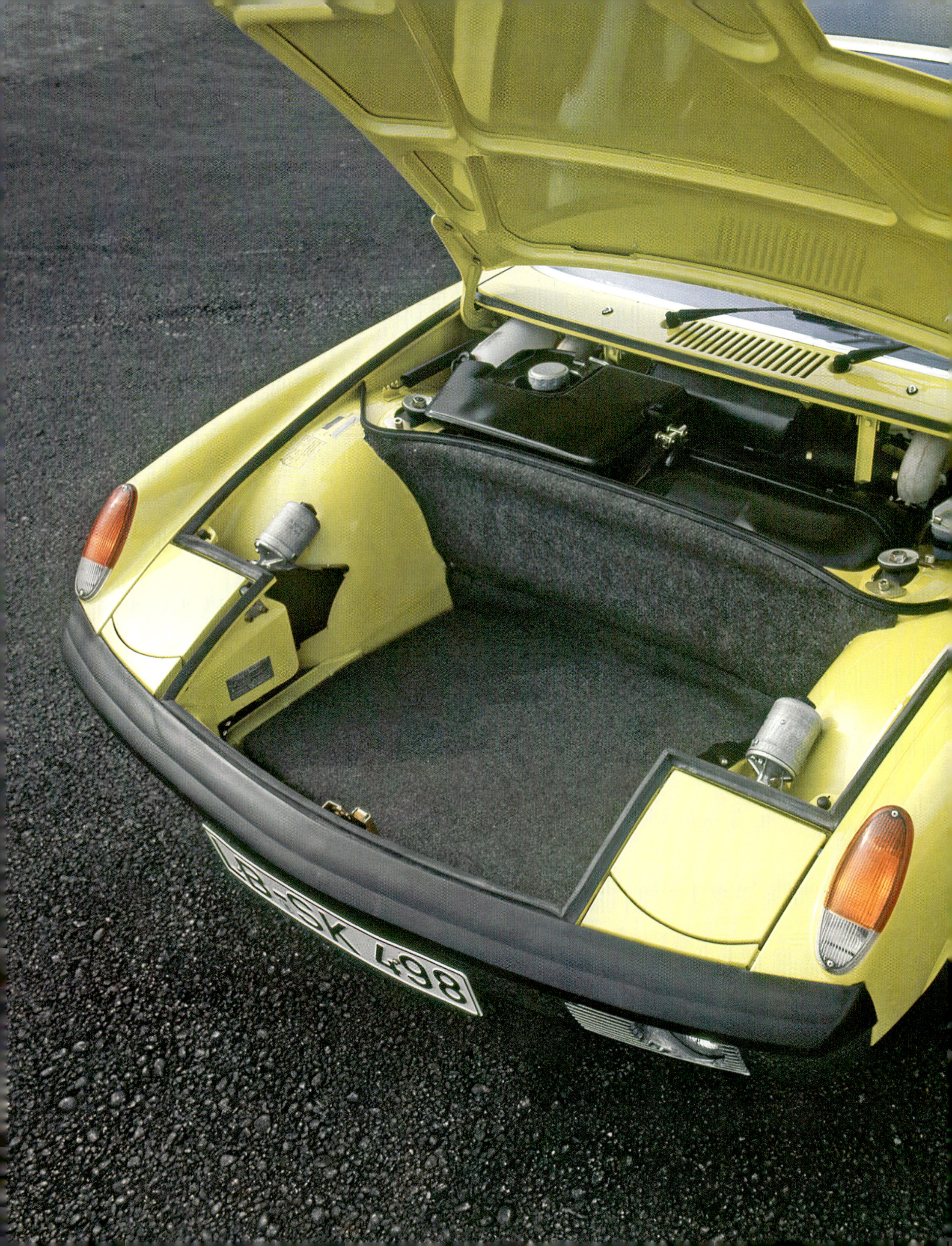

The front compartment of the 1971 model year 914/4. Note the motors for lifting the headlights into place.

When not in use, the Targa top had to be lifted out of the rear compartment if luggage space was to be used. However, few road test reports or owners complained about this.

A 914/6 in use as a pace car at the Daytona circuit in Florida. Note the extra indicator on the front wing. To comply with Federal regulations, a lot of American-spec cars had a reflector on the rear wing as well, but for the 914 series – with the rear light cluster wrapping around the body – it was possible to place a reflector on the lens instead.

car it's just great, as a buy it's a Wagnerian tragedy that just cannot be taken too seriously."

Paul Horrell conducted a test of a late-1971 914/6 for *Supercar Classics* in 1990. Given the amount of progress made by automobiles in the 20 years between the report and the car being built (one need look no further than the Toyota MR2 for a practical, modern mid-engined car), it made interesting reading. He said: "Aesthetics aside, it's a practical shape: visibility is great, the cabin's roomy and there's a big, deep boot at the front and another, shallower one behind. It's aerodynamic, too, low in frontal area and possessed of a very flat floor.

"You sit askew, holding a leathered wheel of the contemporary 911 type. Its left edge is closer to the dash than its right, as the steering column points to a rack in the centre of the car; the floorhinged pedals are offset the same way. Instruments are as per the 911, too, combined fuel and oil temperature gauges on the left, central tacho and right-hand speedo, plus plenty of warning lights.

"It's an airy cockpit, and there's always the option of removing the glassfibre targa panel, not an onerous

The 1971 model year 914/4 in action.

operation. In fact, sunny days present less of a problem to the 914's climate control than cold ones, when you have to wrestle with a heater that varies its output wildly according to engine revs and road speed.

"The monocoque shell is stiffened by four bulkheads, but even so does flex slightly when the targa's off. The fuel tank is ahead of your feet, and contributes to a fairly even-handed weight distribution of 47%:53%, front to rear.

"Being a Porsche engine, durability comes as

standard ... Tickover is soft (compression is just 8.6:1) and uneven (carburation is generous), but any touch of the pedal in neutral sends the little six zinging into life.

"The linkage to the long, floor-mounted gearlever must have presented Porsche's engineers with a problem. They failed adequately to solve it. Though the gearshift is quick when you aim the lever in the correct direction and the synchros are good, the lever flops around in and between gears so badly that, for instance, it can be plumb upright when in either third or fifth, and there's no spring bias to guide you between the 2/3 and 4/5 planes.

"The Porsche relies on low nose weight to bestow light, direct steering that's accurate and full of feel. You drive it on small steering movements, sweeping cleanly around even quite tight bends without handshuffling. Approaching corners, the brakes need a firm squeeze – there's no servo – but they're deliciously controllable, strong and well balanced.

"Turn-in, the very moment when a mid-engined

A 914/6 with the optional Fuchs forged alloy wheels, which came in two sizes: 5.5J x 14 (as seen here), or 6J x 15 when part of the then recently-introduced M471 package.

layout most makes its contribution, is crisp and quick. Even though this car doesn't have the optional anti-roll bars, it hardly leans as the forces build. It clings on well: on Dartmoor's grippy tarmac this one generates impressive lateral forces.

"The central concentration of masses, the wide track and long wheelbase and your low seating position all contribute to a remarkably unperturbed medium-speed ride. Sure, it's joggly going slowly and always firmish, but in dispatching bumps the car never pitches, lurches or runs off course. It's this stable, damped precision that makes the 914/6 feel so modern.

"It weighs less than a ton, so is quicker than a similarly powered 911. The engine is as tractable as you like, but not very torquey. Still, using the revs is no hardship. That makes the 914/6 feel brisker than most four-cylinder cars of similar power-to-weight ratio (Lancia Montecarlo, for example) as you can happily take advantage of the short gearing by holding the

continued page 78

Right & overleaf: The M471 body/wheel package was announced in May 1971, and gave owners the opportunity to acquire a 914/6 GT lookalike that they could use on the road. It was available on the six-cylinder model only.

74

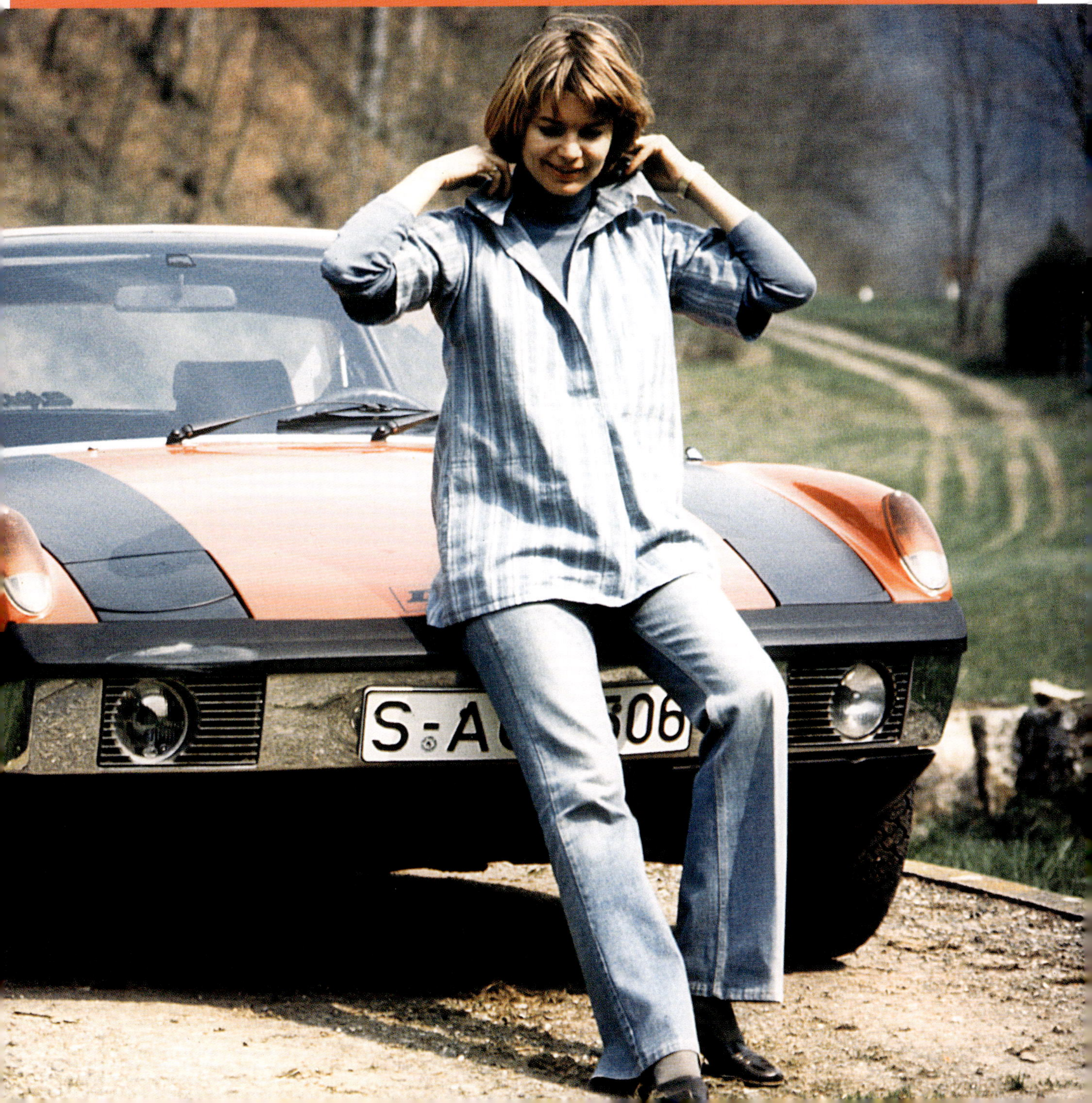

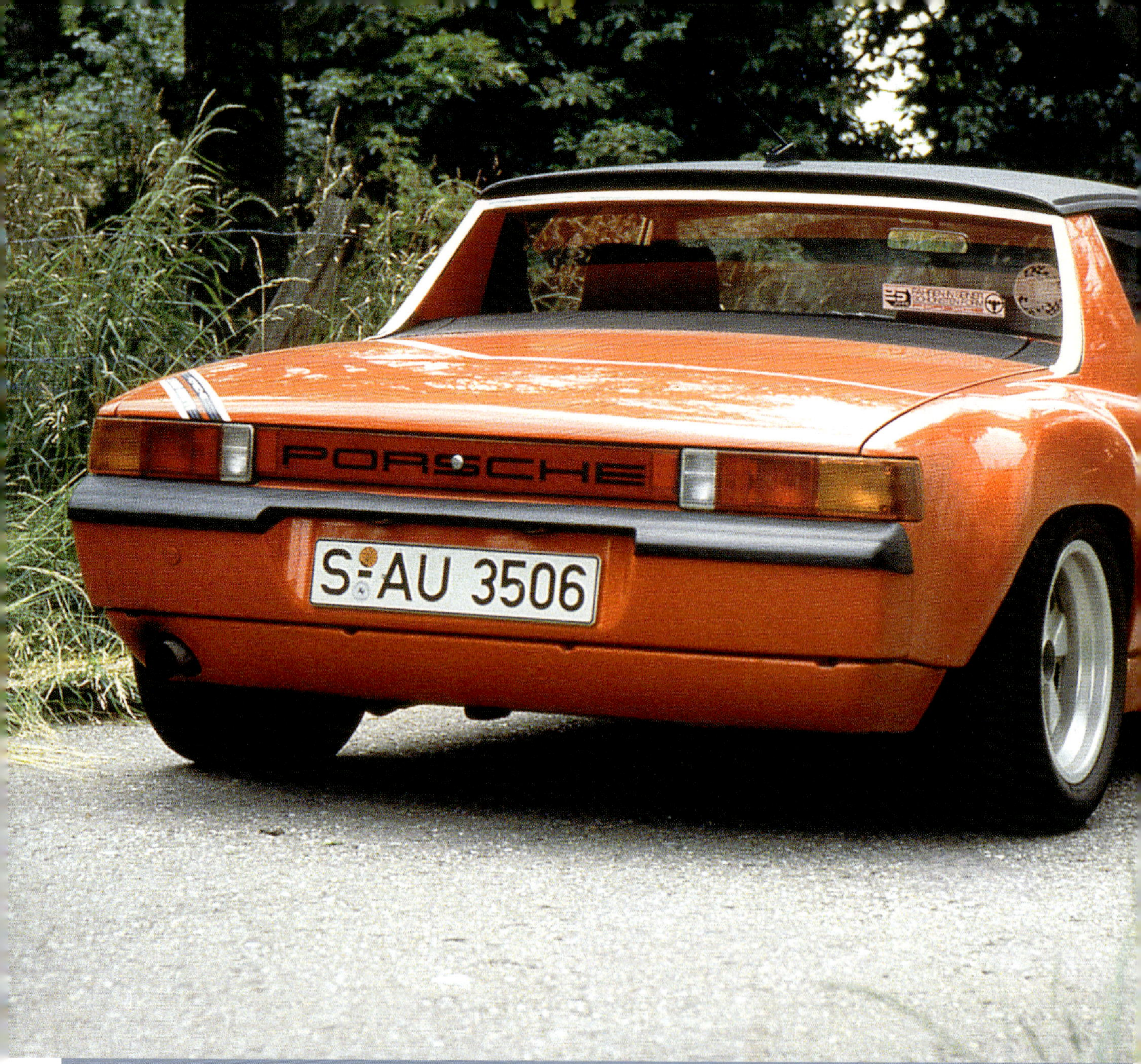
PORSCHE
S-AU 3506

Standard colour schemes, 1972 MY

Standard coachwork colours
Adriatic Blue, Chrome Yellow, Light Ivory, Signal Orange, Irish Green, Tangerine, Bahia Red, and Willow Green

Special coachwork colours
Black, Gold Metallic, Silver Metallic, and Gemini Metallic

Seats
Black, Beige or Brown leatherette. Inlays in Black, Beige or Brown leatherette basketweave or corduroy.

Carpet
Black, Beige or Brown needle loom or pile-type carpet.

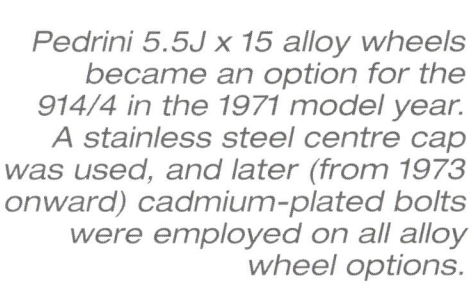

Pedrini 5.5J x 15 alloy wheels became an option for the 914/4 in the 1971 model year. A stainless steel centre cap was used, and later (from 1973 onward) cadmium-plated bolts were employed on all alloy wheel options.

The 914/4 with S-pack in a glamorous setting in the South of France.

engine at elevated revs, swallowing whole chains of bends in third when a four-pot engine's din would have you shifting up.

"It's not just the euphony and smoothness of this engine that distinguish it. It's quiet, too; a surprise given its proximity. In general, this is a refined car, and when the roof is off but the windows wound up, there is little draught to disturb your coiffure."

The same four-cylinder car in the Maritime Alps. As one journalist said: "The secret of a Porsche's effectiveness on the road has always been due to a successful mixing of all the elements that make up 'performance' in its widest sense, and not just brute power."

The 1972 model year

As usual, the next season's models were presented in September of the previous year, so the 1972 model year cars made their debut in autumn 1971. A number of detail improvements were incorporated, along with some modifications to meet the latest exhaust emission laws.

The latter problem was dealt with via the four-cylinder EA80 engine. This was essentially the same as the previous W80 unit, with the same bore and stroke, capacity, compression ratio, and even power. It did, however, lose a fraction of its maximum torque, but this was more than compensated for by coming in further down the rev range. The six-cylinder unit was allowed to continue unchanged.

Body changes included a shorter rear valance to both reduce drag and prevent the apron acting as a snow shovel. It also helped cooling air get to the lower part of the engine; something two small underbody guides were introduced for at the same time. There was better insulation around the engine and, slightly later in the year, a new style and location (though still in the rear compartment) for the wheel jack.

A couple of pieces of contemporary Japanese advertising.

Gold paintwork became available for 1971. This 914/6 looks the part with its Fuchs alloys providing a good contrast to the coachwork colour.

For 1972, the 911 range went to 2.4 litres, taking it even further away from the 914 series in terms of performance. This is the 911 Targa.

Despite the skinny tyres, handling was universally praised. Note the location of the second horn (optional on the 914/4), and the factory-fitted aerial. The works supplied Blaupunkt radios, or, occasionally Becker models, on the six-cylinder cars.

By far the most important feature of the 1972 model year was the introduction of an adjustable passenger seat, thus rendering the controversial footrest unnecessary. Although it was deleted, Porsche placed a foam pad under the carpet to perform a similar task. Seatbelts were changed to the more convenient retractable type a few months later.

The steering column was now standardized across the range, sourced from Volkswagen. The wiper/screen washer controls were moved to a stalk on the steering column for the 914/4, as they had been on the 914/6 since production began. Likewise, the 914/6 ignition switch was moved from the fascia to the right-hand side of the column. The steering wheel rim on the six

The interior of the four-cylinder car (note the Wolfsburg crest on the steering wheel) dating from the 1972 model year. An adjustable passenger seat was the most important change made to the cockpit that year, although vents were also added at each end of the fascia panel.

Dashboard of the four-cylinder car for the 1972 season.

Home market price list & options, (in DM), September 1971

914/4	12,250
914/4 with S-pack	12,995
914/6	19,980
Special paint from list	450
Special paint not listed	650

Option prices (including tax)

	914	*914/6*
M485 Pressure cast wheels 5.5Jx15 with 165 SR15 tyres	650	–
M485 Pressure cast wheels 5.5Jx15 with 165 HR15 tyres	–	799
M976 Chrome wheels 5.5Jx15 with whitewall 165 HR15 tyres	–	299
M577 Gurtel tyres 165 SR15 (as used in the S-pack)	70	-
M433 Halogen H3 driving lights	28	28
M571 Foglights	50	50
M570 Third, centre seat	45	45
M166 Seatbelt (for M570)	50	50
M549 Three-point safety belts (left and right)	111	111

was changed from hard rubber to leather as standard (it had been an option previously).

New air vents were added at each end of the fascia panel, which meant a slightly smaller glovebox and deletion of the 914/4's central vent. Modified wiring allowed the headlights to stay down when the sidelights were switched on, and there was a larger interior mirror. A roof headliner became standard on all models, and the vinyl used for trimming changed in texture from a smooth leathergrain to fine basketweave.

According to the Porsche catalogue, the 914/4 with the optional S-pack had 5.5J x 15 wheels with 165 SR15 tyres (the 914/6 tyres were HR rated), chrome bumpers, a black vinyl roof, two-tone horns, a leather-covered steering wheel, and pile-type carpet instead of needle loom – all standard features on the six-cylinder model.

In the meantime, the standard 911 range for 1972 had received another engine size increase, this time to 2341cc, with three power ratings: 130, 165 and 190bhp. Porsche had already secured approval in the States for the 914/6s to be fitted with 2.4 litre engines for the 1972 model year but, sadly the idea was not followed through when it was realized that the six-cylinder model was getting very close to the end of its shortlived production run.

The four-cylinder car in the USA

For the 1972 model year, the price of the 914/4 was listed at $3755. Early in 1972, the deutschmark stood at DM 3.2 to the dollar – it had been DM 4.0 in late 1969. Not raising the price of the 914 range much meant less profit for VW-Porsche, and the 914/6 became a special order vehicle in the States because of this. As a point of interest, at the same time, a 911T Targa was $7985 ($735 more than the coupé), and the top model, the

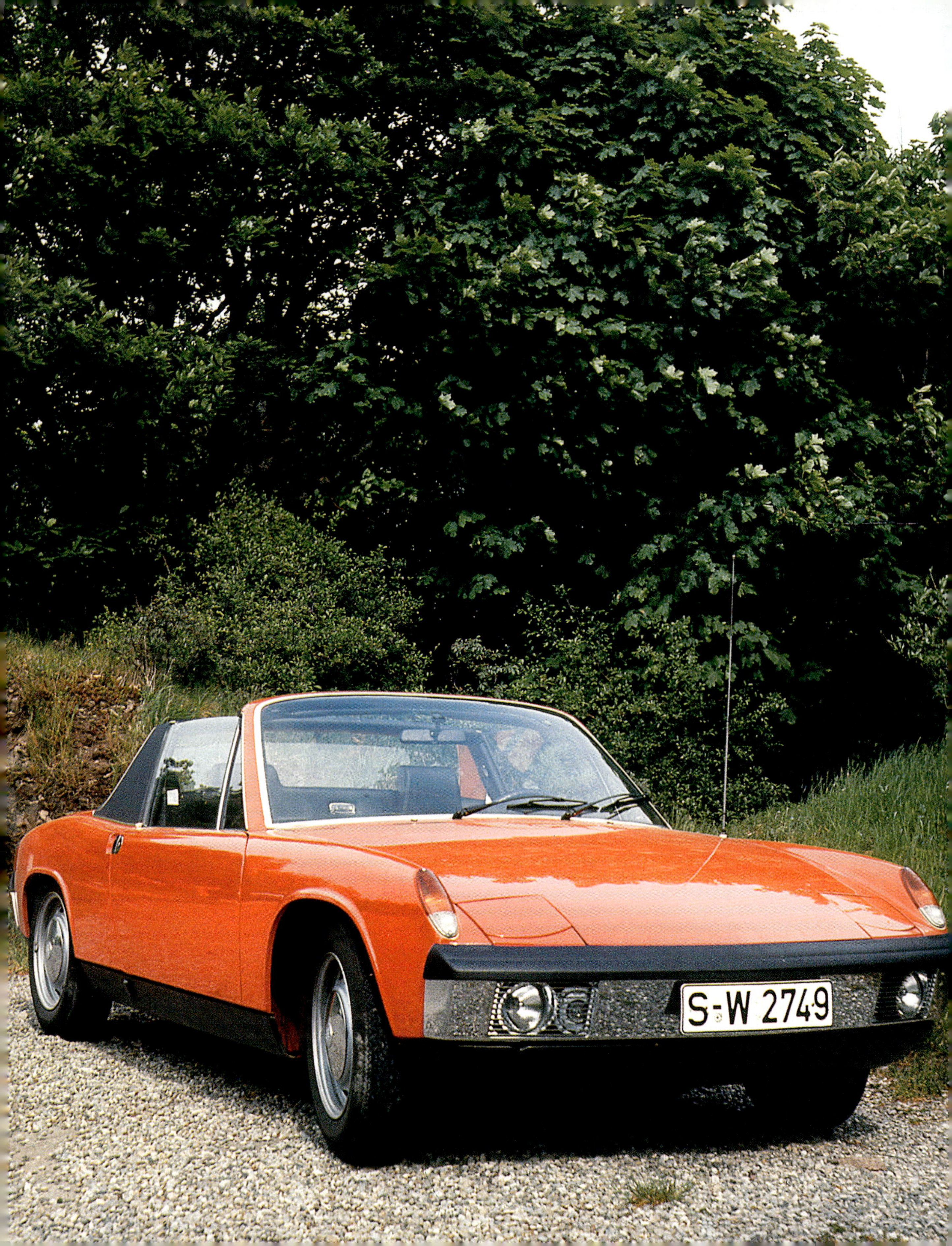
S-W 2749

914/6 production was dramatically cut back. Had it been cheaper and further developed (larger engines were considered), the 914/6 would have offered an excellent package for the enthusiastic driver. Instead, rather unfortunately, it was gradually phased out.

911S Targa, was priced at $10,230. The Appearance Group option for the 914 was $300.

In a February 1972 article, *Road & Track* noted: "The shift linkage is noticeably better than in previous 914s we've driven; it does not seem to be redesigned but rather more carefully assembled and adjusted.

"Surprisingly, the specifications for the 1972 engine list the same 8.2:1 compression ratio; power and torque are the same. The torque curve was the alteration. The minor modifications don't show up at all in the acceleration figures, which are unchanged ... Fuel consumption, however, is about 10% greater; we recorded 22.5mpg compared with 25.5 in our 1970 test. But since the engine now accepts regular fuel, running costs will be almost the same.

"The spacious, comfortable interior is slightly changed for 1972, with new fresh air vents, at each side of the dashboard, that work very effectively. The wiper and washer controls are now on a steering-column stalk, 911 style. The passenger's footrest is gone but the seat has been made fully adjustable fore and aft."

Whilst reviewing the Porsche range in May 1972, *Motor Trend* pulled no punches regarding the 914: "Poor relation, ugly duckling, cast aside by organized groups of *pur sang* Porsche enthusiasts as some sort of bastard offspring of a hasty mismatch between Porsche and the Volkswagen *werke*, the 914 series has had a rough time in its short life. Originally introduced with a choice of either the 911T engine or an injected version of the flat-four VW 411 Squareback engine, the six has been dropped from the normally available US line-up as being, among other things, too expensive for the market. Several variations on the 914/6 theme were considered and then dropped, including a special order 'GT' version with the S engine and flared fenders (for SCCA racing, aborted when that body disallowed the car for insufficient production numbers) and a high-buck, Ferrari-priced luxury number, dropped for lack of sufficient market."

Later, the writer criticized the seating, for although the passenger seat was now adjustable (it wasn't on the earlier models) it had very little lateral support. The gear selector arrangement with a dog-leg first also displeased, described as being "a bloody nuisance on the street, especially in the 914 which hasn't the suds to pull away from a slow roll in second gear."

In general, there were a number of complaints about the dogleg first, although, personally, the author likes this arrangement, having first encountered it in the Maserati Biturbo and, more recently, the Porsche 924.

At least the American journal could be praised for telling it like it was. All too often, modern magazines tend to overlook the less successful models of the prize marques, concentrating only on the vehicles that uphold their legendary status.

In the UK, by the way, the basic four-cylinder 914 was priced at £2302 for the 1972 season, while the 914/6 commanded £3527, or £3696 if it was equipped with a Sportomatic transmission.

Company news

Denis Jenkinson, with his ear always close to the ground, wrote the following for *MotorSport* in July 1972: "Since 1962 Porsche have been quietly, but steadily, building up a private research centre some miles west of Stuttgart near the small village of Weissach, beginning with a circular skidpan on which they could do tests in secret, and gradually enlarging the place with roads and test surfaces until they now have a large and complete circuit to test all manner of cars, even the Can-Am car, with a lap speed on the road course of 118mph [189kph]. At the same time as they built up the test track they began to build laboratory testing equipment, and in the last three and a half years this Research & Development Centre has been completed and is now in full working order, employing 500 workers and 80 engineers.

"It has taken ten years, three and a half of them very concentrated, and something like an investment of £8,000,000 in order to complete this very thorough and all-embracing Research & Development Centre, which can tackle the design, building, developing and testing of anything to do with engineering, not only automobile engineering, and can do research on anything from fibreglass processes, to special space-race metals, and from complete cars to tyres. The growth of the Weissach centre was concurrent with

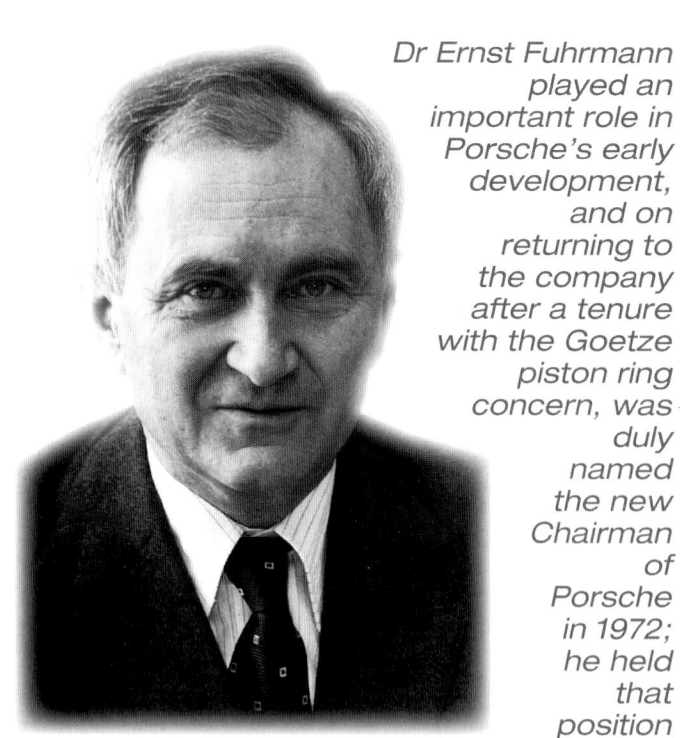

Dr Ernst Fuhrmann played an important role in Porsche's early development, and on returning to the company after a tenure with the Goetze piston ring concern, was duly named the new Chairman of Porsche in 1972; he held that position until 1980.

the all-out onslaught that Porsche made on sports car racing, culminating in the World Manufacturers' Championship for the legendary 917 Porsches, and the growth of the testing facilities was speeded up by the racing programme.

"In the management of the Porsche empire there have been some changes, and Dr Ferry Porsche and his sister Louis Piech and their families still own Porsche, but their sole interest now is in long-term business planning and adjustment of their investments. Since March 1972 all control of the engineering has been taken over by Dr Ing. Ernst Fuhrmann and the business and finance administration has been taken over by Dipl. Kfm. Heinz Branitzki, these two men now being fully responsible for the future of Porsche. Fuhrmann worked at Porsche as a designer from 1947-1956 and then went to the Goetze Werke engineering firm until he returned to Porsche in 1971, and Branitzki was at Carl Zeiss before joining Porsche in 1965.

"Dr Fuhrmann is also looking ahead and can foresee the end of the automobile as we know it today, especially the sports car type of vehicle, and the small-production quality car like the Porsche."

This final statement was an interesting observation, and may have been directed at the 914/6 in particular. Production of the 914/6 was cut back dramatically to let the car sell out; there was simply no profit in so few sales; the figures had all been calculated on a far higher volume and, of course, a weaker deutschmark. However, as is often the case, when the 914/6 was finally deleted from the range, it changed hands at a premium price!

On 1 March 1972 the Porsche company had been reorganized, with all of the members of the Porsche family withdrawing from the car-producing side of the business. Three companies – Dr Ing h c F Porsche KG in Zuffenhausen, the VW-Porsche VG in Ludwigsburg, and the Porsche Konstruktion KG in Salzburg – all came under the control of a holding company, Porsche GmbH, registered in Stuttgart. Ferry Porsche and Louise Piech were joint Managing Directors, with Ernst Fuhrmann responsible for engineering, and Heinz Branitzki appointed Finance Director. The Sales Director was L Schmidt, Development Manager was H Bott; H Kurtz was head of production, and K Kalkbrenner was in charge of the Personnel Department.

As far as the car business in Zuffenhausen was concerned (Porsche per se in the eyes of the public), all of the members of the Porsche family withdrew officially, with Fuhrmann (named as Chairman) and Branitzki in charge. The reorganization was completed when Porsche became a joint stock company, Dr Ing h c F Porsche AG.

After the family split, Butzi Porsche formed Porsche Design, a highly successful consultancy. Ferdinand Piech went to VW-Audi and helped to develop Audi's four-wheel drive system, leading to the world-beating Audi Quattro. Before too long he had become head of the German company ...

In the meantime, important events were taking place at Volkswagen. Kurt Lotz resigned in September 1971, with Rudolf Leiding (a VW stalwart) taking over on 1 October. Volkswagen had once again lost money in 1971, and in 1972 Opel took its position as the leading German manufacturer in terms of output. However, some consolation was to be had from the fact that the 914 became Germany's best-selling sports car, ironically, taking the title from the Opel GT.

Leiding was a production specialist who obviously supported the new direction brought about by the K70. Originally an Audi-NSU prototype, it catapulted Volkswagen into the world of front-wheel drive, water-cooled machines. Introduced as the VW K70 in 1971, it signified the end of the NSU marque, generating uncertainty about the future of an air-cooled, mid-engined vehicle in the line-up. How long would it be before the 914 was axed?

Sadly, these ladies were never listed by Porsche as official factory options, otherwise sales of the 914/6 might have been substantially higher! Most of the six-cylinder cars, like this one, date from the 1970 model year.

Review of the series to date

Wheels magazine noted in March 1970: "As for the individualistic shape of this mid-engined Porsche and/or VW; hate it or hug it but very few will ignore it. Running one of the earliest 914 tests – on a pre-production prototype, in fact – we were even blinked at by new 911s. No finer tribute can a Porsche pay – particularly since no 911 would be caught dead blinking at a VW.

"In short, Porsche people consider this one of theirs, even if the more common class will carry VW four-cylinder engines and VW wheels. After all, those are descended from a Professor Porsche design, too. More directly, perhaps, than the two-litre six."

A large number of improvements were made ready for the 1973 914s. Photographed in June 1972 (three months before the 1973 model year was launched), this is the 1.7 litre version. Note the new Fuchs wheels.

Sadly, the journalist for the magazine was mistaken; the 911 driver must have noticed something wrong with the car and was trying to warn him! Rightly or wrongly, Porscheophiles refused to accept the 914 as a 'real' Porsche simply because it wore a VW-Porsche badge. Call it snobbery or whatever you like, but there was no doubt that it hurt sales, which is particularly ironic in view of the fact that the foundation stone for the Porsche empire had been VW.

The car soon acquired the nickname 'VolksPorsche' (later shortened to VoPo – the name given to the old East German border guards!), which horrified the marketing people. Even in America, where the VW badge was hidden, enthusiasts were well informed via various journals that the car they were driving was not exactly a no compromise thoroughbred Stuttgart machine, though, for the price, it should have been.

The six-cylinder car alone could have carried off the high price as it was a nice package, but the four-cylinder version totally killed its sales potential: the VG partnership should really have realized that such a great difference in price between the 914/4 and 914/6 was always going to spell trouble for the larger-engined version, especially when the cars looked so similar. Few people were going to buy a vehicle that cost the same as a Jaguar E-type but carried VW badges, a marque associated at that time with homely economy saloons rather than high performance sports cars. In the British, Australian and Japanese markets, an additional problem for the six was that a right-hand drive conversion cost three times the difference between the 914/6 and a bigger-engined 911T already with rhd steering. Plus, despite the mid-engined layout, in everyday driving situations the handling advantage over the 911 was fairly marginal at best.

Initial sales of the 914/6 had looked promising, but demand quickly tailed off. In the first year of production 2657 examples were built – well under the expected 6000 sales worldwide. During the second year, it was obvious that the six-cylinder machine was not going to sell and production was dramatically cut back for the 1972 model year. Indeed, only 229 cars were constructed.

Sales in Britain were very disappointing. Between January 1970 and June 1973, only 242 914s were imported, just 11 of which were the six-cylinder model. Officially, the 914/6 didn't appear in the 1973 model year Porsche line-up, and total prouction for the type amounted to just 3318 units.

Preview of the 1973 model year

With no 914/6, a new four-cylinder, two-litre model was intended to take its place and, to comply with ever stricter emissions regulations in the USA, the American market received a new 1.7 litre unit. A new transmission was intended to answer some of the criticism levelled at the old one.

Of the other main features, matt black bumpers were now standard across the range, making the base car look less austere, although, in the USA, rubber bumper guards were added at the front and a chrome blade remained optional; different alloy wheel designs from both Fuchs and Mahle were made available.

There were, of course, a number of other changes, and these are covered in detail in the next chapter. However, it remained to be seen whether or not they made any difference to sales …

www.veloce.co.uk

4
End of
the line

"Interestingly, even Porsche now admits that the first 914s were not up to its standards. While that may not mean much to the early owners, the newer ones can be content to know that Porsche's admitted failure caused them to spend a great deal of time further developing the car. Now some say the 914 may be the best car Porsche makes. While that may be an overstatement, at least the price is Porsche's most attractive." – *Motor Trend*, April 1974 issue.

After the 1972 model year, the 914 range became slightly less complicated. With no 914/6 in the line-up, a new four-cylinder, two-litre model was introduced to bridge the gap between the old 914/4 model and the cheapest 911; to satisfy ever stricter emissions regulations in the USA, there was a new 1.7 litre unit for the American market.

The two-litre power unit was essentially an enlarged version of the existing flat-four. With the bore increased by 4mm to 94mm, and the stroke lengthened from 66mm to 71mm, the new capacity was 1971cc, which added up to 100bhp and 115lbft of torque in European trim, enough to take the car from 0-60 in 9.1 seconds, and on to a top speed of 116mph (186kph).

Engines destined for America had a touch less power and torque due to a lower compression ratio (7.6:1 instead of 8.0:1). However, both engines retained the Bosch D-Jetronic manifold pressure controlled fuel-injection, and a number of other features from the original unit.

American engines were given the GA95 designation, whilst those for other markets had the code GB100. In both cases, the bulkhead between the power unit and the passenger compartment was covered with insulating material to help prevent heat and engine noise from entering the cockpit.

To fall into line with the latest regulations, US 1.7 litre engines were modified and given the new type code EB72. The most obvious change was a lowering of the compression ratio from 8.2:1 to just 7.3:1. Naturally, this reduced maximum power output, which dropped from 80bhp to 72. Torque also suffered: 90lbft on the EB engine compared to 99 on the old EA unit.

There was also a new transmission to answer some of the critics. The type 914/12 transmission was fitted across the range, and had a greatly simplified linkage with less components. Following the test of an early two-litre 914 for *Classic Cars* in 1995, Brian Palmer wrote: "I find myself curiously drawn to its looks, even though this defies all known aesthetic guidelines. Maybe we needed a US West Coast setting rather than a damp, cold autumnal day in Milton Keynes."

However, perhaps the most interesting point to be raised in the article was the almost universal criticism of the gearbox on this four-cylinder car. In a contemporary test, though, *Motor Trend* was a little more complimentary: "Porsche gears are noted for their smoothness, and the 914S has a redesigned gear linkage that has eliminated the former shifting vagueness on this model. Now the gear slots are precise, and one

continued page 97

The latest generation of 914. Very occasionally, the cars had a vinyl covering down the A-posts and front section of the roof.

The Volkswagen two-litre, four-cylinder engine was capable of producing up to 100bhp. It weighed around 145kg (320lb), significantly less than the six, and new engine mountings and extra insulation around the power unit added refinement.

The new engine gave the 914-2.0 some quite respectable performance figures. Top speed was in the region of 116mph (186kph) – not far short of the old Porsche-powered 914.

A 914 in its element: long sweeping bends on open roads. The mid-engined layout endowed the series with excellent roadholding and handling

New Fuchs alloy wheels were a feature of the 1973 model year although they continued to be used until production ended. This is the 914-2.0 model

With the end of the 914/6 model, the 914-2.0 took its place in the 1973 model year line-up. Note the VW steel wheels (these are the optional 5.5J rim version) and the shorter rear apron introduced for 1972. The standard VW wheel changed to a new design for the following season.

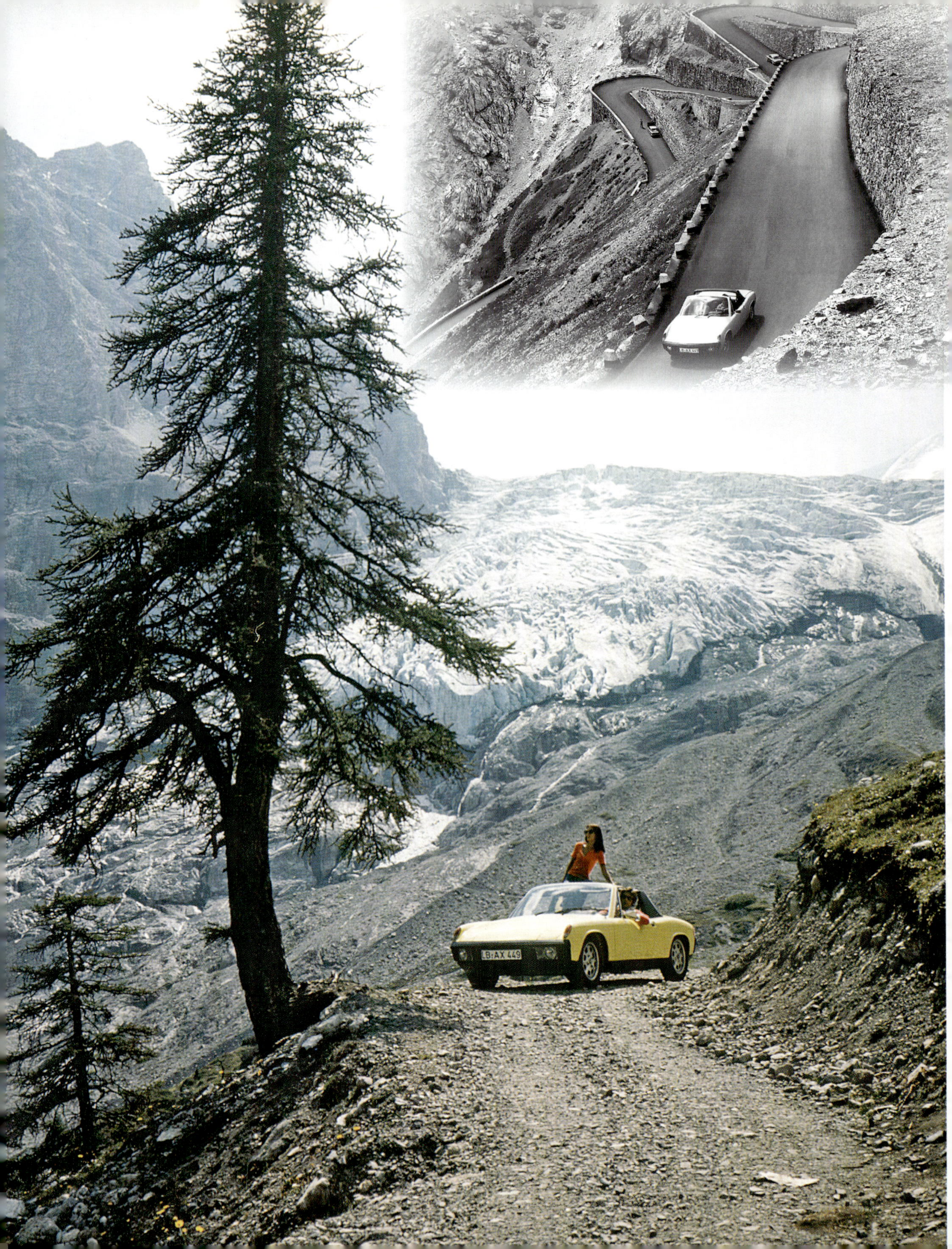
LB·AX 449

Matt black bumpers were fitted across the range, although chrome blades remained an option for all markets. Grilles surrounding the auxilliary lighting were still retained, although were now made of plastic to reduce cost.

quickly gets used to the five-speed pattern, and should never miss the right gear or make a slow shift on the all-synchro box."

Two different alloy wheel designs from Fuchs and Mahle were made available. The 5.5J x 15 Fuchs forged alloy wheel was similar to the usual Fuchs design, and would continue to be used until the series went out of production. The new eight-spoke 5.5J x 15 Mahle cast alloy wheel was similar to the Pedrini design, thus making the latter redundant; it, too, continued to be used until production ended. At the same time, front and rear anti-roll bars were listed as an option; these allowed the ride to be softened for greater comfort without compromising handling.

Matt black bumpers were now standard across the range, making the base car look less austere, although, in the USA, rubber bumper guards were added at the front, and a chrome blade remained optional via the Appearance Group package in America, or as a pure cost option in other markets. To match the colour scheme of the bumpers, black badges were used at the rear. The metal badges read '914' then '2.0' or '1.7' in the USA, or '914 VW Porsche' followed by the engine size elsewhere. In addition, the badges on the engine cover changed from gold to chrome, although this remained a feature unique to cars destined for American shores.

Headlights could now be specified with H-4 bulbs as an option in the Sport pack, replacing the standard Tungsten bulbs. The US still had sealed beams, but they were now at least slightly stronger – the use of Halogen bulbs was not allowed in America at the time. Cars delivered to France continued to have yellow glass, whatever the bulb.

Inside the car, a conventional handbrake replaced the original to make its use more agreeable, mounted

Opposite: Porsche commissioned a whole series of stunning shots with the 914-2.0, but few have been seen before. By comparison, some of the pictures used in the catalogues were quite boring.

lower but in roughly the same place close to the sill. In view of the increased speed capability of the 914-2.0, a 150mph (or 250kph) speedometer was fitted, even though this figure was somewhat optimistic.

Following on from the steering column change for the 1972 model year, an intermittent wipe became available for 1973. For the two-litre car, there was also the option of a centre console with three auxiliary gauges – a clock, oil temperature gauge, and voltmeter. If not specified, the oil temperature gauge was fitted in the left-hand dial in the main group, as it had been in the 914/6 model.

An upholstered hinged lid was now available for the moulded tray between the two seats if a third seat option was not taken up. To reduce production costs, the old VW chrome window winders were dropped in favour of black plastic ones, and the interior door handles changed from chrome to black to match. A further saving was made by supplying a six-piece tool kit instead of an eight-piece (incidentally, the 914/6 had had a 15-piece kit).

The model in Europe

At the same time as 1973 model year details were issued, Porsche furnished its dealers with the prices and specifications of competitive vehicles. A selection of the more interesting models are listed in the table on page 102, although, in reality, not all of them posed a true threat, even in this condensed listing. For instance, the buyer of a Mercedes-Benz coupé is unlikely to be in the market for a mid-engined sports car. It does, however, throw up one or two points. It is often easy to forget in England that the Lotus Europa was expensive

continued page 101

Right: The matt black bumpers prompted Porsche to change the badge on the tail to black. Note the latest badge arrangements with the engine size displayed, this is the 1.7 litre.

(and above) A couple of publicity shots with LB-SC 717 in more relaxed settings

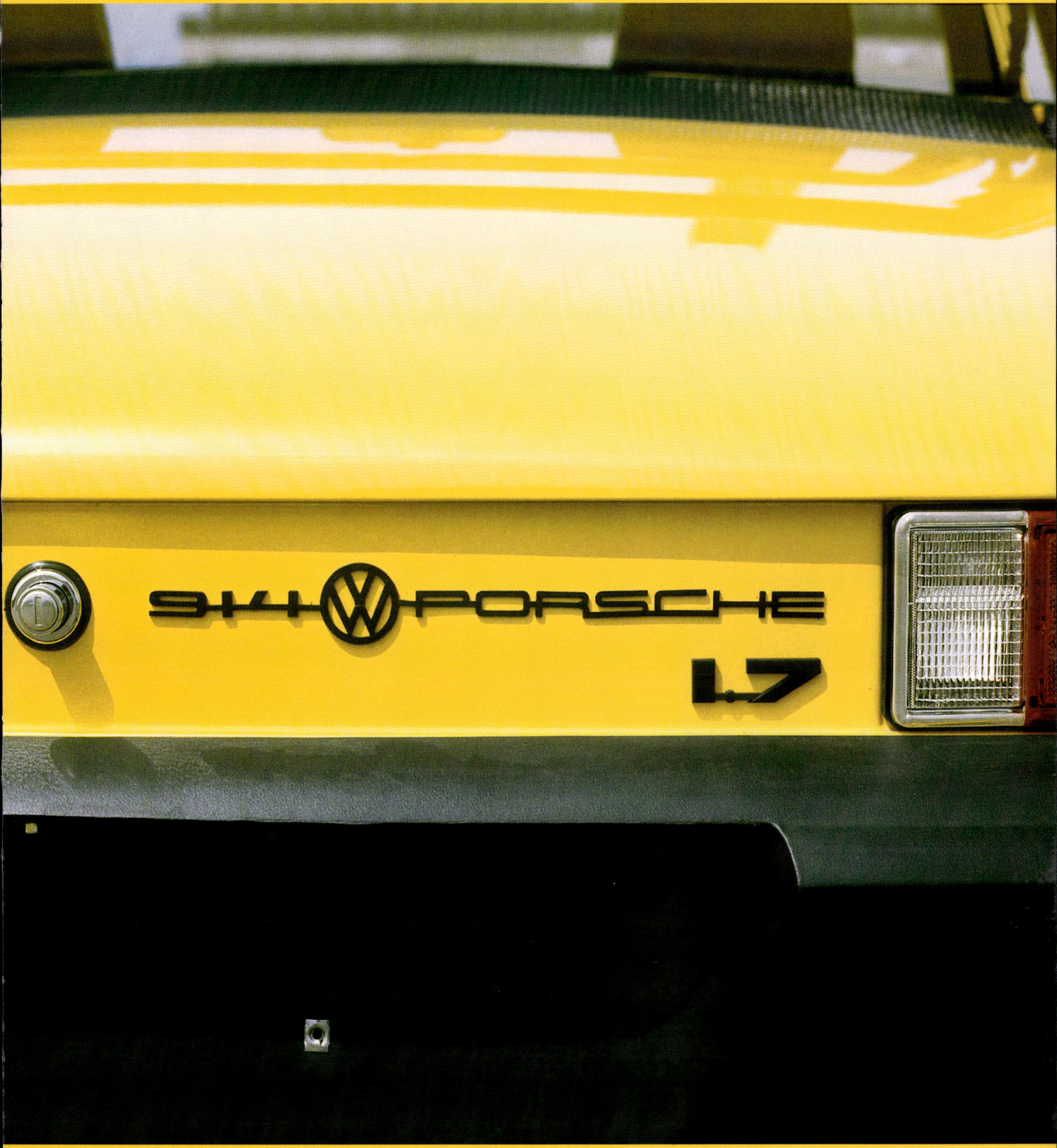
914
PORSCHE
1.7

Home market price list (in DM) & options, August 1972 (1973 MY)

1.7 model	13,360
2.0 model	13,760
Comfort package	400
Sport package	650
Comfort and Sport pack combined	990
Special paint from list	480
Special paint not listed	750

Options:

M102	Heated rear screen	105
M166	Seatbelt for M570 (not supplied in Comfort pack)	55
M285	Chrome bumper	300
M404	Anti-roll bars (as used in Sport pack)	300
M485	Pressure cast wheels 5.5J x 15 (not supplied in Sport pack)	615
M549	Three-point safety belts	118
M568	Tinted glass (except rear)	288
M570	Third, centre seat (as in Comfort pack)	48

The front compartment contained the fuel tank, spare wheel (with tool kit inside the well, although the jack was housed in the rear compartment), window washer system and, if air conditioning was fitted, a condensor. Both luggage spaces had grey carpet on the floor.

as a fully built car (it could be bought in kit form in the UK to avoid expensive purchase tax). In fact, in America, it was nearly $1500 dearer than a 914-2.0, despite being a slower machine.

The Comfort package included pile carpet, a leather-rimmed sports steering wheel, leather gearlever

A new option for the two-litre machine was this centre console. The uppermost dial was a clock, with an oil temperature gauge in the middle, and voltmeter at the bottom.

Marque	Model	PS	Price (in DM)
Porsche	914-1.7	80	13,360
	914-2.0	110	13,760
	911 T	130	23,480
	911 E	165	27,775
	911 S	190	31,500
	Carrera RS	210	33,000
	911T Targa	130	25,700
	911E Targa	165	29,995
	911S Targa	190	33,720
Alfa Romeo	GT1600	109	14,490
	2000GTV	131	16,790
	GTA Junior	100	18,950
	1600 Spider	109	14,490
	2000 Spider	131	16,790
BMW	3.0 CS	180	28,950
	3.0 CSi	200	30,650
Fiat	Dino Coupé	180	29,500
	124 Sp. Spider	100	12,300
Jaguar	E-type V12 dhc	272	36,360
Lancia 2000HF		125	20,750

Marque	Model	PS	Price (in DM)
Lotus	Europa TC	106	19,314
	Elan +2S 130	126	24,642
	Elan Sprint	126	20,868
Matra	530 SX	75	11,690
	530 LX	75	12,890
Mercedes-Benz	250C	130	20,313
	280CE	185	22,977
	350SL	200	31,413
MG	MGB-GT	95	13,990
	MGB	95	11,950
Opel	Opel GT/J	90	10,990
	Opel GT	90	12,845
Triumph	GT6	96	12,950
	TR6	152	16,025
	Stag	147	23,890
Volvo	1800E	124	21,900
	1800ES	124	25,150

boot, two-tone horns, a centre console (with voltmeter, clock, and oil temperature gauge), a centre armrest/storage compartment with upholstered lid, and black vinyl-covered roll bar. The Sport package included forged light alloy wheels by Fuchs, front and rear anti-roll bars, and Halogen bulbs in the headlights.

For comparison, the contemporary Appearance Group Option package for the USA included a black vinyl-covered roll bar, two-tone horns, chrome bumpers, foglights, 5.5J x 15 steel wheels fitted with 165 SR15 tyres, a leather-rimmed steering wheel, pile carpet, centre console, and the centre armrest/storage compartment. The

continued page 107

Dashboard details of the two-litre machine.

A 1973 model year car with the Fuchs alloy wheels. Note the Ludwigsburg number plate and white headlight surrounds, which changed to black the following year.

Another view of the same car, pictured in November 1972. The coachwork colour schemes and fashions are typically seventies style.

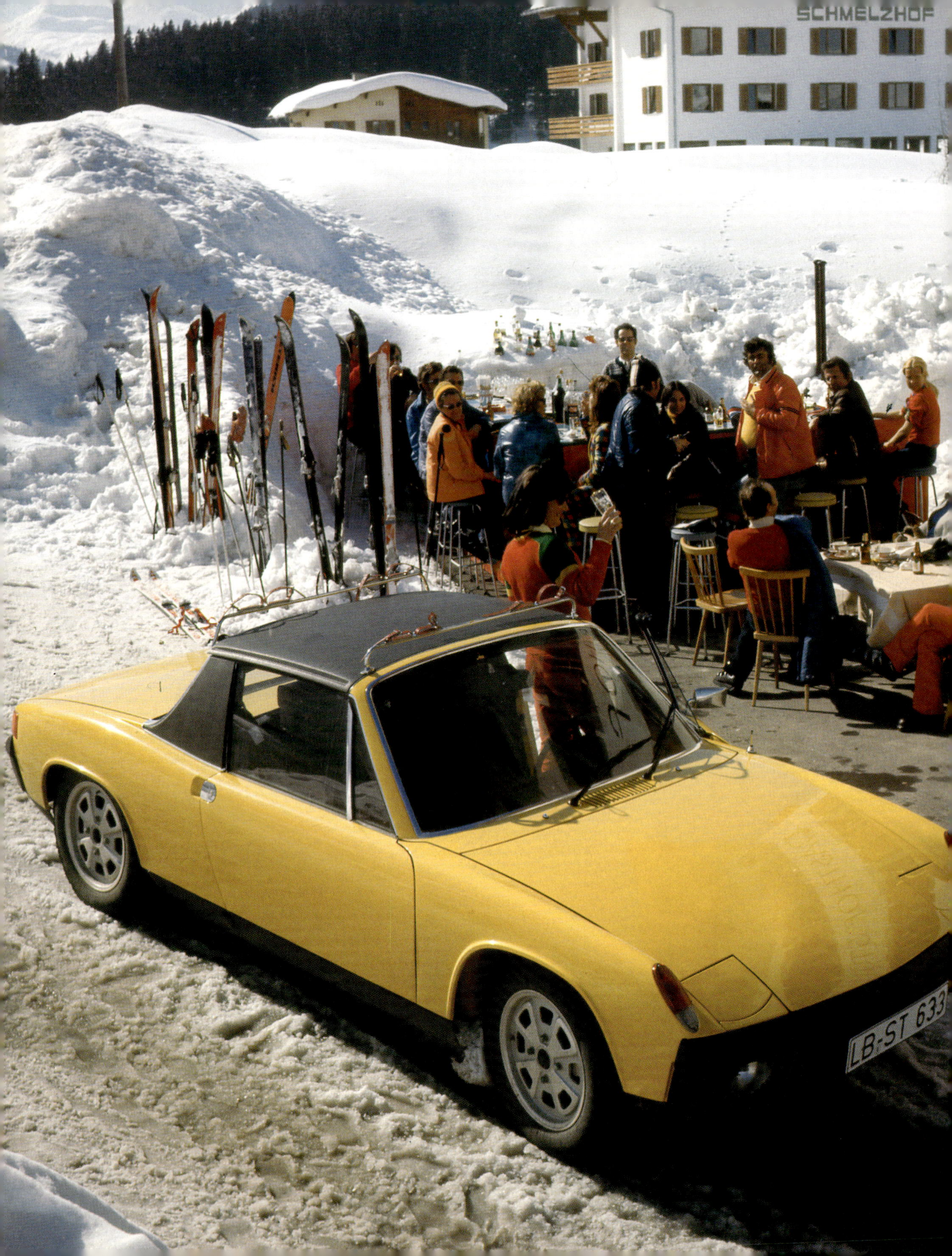
SCHMELZHOF
LB-ST 633

(and main pic) The fun theme was continued in these 1973 model year publicity photographs taken at various European skiiing resorts in the Alps. The whole idea was that the car should appeal to a younger generation. Combined with various improvements, the result was the best season of 914 sales to date.

With the six-cylinder machine dropped from the range, the 914 series was now far cheaper than the 911s. Above all, it was promoted as an affordable fun car.

A couple of 1973 model year cars at St Moritz in the Swiss Alps.

Another shot from the same series as the previous picture. Note the skis anchored to the roof, something the Targa top would have made quite difficult in reality. A roof rack was not a listed option, by the way.

vast majority of these items were standard on the two-litre model anyway, and surpassed in some instances, as with the wheels which were Fuchs alloys.

The 914-2.0

In January 1973, the American magazine, *Motor Trend*, announced the 914S with the two-litre version of the flat-four engine. It was noted that the 914S the magazine tested had a centre console, modified bumpers, anti-roll bars, and wider 165 SR15 tyres on 5.5 inch alloy wheels (which, in turn, gave the car a 25mm, or one inch, wider track at the front). The anti-roll bars (15mm diameter at the front, 16mm at the rear – the equivalent to 0.59 and 0.63in respectively) and forged Fuchs alloys were a standard feature on American two-litre models.

The 0-60 time was cut from 12.5 to 10.5 seconds, and top speed increased by 3mph (5kph) to a recorded 112mph (179kph). Thanks to the extra torque

The Americans were also treated to a higher profile advertising campaign. The 'Weather Porsche' emphasized its safe handling in all conditions. Note the rubber guards added to US-spec cars in 1973, even when the optional chrome bumper blade was specified.

The 'Action Porsche,' with performance as the main objective. Note the 'positive' Porsche stripes (ie the Porsche script is the same colour as the stripe itself) often fitted by dealers in the USA. These stripes, when fitted, changed to a 'negative' type for 1974.

City Porsche

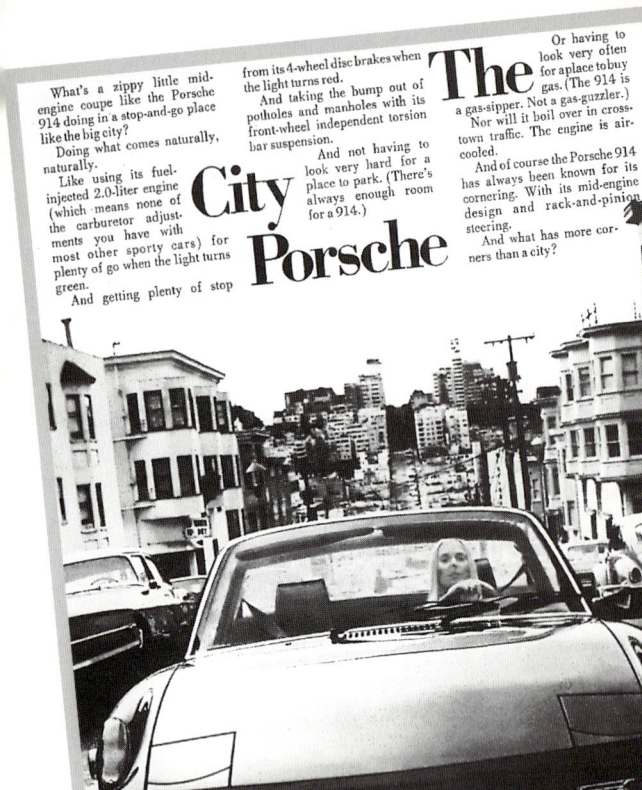

What's a zippy little mid-engine coupe like the Porsche 914 doing in a stop-and-go place like the big city?

Doing what comes naturally, naturally.

Like using its fuel-injected 2.0-liter engine (which means none of the carburetor adjustments you have with most other sporty cars) for plenty of go when the light turns green.

And getting plenty of stop from its 4-wheel disc brakes when the light turns red.

And taking the bump out of potholes and manholes with its front-wheel independent torsion bar suspension.

And not having to look very hard for a place to park. (There's always enough room for a 914.)

Or having to look very often for a place to buy gas. (The 914 is a gas-sipper. Not a gas-guzzler.) Nor will it boil over in cross-town traffic. The engine is air-cooled.

And of course the Porsche 914 has always been known for its cornering. With its mid-engine design and rack-and-pinion steering.

And what has more corners than a city?

And the 'City Porsche,' with fuel economy as its main attraction.

Opposite: Contemporary American lighting arrangements.

compared with the old 1.7 litre unit (108lbft at 3500rpm against 99lbft at the same engine speed), the car was also more tractable. However, fuel consumption suffered slightly, by about 2mpg on average.

The standard 914-1.7 was $4499 while the two-litre cost $5049. At the same time, a 911T Targa would have cost $8760. The 914S tag was soon dropped – Porsche didn't like the S designation being used – and the official 914-2.0 name was adopted by Porsche+Audi. Nevertheless, it should be noted that concessionaires in Britain and Australia called the 914-2.0 the 914SC, a title that, strangely, was allowed to continue.

The March 1973 edition of *Motor Trend* noted the following: "Driving is what a Porsche is all about; it is one brand of automobile that is sold primarily to the

A US spec 914 for the 1973 season.

true enthusiast. The 914 has acquired a good bit of refinement in its few short years of existence, and with the two-litre engine, the model now deserves to wear the Porsche emblem.

"The Targa style roadster has a removeable fibreglass top, which is easy to remove and install,
continued page 112

109

Another American specification 914 from 1973. Note the lack of a VW emblem on the hubcaps, the Porsche script on the engine cover, and the additional indicator light on the front wing. The Targa top was covered in a black textured coating, incidentally.

Right: A final shot from the 1973 season; one of a series of stunning publicity shots taken in November 1972.

Home market price list & options (in DM), February 1973

914-1.7	13,990
914-2.0	14,450
Comfort package	650
Sport package	990
Special colour on list	480
Special colour not listed	750

Options:

M404 Anti-roll bars (as in Sport pack)	300
M474 Bilstein shock absorbers	295
M485 Forged alloy wheels 5.5J x 15 (as in Sport pack)	650
M220 Sperr differential (80%)	650
M102 Heated rear screen	105
M285 Chrome bumper	300
M567 Laminated tinted windscreen	220
M568 Laminated tinted glass (except rear screen)	310
M089 Tinted windscreen	149
M572 Two-tone horn (as in Comfort pack)	32
M640 PVC underseal	60

Home market price list & options (in DM), February 1973

M166 Seatbelt for M570 (not supplied in Comfort pack)	55
M549 Three-point safety belts	118
M565 Padded steering wheel (as in Comfort pack)	110
M570 Third, centre seat (as in Comfort pack)	48
M591 Centre console (as in Comfort pack)	53
M490 Electric aerial	118
M095 Wolfsburg radio (MW/LW)	288
M097 Emden radio (MW/LW/UW)	365
M587 Hannover radio (MW/LW/UW) with automatic aerial	640
M433 Halogen driving lights	30
M551 Halogen headlights (as in Sport pack)	115
M571 Foglights	53
M659 Halogen fog and driving lights	83
M652 Intermittent wipers	29

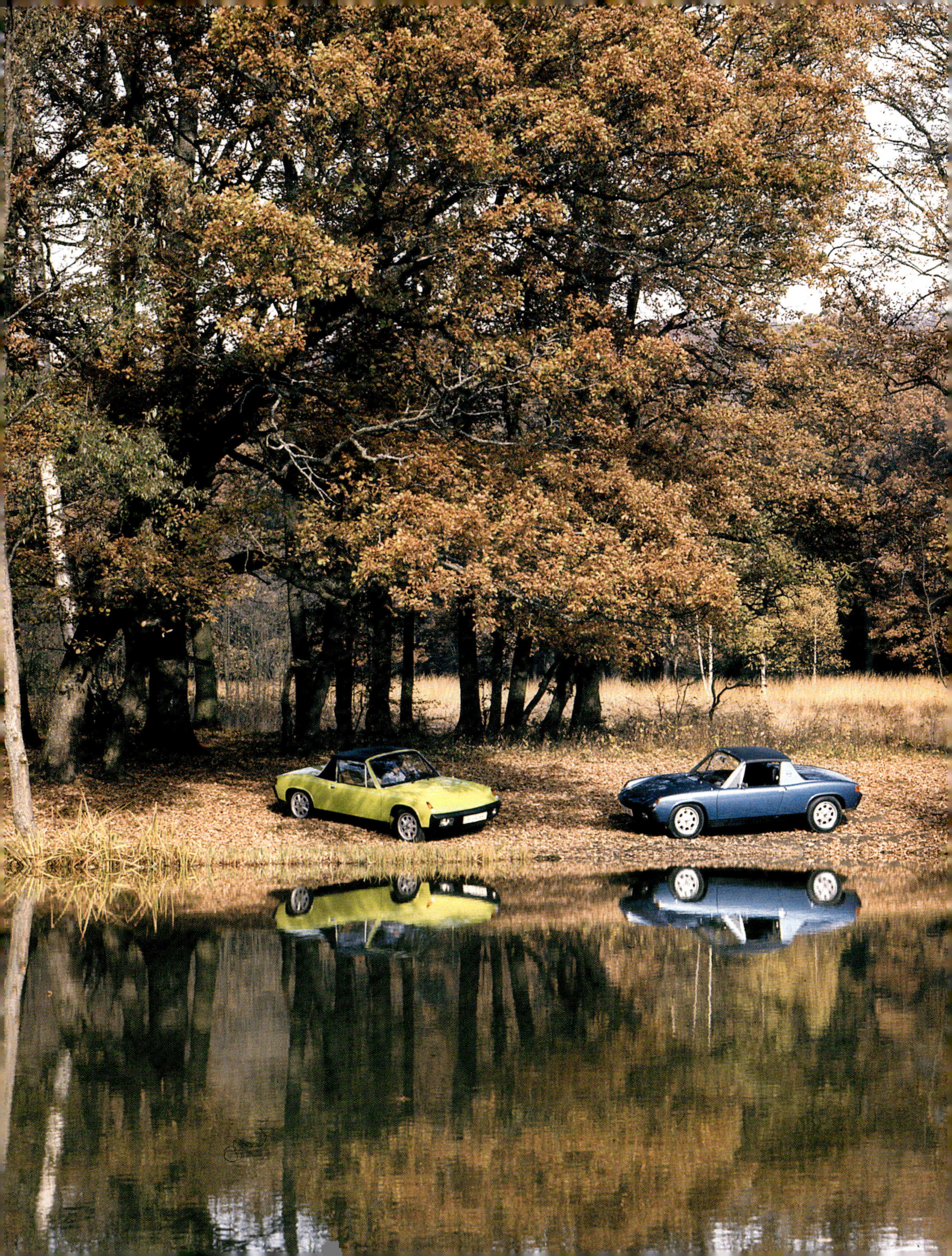

fits in the rear trunk for carry along convenience, but it does seem that it could be finished a little better on the outside. Inside, we discovered during a rainstorm that the roof leaks at the edges right onto the driver or passenger outboard arm. The top fits tightly, doesn't rattle, so we couldn't trace the pesky water hole to any flaw in the top – it just leaked.

"Summing up, the new 914S is simple. Drive it and drive it hard to appreciate its virtues. We think the car, be it a Porsche or a VW, embodies some of the best ideas from both companies. After all, the same man designed the original model of both makes."

Road Test magazine declared that the early cars had excessive noise levels, poor performance, roof leaks, and a gear linkage that left something to be desired, but that the early problems had "subsequently been taken care of ... The big improvement in the 914 came with the introduction of the two-litre model early last year, with little changing since but the price."

In conclusion it said: "The 914, then, can be looked upon as both the wave of the future and the 911 of a few years ago, to which it is now similarly priced. When the 914 is seen for what it is: the best combination of performance, handling, fuel economy and utility available in a sports car today – a mantle the original 911 would have been hard put to lay claim to in its time, things are put properly into perspective."

Midway through the 1973 model year, the treadplates were changed from aluminium to black plastic to further cut costs, though there were improvements to hush the criticism of owners with leaking roofs. The side windows and their frames were slightly modified and, later in the year, the Targa top mountings and seals were revised. Cars sent to the United States now featured steel door beams to comply with the most recent Federal regulations.

Thanks to the new two-litre 914 and improvements to the range in general, the 1973 model year was to be the 914's most successful sales period, with annual production ending just 10 per cent short of the original target of 30,000 units a year. With most of the cars going to America, this was no mean feat, as the exchange rate was now less than DM 2.5 to the dollar.

The 1974 model year
The Volkswagen Type 412 had been introduced for the 1973 model year. It was available as either a two- or four-door saloon, or an estate car, and initially retained the engine of the 411 (Type 4). The 412 power unit went to 1795cc (93mm bore x 66mm stroke) for 1974 in the heavier four-door and estate models, and it was

continued page 117

Standard colour schemes, 1973 & 1974 MY
Standard coachwork colours
Chrome Yellow, Light Ivory, Signal Orange, Bahia Red, Summer Yellow, Forest Green, Olympic Blue, Phoenix Red, and Ravenna Green

Special coachwork colours
Black, Metallic Chrome Yellow, Metallic Marathon Blue, Delphi Green Metallic, Silver Metallic, and Metallic Ocean Blue

Seats
Black, Beige or Brown leatherette. Inlays in Black, Beige or Brown leatherette basketweave or corduroy

Carpet
Black, Beige or Brown needle loom or pile-type carpet.

Notes: The brown listed on interior colours for 1971, 1972, 1973 and 1974 was a mahogany-type brown.

The interior of the 914. Note the black door handles and window winders, as well as the upholstered lid for the centre compartment. Note also the red ignition key intended for the starter only; the black key, also supplied with the car, was the master key.

Changes for the 1974 model year were confined mainly to engine specifications and reducing production costs. The new 914-1.8 is nearest the camera with the latest design of standard Volkswagen wheels, whilst in the background is the two-litre model.

Overleaf: The 1974 model year was the last season in which this style of bumper was seen. A chrome bumper blade was still an option until the new bumper design was introduced for 1975. By now, the smaller engine had been increased in size from 1.7 to 1.8 litres, although the two-litre capacity was unchanged.

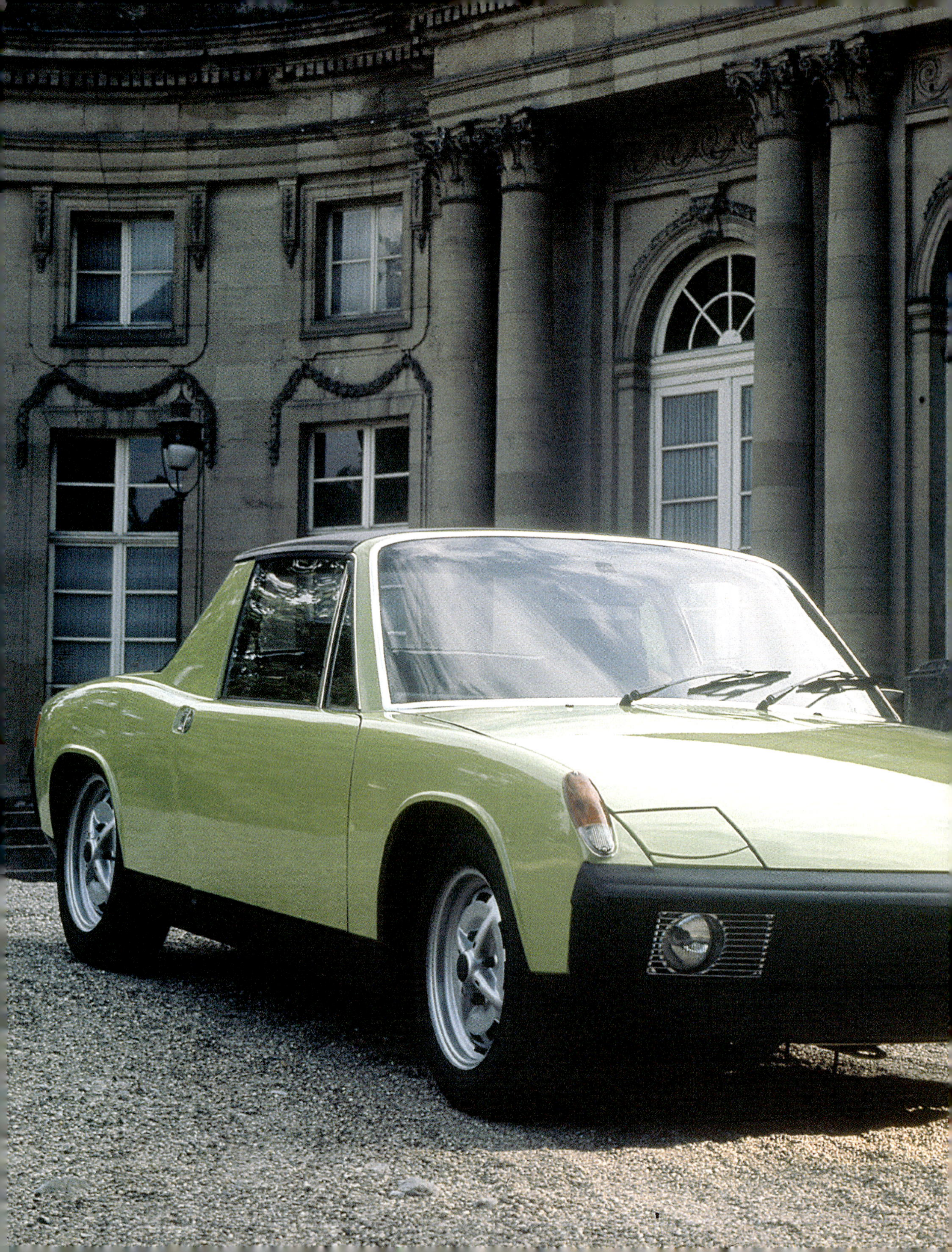

(and overleaf) A couple of tasteful publicity shots from the 1974 season.

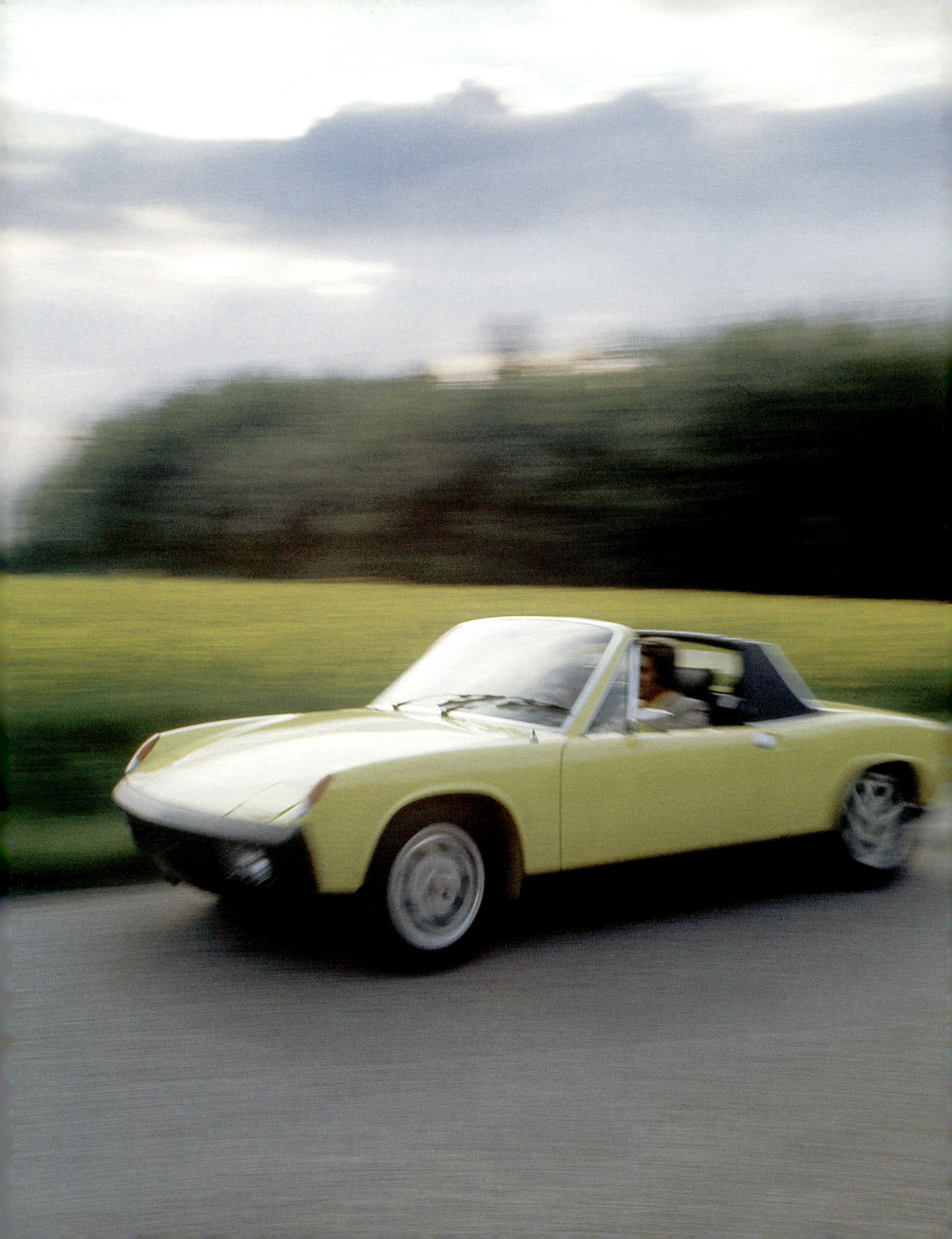

also used in the Transporter light commercial series. The same lump replaced the 1.7 litre engine for the 914 series, too.

There were two versions, one for America (the EC76) and one for other, mainly European, markets (the AN85). The American engine, with Bosch L-Jetronic airflow controlled fuel-injection, was sadly suffocated by Federal exhaust emission regulations. Introduced slightly later than the European-spec unit, in November 1973, it produced just 76bhp at 4800rpm – less power than the original 1.7 litre engine had despite both a larger capacity and bigger valves – and torque was also down.

The AN85 engine was not subjected to such strict rules and, realizing that enthusiastic drivers in Europe would not be impressed by such meagre bhp figures, the VG decided to produce the 1.8 litre unit equipped with two twin-choke Webers running on a far higher compression ratio (8.6:1 against just 7.3:1 in the States). This added up to a far livelier 85bhp and 105lbft of torque.

The standard Volkswagen wheel design was changed to that used by the Kafer Cabriolet, Jeans Beetle and Super Beetle. With a 5.5J x 15 rim, it made the old 4.5J and 5.5J VW wheels redundant, and they were deleted from the range. At the same time, the brake calipers were modified to take thicker pads. This design, with four large ribs, was retained until production came to an end.

To reduce costs, the rear badges were now in black plastic, and even the aluminium screenwash nozzles were changed to black plastic the following year (the windscreen wipers had always been black). The metal surround to the three main gauges on the fascia was also changed to plastic, and when the optional steering wheel was chosen instead of the standard hard rubber item, leatherette was used instead of genuine leather.

A useful distinguishing feature on the 1974 MY-onward cars was that headlight surrounds were now black (they used to be white), and the headlight retaining ring was also in black where it used to be chrome. The fuel tank was revised slightly, with a new location for the filler, although the tank itself remained in the same place, and the front compartment lid still had to be opened to fill up with petrol. For the sake of standardization, both models were fitted with 150mph (or 250kph) speedometers.

Ever-changing American regulations now dictated that black rubber guards be fitted on the bumpers at both front and rear for the US market (Swedish cars also had unique bumpers incorporating headlight

continued page 121

The 914-2.0 being pushed hard on American roads. It took some quite spirited driving to make a 914 roll as much as this in a corner.

For 1974, American cars gained rubber guards on the rear bumper in addition to the existing ones at the front. Note the New Jersey number plates.

Dashboard detail of the American spec 914, with the seatbelt warning light positioned above the heater controls.

This American-spec 914-2.0 dates from the 1974 model year. The engine grille lettering officially appeared only on production cars destined for the USA, and there were different lighting arrangements, such as reflectors on the outer edge of the all-red rear light cluster, and an extra indicator on the front wing.

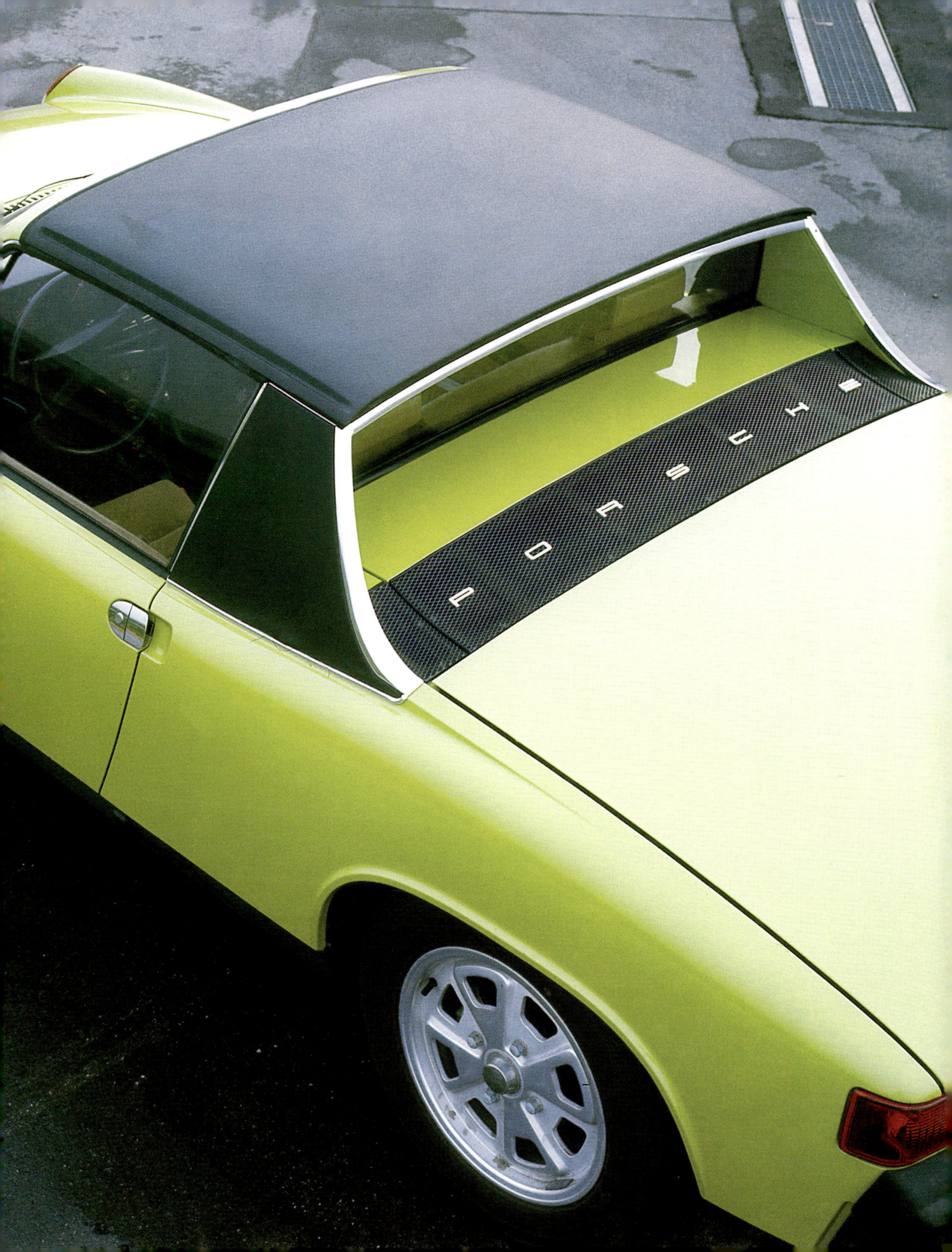
PORSCHE

Right: A final view of the American 914-2.0 for 1974. The alloy wheels and chrome bumper blade alone added over $500 to the car's purchase price.

A couple of pieces of American advertising showing the 1974 914 – one issued by Porsche, the other by the Firestone tyre company.

washer jets), and they also gained a seatbelt warning buzzer with an ignition interlock.

Matters of the moment
When the new generation of 911s with impact bumpers was launched in September 1973, it was noted that engine sizes had increased again, this time to 2.7 litres for mainstream cars, with three-litres specified for top models. This took them even further away from the 914 series in terms of performance and refinement.

On the home market, the 1.8 litre model was priced at DM 13,990 with the two-litre at DM 14,990. All cars now had three-point seltbelts as standard, with the two-litre model also gaining a vinyl roll-over bar covering and a laminated windscreen. The popular Comfort pack was DM 700 at this time.

On the East Coast of America, the 1.8 litre 914 cost $5400 – $650 less than the larger-engined version. Out of interest, the basic 911 was $9950, whilst the

Sales continued to fall, generating speculation about how much longer the model could survive ...

The 911 range moved even further away from the 914 series for 1974 when it went to 2.7 litres. All the time, the Porsche 911 line was becoming faster and more refined, while the 914s were getting slower and more spartan.

Targa-bodied variant was priced at $10,800.

With a poor exchange rate for sales in the USA (at least as far as the VG was concerned) on such a relatively low-priced vehicle, another batch of cost cutting measures (which rather went against the grain) was introduced for the American market to ensure at least some profit. Black bumpers were fitted to all cars, and both the centre console and Fuchs alloy wheels became a cost option (a chrome bumper blade, centre console and the Fuchs forged alloys had all been standard on the US-spec 914-2.0 for 1973). To go some way toward making up for these reductions, pile-type carpet became standard on all American models, as did the vinyl-trimmed roll bar.

The American option list was now as extensive as the European versions. 1974 options included air conditioning at $650, anti-roll bars ($145), Bilstein shock absorbers ($150), an AM/FM radio ($289), cast alloy wheels ($325), forged alloy wheels ($380), chrome bumpers ($145), a heated rear window ($50), front

In an attempt to boost sales, a number of special editions were launched. This is the G-pack option dating from January 1974, forerunner of the 914 GT and Limited Edition.

The 914 GT with colour-coded painted bumpers, sills, front spoiler and Mahle cast alloy wheels. There was also a side stripe, plain on the GT, but with Porsche script in America, where the model was known as the 914 Limited Edition.

spoiler ($115), tinted glass (also $115), and metallic paint at $270. The Appearance Group Option package, priced at $300, included two-tone horns, foglights, a leatherette-covered steering wheel, centre console with gauges, and the combination central armrest with storage compartment. The latter package remained the same until production ended.

The only saving grace for the 914 series was that its main competitor, the Opel GT, had been taken out of production. The final example left the line in August 1973, the 103,373rd built; it wasn't until May 1974, that the 100,000th 914 rolled off the production line. The Matra M530 had also been killed off when Simca-Chrysler took over the Matra concern. Only 9609 had been built between 1967 and 1973. Despite an excellent race pedigree, like the 914/6, it had been launched at a far higher price (almost 60 per cent greater) than originally intended.

Still sales fell, however. Mike Lawrence, in his book *A-Z of Sports Cars* wrote: "Despite awful styling and an inflated price tag it sold quite strongly in some markets, but not at all well in others such as Britain. The 914SC (lhd only) had a 1971cc engine and 120mph/195kph was claimed, but that did not improve the beast's looks, lower the price, or erase the VW badge."

In fact, between 1970 and 1974 AFN Ltd sold just 85 examples of the 914 in the British Isles. UK list prices were later reduced slightly to try and boost sales, but without much effect. Most of the 914s in Britain today have been imported from the USA after production ceased!

The 914 GT & Limited Edition

At the Paris Salon in October 1973, Karmann displayed two 914s with striking coachwork colour schemes and contrasting stripes. The theme was taken into limited production in spring 1974 using the top spec 914-2.0 as the basis.

Porsche was originally going to call this new model the Can-Am, in recognition of the marque's success in the series during 1972 and 1973, but when the company withdrew in 1974 because of a change in the rules, it all seemed rather pointless. Instead, in Europe the car was called the 914 GT, and in America it was known as the 914 Limited Edition. Both featured Mahle cast alloy wheels, a front spoiler, anti-roll bars, and dramatic coachwork that could be described in a number of ways; very 1970s, is probably the least likely to offend ...

The colour schemes offered were black (usually a cost option) with yellow bumpers, sills, wheel centres,

123

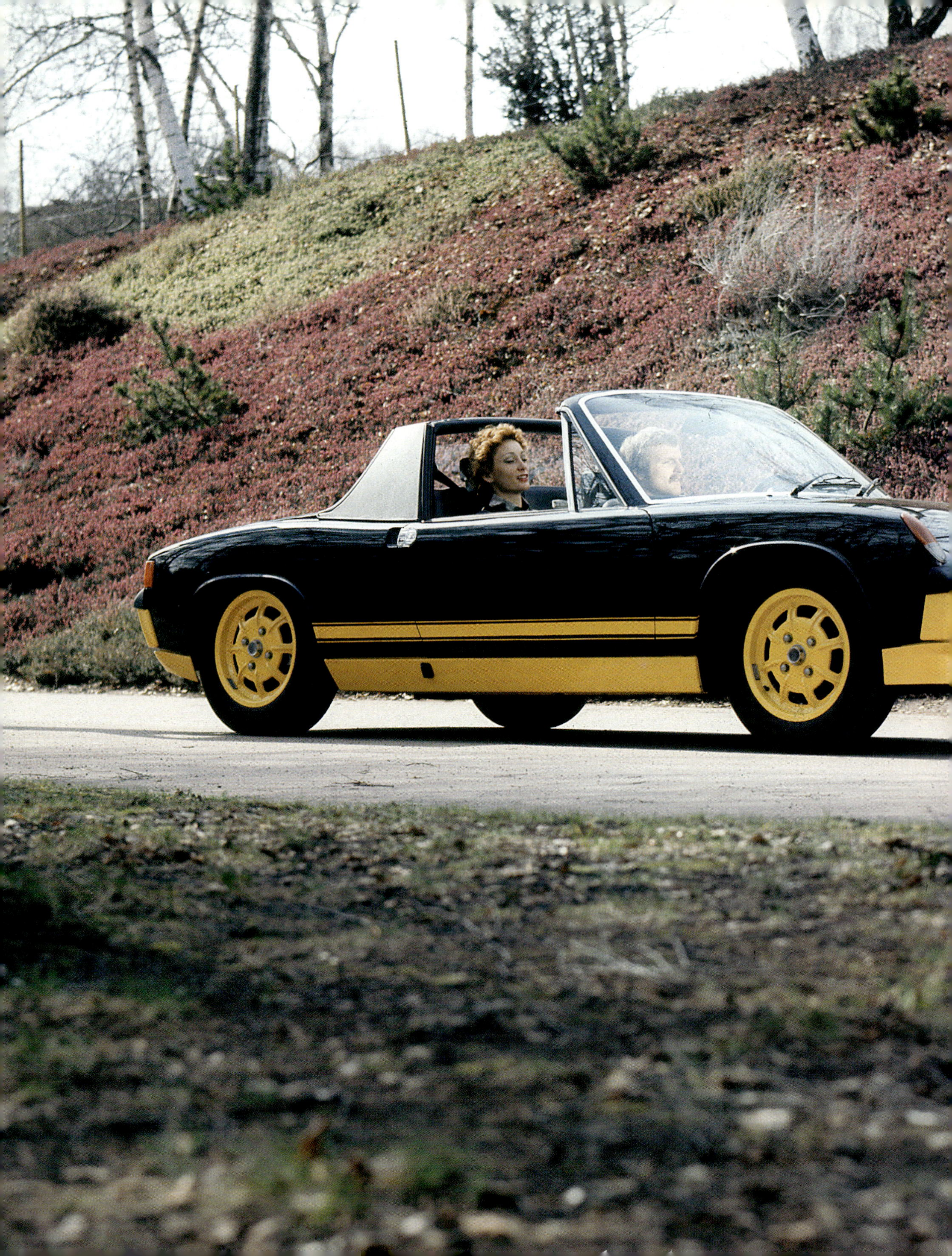

The days of air-cooled Volkswagens were numbered. This 1303S Beetle, which came tenth on the 1973 Austrian Alpine Rally in the hands of Tony Fall, had already ceased production at Wolfsburg, although a number of other plants continued limited production. One by one, the air-cooled models were falling by the wayside, with the Karmann Ghia the victim in 1974.

valances, front spoiler and side stripes, or light ivory with green or orange accents. The special feature on the 914 Limited Edition was the 'negative' Porsche side stripe (ie the Porsche script was in body colour) instead of a plain coachline.

What it added up to in reality was the chance to offer a completely different model without having to invest any money to get production under way. The GT was fairly shortlived, but the $6670 Limited Edition ran into the 1976 model year, despite there being only 1000 available.

In America, where cars actually produced in the USA have always been extremely cheap for the home

Another view of the limited production 914 GT, introduced in 1974.

Home market price list & options (in DM), May 1974

914-1.8	15,750
914-2.0	16,870
Comfort pack	800
Grand Tourisme pack	990
Special paint on list	610
Special paint not listed	894

Option prices including tax:

	1.8L	2.0L
M474 Bilstein shock absorbers	337	337
M485 Pressure cast alloy wheels 5.5J x 15	726	726
M596 Forged alloy wheels 5.5J x 15	842	842
M220 Sperr differential (80%)	726	726
M404 Anti-roll bars	316	316
M102 Heated rear screen	118	118
M285 Chrome bumpers	316	316
M568 Laminated tinted glass (except rear)	410	252
M089 Tinted windscreen	167	–
M567 Laminated tinted windscreen	316	158
M640 PVC underseal	68	68
M591 Centre console (as in Comfort pack)	62	62
M166 Seatbelt for M570	58	58
M570 Third, centre seat cushion	53	53
M565 Sports padded steering wheel (as in Comfort pack)	116	116
M490 Electric aerial	135	135
M097 Emden radio with electric aerial	365	365
M095 Wolfsburg radio	288	288
M572 Two-tone horn (as in Comfort pack)	37	37
M551 Halogen headlights (as in Comfort pack)	121	121
M433 Driving lights	37	37
M659 Fog and driving lights	95	95
M571 Foglights	63	63
M652 Intermittent wipers	37	37

The Scirocco, launched in 1974 and styled by Giugiaro, not only replaced the Karmann Ghia, but almost certainly took a large chunk of 914 sales. The 914-1.8 was priced at $6300, while the Scirocco – not far behind on performance and undeniably prettier – cost less than $5000 in the same period.

market, the subject of pricing again raised its ugly head. In the July 1974 edition of *Road Test* magazine it was noted: "The 914 was branded 'overpriced' when it was $2000-$3000 cheaper than it is now, which supposedly elevates it into the outrageously overpriced category, and the 911, which costs about twice as much, into the scandalously overpriced bracket."

Nothing could be done: after all, exchange rates dictated the price and the Porsche range was barely in line with them. Perhaps the most interesting line in the article, knowing what we know today, concerned the fate of the 914 since Volkswagen had started using water-cooled engines for its Dasher (Passat) and Scirroco models. Behind the locked doors of the Porsche design office, plans were already afoot for the 924 model, but more on that particular vehicle later.

Company news

In 1974, VW had been obliged to cut back its workforce, despite the launch of the new Passat (known as the Dasher in the USA). New generation cars (and the Audi range) eventually pulled the company out of trouble, but, for a moment, there was a serious danger that the business might fail and have to close its doors completely.

After Nordhoff passed away, the relationship between Porsche and Volkswagen was never as close, and the 914 project put a great deal of strain on the partnership. Promoted from within the VW organisation, Rudolf Leiding took over from Lotz in October 1971, and soon afterwards decided in favour of moving toward a range of models with water-cooled, front-mounted engines.

By July 1974, when Karmann Ghia production ceased, over 360,000 coupés and more than 80,000 cabriolets had been built. The model was replaced by an altogether more modern vehicle – the Volkswagen Scirocco – which entered production at the Karmann works during the spring of 1974.

The 412 was scheduled to be deleted for 1975. The Passat, Scirocco and Golf (the Scirocco and Golf had been styled by Giugiaro as part of the EA-337 project) all used transverse water-cooled, in-line fours of 1471cc, although the Scirocco was soon given a 1.6 litre engine to maintain its sporty image.

As Ferry Porsche stated in his fascinating book, *Cars Are My Life*: "This complete change of policy by VW naturally called into question the existence of the joint distribution company, the break-up of which had already been recommended by members of the VW supervisory board. Finally, on 8 May 1974, an agreement to that effect was signed. We acquired VW's stake and moved our sales department into the VG building in Ludwigsburg."

The agreement was retroactive to 1 January 1974, bringing to an end a very uneasy alliance in which the parties involved seemed to be pulling in opposite directions. Full control of the 914 shifted to Porsche, although a clause in the new contract ensured that, from the outside, it would seem as though nothing had changed.

The cars were still known as VW-Porsches everywhere (except in the United States, that is), and VW power units would continue to be used until the model ceased production. A number of development contracts were cancelled, although Volkswagen and Porsche did not entirely forsake their long-running relationship.

The age of the four-wheel drive rally car came with the launch of the Audi Quattro in March 1980. Ferdinand Piech, Audi's Technical Director at the time, approved the project, with the first prototype being ready in late 1977. Its World Rally Championship debut came on the 1981 Monte Carlo Rally and, from 1982 to 1984,

A couple of shots of the 1975 car on test. By the mid-1970s, a number of companies were offering 914 accessories. One American firm, for instance, sold a 916-type front spoiler, and a rear reflector panel like that found on the 1974 911s.

The main change for the 1975 model year was adoption of the so-called 'crash bumpers' to meet latest Federal regulations, first proposed for 1974 but then postponed until the following season. Square lights were used with the new bumper design, usually sourced from Bosch, and, again, fog or driving lights were available (both with H-3 bulbs). If no auxilliary lights were specified, the bumper remained plain with no openings as the horns were now mounted behind the front valance. This car has the optional front spoiler.

Audi dominated the rally scene. It is interesting to note that Ferry Porsche had suggested a 4WD Passat to Volkswagen as early as 1974 ...

The 1975 model year

An owner's survey carried out by *Road & Track* in November 1974 made interesting reading. When asked to give the five best features of the 914 range, the average answer included handling, good fuel economy, comfort, high speed cruising ability and reliability – virtually everything the catalogues had promised.

However, the five worst features included a lack of punch in the smaller four-cylinder cars (the American emission regulations stifled engine power on vehicles destined for the USA, getting progressively stricter as the car was developed), workmanship, the linkage to the gearbox, engine access (causing maintenance difficulties), and annoying roof squeaks.

The burning question, of course, was would customers buy another? An overwhelming 89 per cent of those asked said yes, they would, with the remainder giving a definite no; not one person taking part in the survey was undecided. The only conclusion to be drawn from this is that buyers were happy enough with the car despite the high price; it was simply a matter of persuading the potential purchaser to go to the showroom and try the vehicle, rather than make a decision based on looks alone or hearsay.

Changes for 1975 kicked off with a different

The new bumpers undoubtedly improved the car's aesthetics, although fewer than 16,000 vehicles were destined to wear them. This model had the Fuchs forged aluminium alloy wheels, the same design as that used from 1973 onward.

Standard colour schemes, 1975 MY

Standard coachwork colours

Berber Yellow, Light Ivory, Nepal Orange, Scarlet, Malaga Red, Summer Yellow, Forest Green, and Lagoon Blue

Special coachwork colours

Black, Copper Metallic, Ancona Metallic, Palma Metallic, and Silver Metallic Diamond

Seats

Black, Opal or Yellowstone leatherette. Inlays in Black, Beige or White leatherette basketweave or corduroy. Alternatively, inlays could be specified in Tartan cloth, available in Green, Black/Grey, Yellow, Greenish-Yellow, Orange, Bright Red, Burgundy Red, Ski Blue or Matisse Blue

Carpet

Black, Beige or Brown needle loom, or Black or Beige for pile-type carpet

Notes: The brown listed on interior colours (opal) was a light brown as 1970, but carpet was maroon in reality. Yellowstone was basically last year's beige.

bumper design. These so-called 'crash bumpers' were introduced to comply with the latest US regulations, and actually improved the looks of the car by quite some degree. The slim black rubber bumpers looked the same for American cars, but had shock absorbers behind them, and Californian and Maryland cars had small rubber guards in addition.

The optional fog/driving lights were now rectangular, and a front spoiler was made available to special order. Another consequence of the new bumper design was that the rear number plate lights were positioned to the side of the plate, and the horns situated behind the front apron.

Although the GB100 continued for most markets, a modified two-litre engine – the GC88 – had to be introduced for the States to satisfy even stricter emissions regulations. It retained the Bosch D-Jetronic fuel-injection and virtually the same specification, but the latest emissions equipment further drained power: maximum was now just 88bhp and torque was reduced

continued page 134

(and overleaf) Three superb publicity shots of a 1975 model year 914. Note the Mahle cast mag-alloy wheels, used from 1973 on, and the standard front apron arrangement.

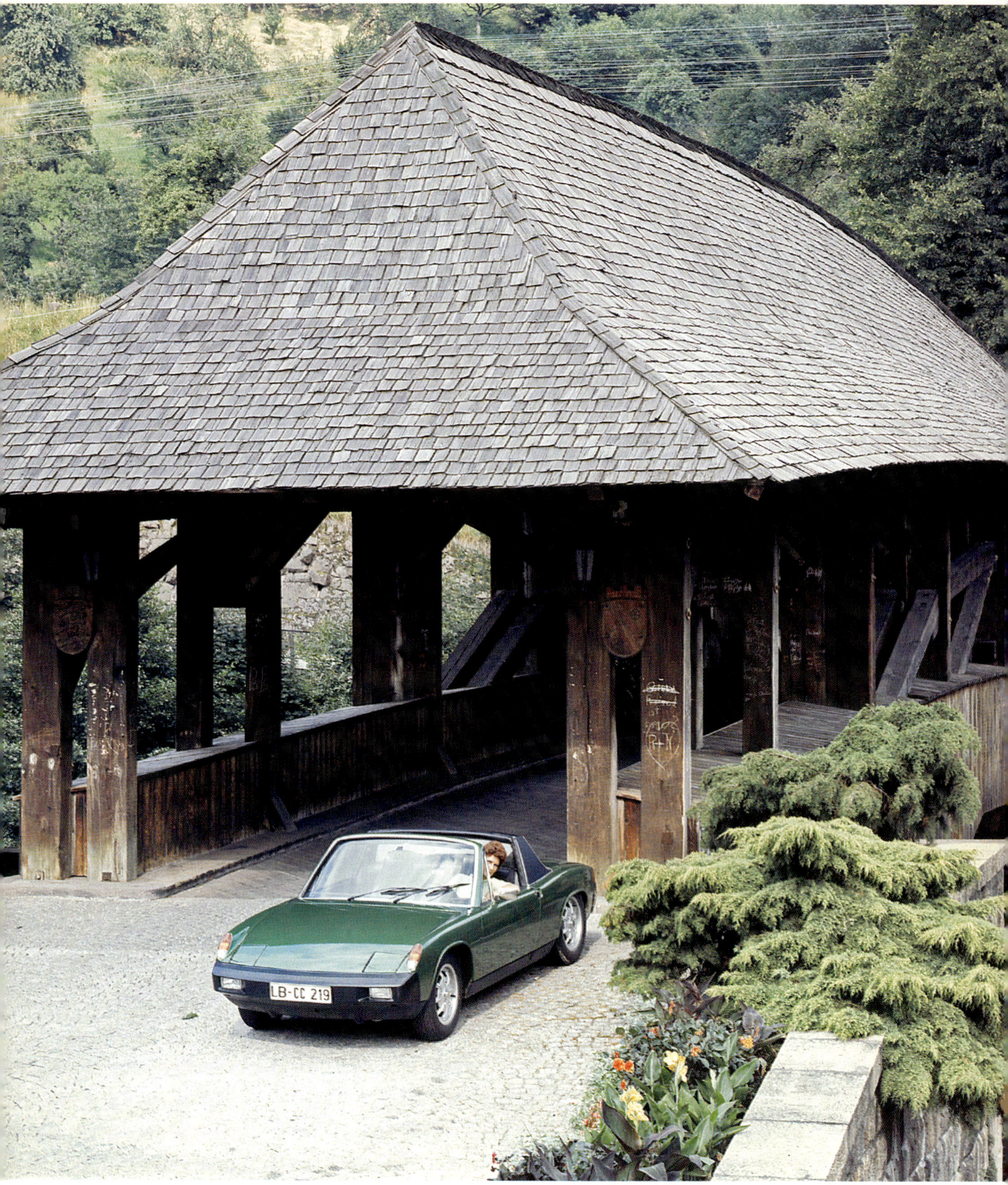
LB-CC 219

A couple of views of the 1975 interior.

to 105lbft – figures only just above those quoted for the original 1.7 litre engine.

The 1.8 litre EC76 unit was largely unchanged, but a new exhaust system meant that an extra 100rpm was needed to reach the same peak power, and there was less torque available (89lbft instead of 94). In California, catalytic converters and extra anti-pollution equipment were fitted on both engines, making them costlier to produce.

The vinyl used to trim the interior was now a heavier basketweave pattern instead of the fine one used previously, and various tartan check patterns were made available for the seats. Fatter black plastic VW window winders were used to standardize them with contemporary Volkswagen models.

Another special edition, known as the 'Silberseries', was introduced for Europe. Basically a 914-2.0 with silver coachwork, a large number of options were included, such as tinted glass and alloy wheels, in a bid to attract sales. In Germany, the price was held on standard models, but in America the exchange rate and additional costs involved in meeting the emission regulations pushed even the basic 914-1.8 to $6300. Adding on the cost of options meant it became a very expensive car.

For the American market, the 1975 Appearance Group included a steering wheel with leatherette cover, the centre console (with clock, oil temperature gauge and voltmeter), a leatherette boot for the gearlever, two-tone horns and front foglights. The 1975 Performance Group contained Mahle cast alloy wheels, anti-roll bars, and a front spoiler.

In Australia, *Modern Motor* opened an April 1975 article on the 914SC with the statement: "Labelled alternatively as a 'bathtub on wheels' and 'VW's very worst shape' the VW-Porsche is one of those cars which failed to stir much initial enthusiasm both at home and abroad – it was your actual 'slow starter'. The model hardly caused a ripple of interest in Australia – because the only cars to come here had to be specially converted to rhd which, on a one-off basis, is hideously expensive."

However, by the time the testers had finished with the two-litre four-cylinder car, they had grown to like it. More historically significant, though, was the fact that no more of the 914 series models were going to be sent to Australia as the Design Rules Council in that country did not allow it.

Markets were either shrinking, disappearing, or becoming increasingly difficult to satisfy legally. Because of this, the decision was taken to run down production

The American spec dashboard, readily identified as a car destined for the USA by the Porsche badge on the steering wheel: all other markets had a Wolfsburg badge in the wheel centre.

to an absolute minimum, and to sell the 914 series only in America for 1976 – about the only country where any sort of demand existed, at least at a level where a profit could be seen.

The final year
On 10 February 1975, Toni Schmucker – who had spent 33 years with Ford Germany – took over from Rudolf Leiding at Volkswagen. Carrying on from where Leiding left off, use of the 1795cc VW engine was discontinued for the 1976 MY in the VW range when the Transporter series (the only model other than the 914 to still use it) went to two-litres, using essentially the same engine as in the 914. For this reason, only the GC88-powered 914-2.0 was offered for 1976.

In 1976 *Sports & GT Cars* noted: "As the indignities of smog gear enfeebled the 1.7 litre engine, we got two larger versions, a 1.8 and a 2.0. The 1.8 was with us in 1974 and 1975 but has now been discontinued. And why not?"

Trick photography. The car on the left is destined for Europe, whilst the one in the picture below is US-bound. Vehicles destined for California and Maryland had extra small bumper guards front and rear.

Regarding the Targa top: "For open-air motoring, the fibreglass top comes off when four clamps are undone. This stores in the rear trunk, taking little space as it nestles on its padded fittings. This top is a bit large and awkward for one person to remove and stow (or un-stow and install) but it can be done. With the top off the open-air motoring is delightful, especially since the fixed rear window keeps the draft off the back of your neck."

As mentioned earlier, all 1976 model year production (a total of 4075 cars) was exported to the United States. About the only change from the previous year was that the script on the rear panel was created via self-adhesive black transfers instead of a plastic badge!

The two-litre 914 was priced at $7250, compared to $10,845 for the 912E. Whilst the latter could hardly be classed as cheap, it should be remembered that the 911S coupé was $13,845 at the time, and the Targa-bodied version $14,795.

Road & Track carried out a test on the two-litre machine, and recorded a maximum speed of 107mph (171kph) after covering 0-60 in 12.7 seconds, and the standing-quarter in 19.2. Average fuel consumption was quoted as 26.5mpg.

Speed in gears:
1st	29mph (46kph) at 5600rpm
2nd	46mph (74kph) at 5600rpm
3rd	71mph (114kph) at 5600rpm
4th	96mph (154kph) at 5600rpm
5th	107mph (171kph) at 4700rpm

These figures were just about on a par with those quoted for the original 914/4, and a number of journalists picked up on that fact. *Motor Trend* had at first claimed that the 914 was a very forgiving car although, in later tests, one of the problems with mid-engined cars became apparent: when pushed too far, the car spun round and round. However, with such good cornering ability, the average owner should never have to experience this phenomenon, and most tests were full of praise about this aspect of the machine.

Production finally came to an end in the early part of 1976, although no announcement was made; it was simply allowed to fade away with final sales being completed in June that year. Although considered a flop by many, it should be remembered that production rates were similar to those of the contemporary MGB, which hardly equates to a disaster. For all its problems, the 914 series has a unique place in the history of Porsche in that it was the only mid-engined production road car built by the Stuttgart firm until the recent introduction of the Boxster.

Standard colour schemes, 1976 MY

Standard coachwork colours
Light Ivory, Nepal Orange, Scarlet, Malaga Red, Summer Yellow, and Lagoon Blue

Special coachwork colours
Black, Viper Green Metallic, Ancona Metallic, and Silver Metallic Diamond

Seats
Black, Tan or White leatherette. Inlays in Black, Tan or White leatherette basketweave or corduroy. Alternatively, inlays could be specified in Tartan cloth, available in Green, Black/Grey, Yellow, Orange, Bright Red, Burgundy Red or Blue

Carpet
Grey, Tan or Brown needle loom, or Grey or Tan for pile-type carpet

The car continued almost unchanged for 1976 (this is actually a 1975 model). Sadly, just as it was reaching the height of its development, the 914 series was gradually phased out in the early part of 1976, with final sales occuring June that year. All of the last season's production – purely two-litre cars – went to America.

5
The model in competition

Porsche had a reputation to uphold. The company had won the Manufacturers' Championship in 1969 and, in May of that year, built 25 examples of a model known as the Type 917.

Victory came first in a minor race at Zeltweg towards the end of 1969, but a revised version called the 917K arrived in time for the 1970 Daytona 24-hour race. There was no looking back after that, as the car totally dominated the racing scene for the next four years.

In a bid to promote the 914 series, the decision was taken by the management at Stuttgart to develop the machine for competition; after all, sales would undoubtedly increase on the back of any successes, just as they had done with all previous Porsche production models.

The 914/6 GT
This was officially nothing more than a standard 914/6 fitted with the optional R-package; indeed, to prove the point, all 12 of the works-prepared cars carry production 914/6 chassis numbers. However, because of its FIA homologation in the two-litre category for Special Grand Touring cars, the name 914/6 GT was quickly coined.

In addition to the works vehicles, a large number of cars were converted to GT specification for customers, either by the factory or privateers from Porsche-supplied parts. The 914/6 GT was available in three versions: a customer car for competition/fast road work; a track racer developing 220bhp, and a rally model with around 160bhp at the wheels.

These models were not cheap. At a time when the standard 914/6 cost DM 19,980 (quite a lot of money), the basic customer car was priced at DM 24,480, whilst the full-blooded racer was nearly double that at DM 44,480. The rally car was somewhere between the two, costing DM 38,480, but specification was high in all cases.

On the racer, the two-litre Carrera 6 engine was used with Weber carburettors and twin spark ignition. The internal dimensions were the same as those already in use on the 914/6 (ie an 80 x 66mm bore and stroke giving a 1991cc displacement), but the cylinder bores, heads, cams, cranks, conrods and pistons were all substantially different, and the compression ratio was far higher. Power was transmitted through a transaxle sourced from the 904.

Throughout the GT series, many braking components were sourced from the 911 range, although the front brake calipers came from the 908 on works-built racers. Heavier lower wishbones were developed for the front suspension, and various anti-roll bar combinations were made available. Uprated shock absorbers and a slightly different suspension geometry completed the transformation.

The wheels were Fuchs forged alloys (usually 7J width at the front, 8J at the rear) hidden under steel wheelarches 50mm (two inches) wider than those found on the standard cars (this being the limit allowed by FIA regulations). A 100 litre (22 Imperial gallon) petrol tank was added on the racer, leaving little room in the

Shell
TEXACO
TEXAC
ESSO
Coca-Cola
Ford Capri GT
BP
Gulf
Chevron
UNIROYAL
STELLA ARTOIS
Shell
Castrol
Gulf
20
GULF

Left: One of the all-conquering Porsche 917Ks (in John Wyer/Gulf colours) pictured alongside a 914/6. The picture was one of a series taken by the works but, sadly, in terms of sales, the 917's success did not rub off on its mid-engined cousin.

Right: The 914/6 GT prototype (chassis number 9140430019). Completed in the first week of October 1969, it was built on one of the earliest 914/6 chassis and was the first of 12 works GT models. Other test cars carried the chassis numbers 9140430983 and 9140431640; the latter was used for endurance trials.

Porsche made a great effort to cash in on the GT model's racing success: this photograph, used in the 1972 model year catalogue, was entitled "The Sports Car with the Race Car Design."

Bjorn Waldegaard on his way to victory in the 1970 Austrian Alpine Rally. The car was an Austrian-entered 914/6 GT but, despite this win, the Porsche works drivers were less than happy at having to use the 914 for the Monte – they much preferred the 911 for snowy conditions.

Motorsport in 1970

After the 1970 Targa Florio, the headlines carried the news that Jo Siffert and Brian Redman had won the event for Porsche in a special lightweight 908/3. However, in the background there was also a works entry of two 914/6 GTs (chassis numbers 9140430705 and 9140430709); not for the race, though, but just the practice session in order to gain some valuable experience of how to set up the cars in real life situations.

The Nürburgring 1000km Race, held on 31 May 1970, saw the International debut of the 914/6 GT. The four cars managed to secure second, third, fourth and fifth in the two-litre GT Class, but this achievement was not widely reported, the glory, naturally, going to Elford and Ahrens for their outright win in a 908/03.

At Le Mans in 1970, the Porsche marque dominated the legendary 24-hour race to take the first of many overall victories at the Sarthe circuit. Porsche veteran Hans Herrmann and Britain's Richard Attwood took their Austrian-entered 917K to victory, followed home by two other Porsches.

The excellent performance of Guy Chasseuil and Claude Ballot-Lena was again somewhat overshadowed, but their win in the Grand Touring category was a significant result for the lone 914/6 model, not least because this equated to sixth overall. Entered by Sonauto, the French Porsche importer run

continued page 146

front compartment for anything other than the spare wheel.

The chassis was braced at front and rear with six extra strengthening plates; the roof panel was bolted in place to add rigidity to the structure and give the car better claim to being a true GT: after all, if the roof could be removed, it wasn't a closed car. In addition, a bar running across the suspension towers braced the chassis at the front, and stabiliser bars were fitted in the rear compartment.

The front and rear lids (the latter with larger grilles) were made of fibreglass with balsa wood members in order to make them lighter, and perspex side and rear windows were often used for the same reason. Fibreglass one-piece bumpers replaced the originals, and the interior was naturally stripped-out to the bare minimum (even the inner door handles were replaced with a simple leather strap), racing seats, and a roll bar.

The 914/6 GT was homologated in the FIA's Group 4 on 1 March 1970 after the minimum 500 standard 914/6s had been completed. The 12 works cars were built in Zuffenhausen's Competition Department between 3 October 1969 and 27 November 1970.

The 1970 Nürburgring 1000km Race was held on 31 May. This 914/6 GT, driven by the Kaiser and Steckkonig pairing, came home 20th overall, third in Class at its international track debut.

Just behind car number 93 was this 914/6 GT driven by Nolte and Christmann. The top Porsche 914 finisher in the 1000km Race came 19th overall (second in Class) with Robert Huhn and Gunther Schwarz at the wheel, narrowly beaten for Class honours by a 911L.

A lone 914/6 GT was one of 24 Porsches at Le Mans in 1970 – it easily won its Class and finished an amazing sixth overall. Racing versions of the 914/6 GT rode 50mm (two inches) lower than standard cars.

The Sonauto car averaged 99.27mph (158.8kph) for the 24 hours – a remarkable achievement by any standards, made all the more impressive by the fact that it completed the course on its original tyres and brake pads.

In addition to a fine finish in real life, the Sonauto car was actually seen a number of times in the classic Steve McQueen film called Le Mans – all racing fans should have a copy.

Opposite, inset: Some of the GT (racing version) modifications in detail. This picture shows the 100 litre fuel tank and spare tyre mounted above the supplementary oil cooler ...

Preparation for the 1970 running of the Marathon de la Route. As always, the works cars received meticulous attention from a hand-picked team of engineers.

... and this is the stripped-out interior. The GT weighed around 90kg (200lb) less than the standard 914/6.

With a raised compression ratio of 10.3:1, the Carrera 6 1991cc unit gave a reliable 220bhp at 8000rpm. Depending on the gearing, the car should have been capable of around 150mph (240kph). However, for the Marathon, in order to comply with the regulations, only 160bhp was possible.

The three works GTs at the factory before the 1970 Marathon.

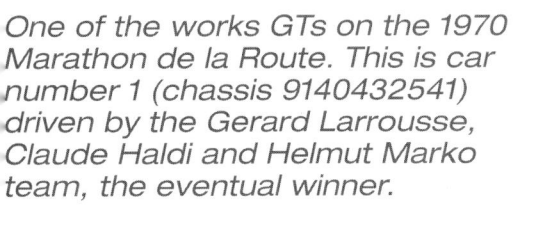

One of the works GTs on the 1970 Marathon de la Route. This is car number 1 (chassis 9140432541) driven by the Gerard Larrousse, Claude Haldi and Helmut Marko team, the eventual winner.

Car number 2 (running in Group 4 trim) in the pits. Driven by Ballot-Lena, Steckkonig and Koob, it finished third overall behind its two sister cars, entered in Group 6 because of the even wider rear wheelarches employed for the event.

Night time on the Marathon. In daytime only events, the headlamp mechanisms were often removed to save weight, but they were obviously necessary during endurance events such as this. Note the fuel filler hole location on the GT's bonnet, and the different colours on half of each of the works cars' bumpers.

145

This was the way the 1970 Marathon de la Route finished, with car number 1 followed home by car number 3. The latter (chassis 9140432543) was driven by the Waldegaard/ Andersson/Chasseuil team. Car number 2 was next, making it a Porsche one-two-three.

(and overleaf) A couple of contemporary shots showing the works cars being prepared for the 1971 Monte Carlo Rally

by that great stalwart of the Stuttgart marque, Auguste Veuillet, it was one of the 12 Porsches that finished the event (no fewer than 24 had started).

The Marathon de la Route at the Nürburgring was to be a Porsche 914/6 benefit. Run in August over no less than 84 hours, the works entered three 914/6 GTs (chassis numbers 9140432541, 9140432542 and 9140432543 – all built in March 1970) to be driven by team leaders Gerard Larrousse, Claude Ballot-Lena and Bjorn Waldegaard respectively. The orange-red 914/6 GTs finished first, second and third.

A one-two Class win at the Österreichring in October gave Porsche some more valuable points in the GT Championship; the first 914/6 GT home (12th overall) was driven by Gunther Steckkonig and Prince von Hohenzollern. This was enough to secure the 1970 International GT Trophy for the Stuttgart marque by a comfortable margin: Porsche had 57 points at the end of the season, its nearest competitor just 36.

Motorsport in 1971

The 914/6 made its official works rally debut on the 1971 Monte Carlo Rally, run from January 22 to 29, although a single entry had been made in the 1970 RAC Rally as a trial run for the most prestigious event on the rallying calendar. Driven by Claude Haldi and John Gretener, the 914/6 (chassis number 9140431732, and registered S-X 7495) came 12th, only six places behind the only other Porsche to finish – a 911S in the hands of Gerard Larrousse.

Using the same drivers – Bjorn Waldegaard, Gerard Larrousse and Ake Andersson – who had brought the Stuttgart firm first, second and fourth places on the 1970 Monte, Porsche prepared three new 914/6s for the 1971 event (completing them in the last week of November 1970). However, competition was going to be stiff with seven Renault-Alpine A110s, five Lancia Fulvias, three Datsun 240Zs and a couple of Fiat-Abarth 124s at the head of the start list.

Setting out from Warsaw, Bjorn Waldegaard and Hans Thorszelius did take the fastest time on one stage, but Ove Andersson (later to become Toyota Team Europe's boss) led all of the way to give a Renault-Alpine victory, followed by Therier and Andruet in similar cars.

Ultimately, Waldegaard finished first in Class and a highly respectable joint third place overall in chassis 9141430139, although the staff at Porsche had hoped for an even better result to help boost sales. Sadly, the other two Porsche 914/6s (chassis numbers 9141430140 and 9141430141 respectively) struggled with transmission and clutch trouble before retiring. When the cars were returned to the workshop, the problem was identified as a glued-in pin on the clutch release lever coming loose.

The works never used the model again for rallying afterwards, despite its layout being ideal for this branch of motorsport. It seems as though the rear suspension was not up to the job, and a number of questions were raised about body stiffness.

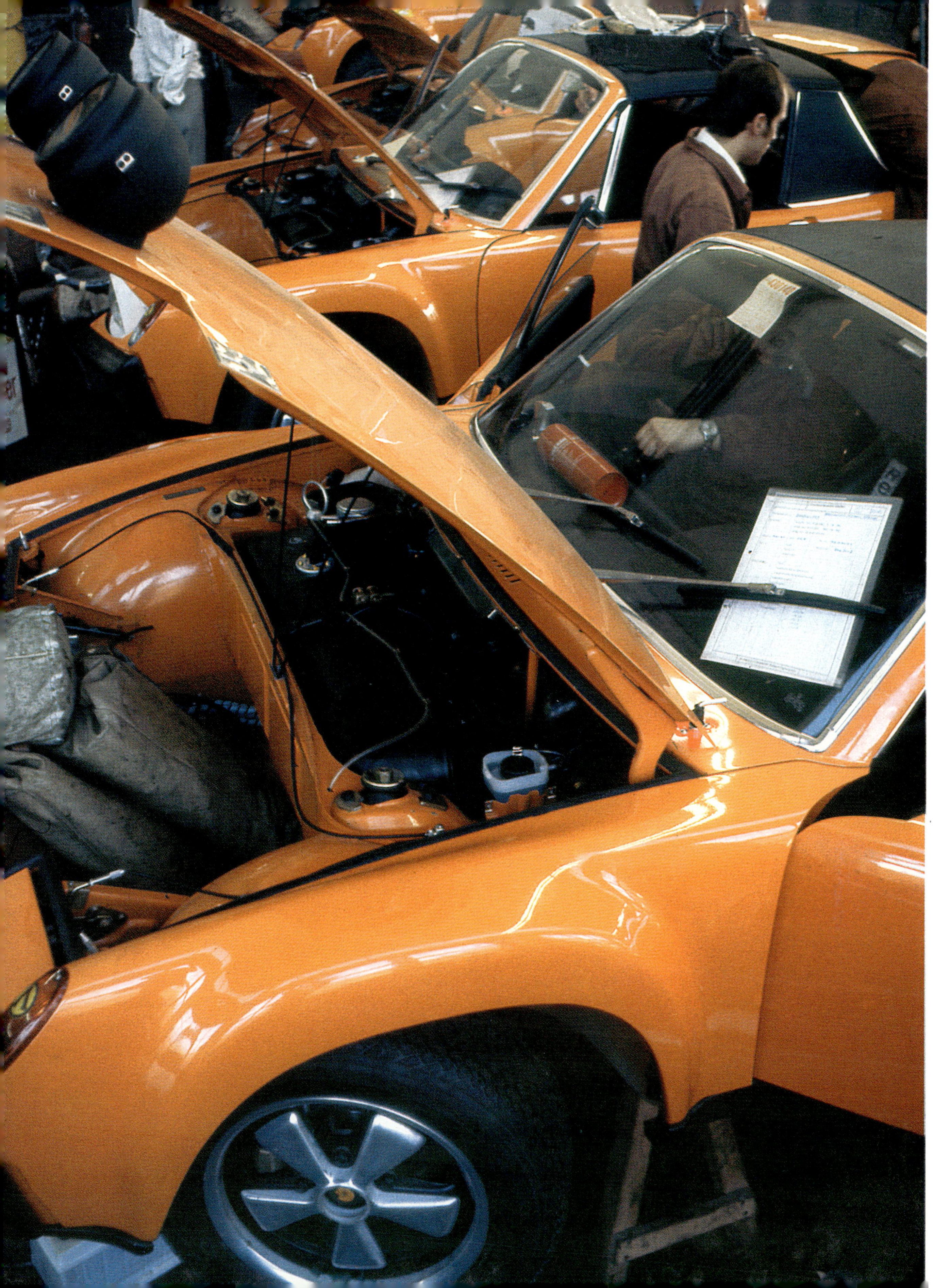

In racing, the season opened with the Daytona 24-hour Race and, like the previous year, a Class win (seventh overall) for the 914/6 GT. Two months later, another Class win was achieved, this time at Sebring for the 12-hour Race and with the Locke/Everett pairing at the wheel.

The International Motor Sports Association (IMSA) Championship had just been established in America. Of the four general Classes, the one which interested Porsche was the GTU (Gran Turismo, under 2.5 litres) category in relation to the 914/6 model. The car that won its Class at Sebring had been entered by Peter Gregg, and Gregg also campaigned the IMSA series. With the support of Porsche+Audi, Gregg's 914/6 GT claimed outright victory at three of the IMSA races and Class wins in the remaining three – enough to take the 1971 IMSA GTU Championship.

Porsche took the flag once again at Le Mans, thanks to Helmut Marko and Gijs van Lennep repeating its overall success of the previous year. However, the two 914/6s entered fared less well: car number 46 was entered by Club Porsche Roman, but the pairing

148

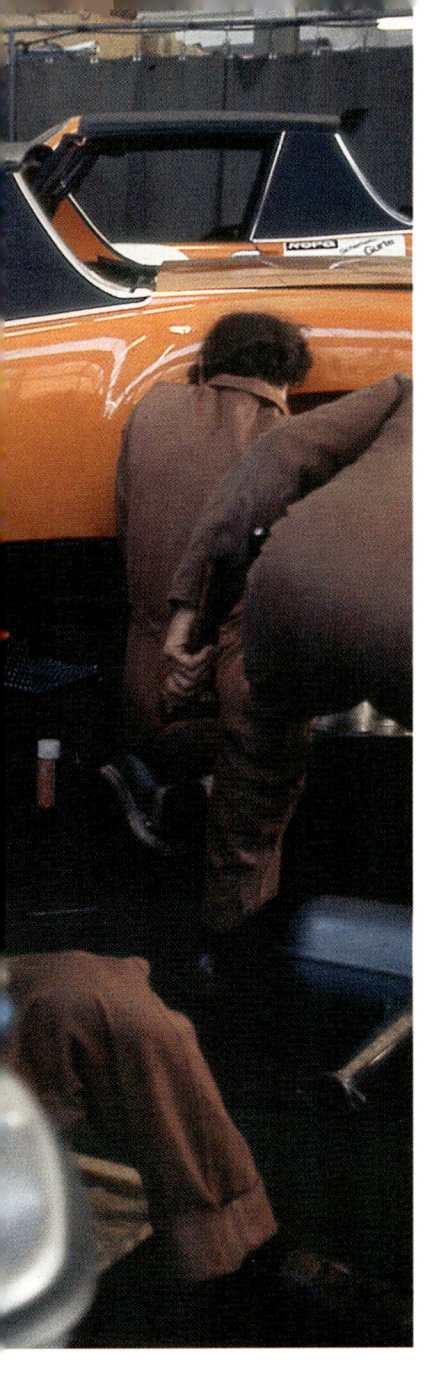

The works entry for the 1971 Monte lined up for publicity shots at Zuffenhausen. The rally cars had 160bhp 911S engines from the 1968 model year, with stoneguards to protect the powerplant and transmission. They also had a unique braking system on the rear to allow for handbrake turns on hairpin bends.

The drivers on the Monte were greeted by awful weather conditions, better suited to the 911 with the weight above its driving wheels ...

149

The prize giving at the end of the 1971 Monte Carlo Rally. For the 1972 event, Waldegaard and Thorszelius teamed up once more, but this time in a works 911S; the 914 series was never used again by the works for rallying.

... nonetheless, Bjorn Waldegaard and co-driver Hans Thorszelius did manage joint third overall. Thorszelius (left) looks happy that it's all over!

of Sage and Keller retired in the ninth hour when a con-rod broke in the engine. The other 914/6 (heavier by about 70kg, or 155lb, for the 1971 event) was entered by Autohaus Max Moritz. Driven by Quist and Krumm, it made it to the fifteenth hour before gearbox trouble sidelined the car (they had been in 15th place). This was to be the 914's last appearance at the famous Sarthe track.

By the end of the year, the 914/6 GT had once again clocked up a vast number of Class wins in Europe and America, notable results coming at Monza, Spa and the Österreichring. The many victories in minor events were thanks to the efforts of privateers and smaller racing teams such as those run by Strahle, Jurgensen, and the Max Moritz Racing Team.

In the meantime, in May 1971 Porsche launched the M471 body/wheel package which gave 914/6 owners the chance to own a GT lookalike to use on the road. The option included steel wheelarch extentions to cover the 6J x 15 Fuchs alloys (used with spacers at the rear), new fibreglass sills and a front spoiler. The M471 option was deleted with the 914/6's passing at the end of the 1972 model year.

R Meaney, B Bean and G Wright: the team (seen here) that came away with a Class win in the 1970 running of the Daytona 24-hour Race, were beaten in 1971 by fellow Porsche drivers J Duval, B Bailey and G Nicholas. Held on the last day of January, a Porsche 917 won the event overall.

Japanese advertising making the most of Porsche's competition activities.

151

Gerd Quist and Dietrich Krumm drove this 914/6 GT on the 1971 Nürburgring 1000km event, held over May 29-30. The pair took a Class win and finished 14th overall.

The twilight years

Apart from the occasional Class win in minor events and appearances in SCCA races, the 914 series was being seen less and less. The 914 had come 13th overall and second in Class in the 1971 Targa Florio, and, in the following year's event, took a Class win (ninth overall) courtesy of Schmid and Floridia.

Appropriately, in 1973, Porsche won the final Targa Florio event, not with one of its all-conquering sports racers but a works 911 Carrera RS driven by Herbert Muller and Gijs van Lennep. In the background was also a fairly standard 914 wearing number 127; unfortunately, in the background is where it stayed and didn't figure in the final placings.

As a matter of interest, it should be noted that Porsche failed to contest the 1972 World Championship as the new regulations – which introduced a three-litre engine capacity limit – didn't suit the Zuffenhausen firm. Instead, Porsche turned its attention to the Can-Am series, the works cars proudly displaying the Porsche and Audi names side-by-side on their coachwork. The German company easily won the series in 1972 and repeated this success the following year. With the 917 now producing over 1000bhp, Porsche laid claim to no

One of the many 914/6 GTs running at the Nürburgring in 1971. Porsche had an excellent event, winning overall, claiming no fewer than five Class victories, in addition to that covered by the winner (driven by Vic Elford and Gerard Larrousse).

The 1971 Österreichring 1000km Race. The 914/6 GT took ninth overall and a Class win, thanks to the Schickentanz/Kersten pairing.

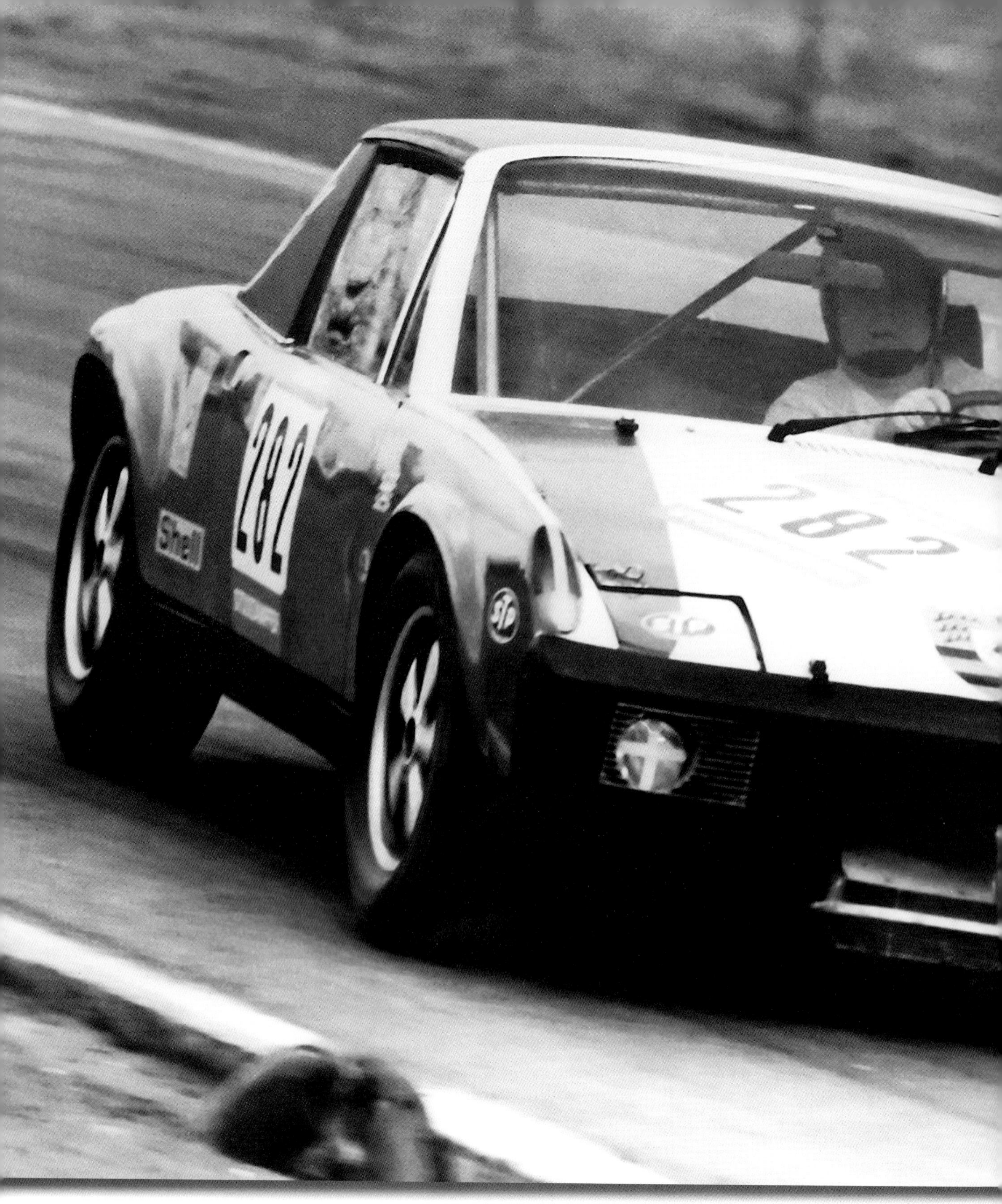
282
Shell
282

Christian Jurgensen, seen here in action, was a fine 914/6 GT driver and later team owner from Switzerland – he did a lot to promote the 914 series' cause.

fewer than eight overall victories in the Can-Am series to take another well-deserved title in America. For 1974, however, the rules changed and the Stuttgart marque stayed away ...

SCCA racing in America

The Sports Car Club of America (SCCA) ran a high profile racing series that was undoubtedly an excellent showcase for sports cars. Success on the track meant success in the sales room, and a Class title at the end of the year was an enormous boost to dealer fortunes. It was an obvious move for Porsche to enter the fray.

Early speculation in America had the 914/6 in SCCA Class D production racing and the 914/4 in Class E. The latter wasn't expected to fare very well against the competition and, indeed, didn't, but many had high hopes for the six-cylinder vehicle. In the end, the 914/6 was put into the faster and more competitive Class C section.

The 1970 SCCA Class C season was supported by Triumph (through Bob Tullius on the East Coast and Kas Kastner on the West), Datsun (with Peter Brock running his famous BRE-Datsuns), and Porsche. Porsche+Audi decided to run three teams of 914/6s, with Josef Hoppen acting as Competitions Manager.

Ex-Grand Prix driver Richie Ginther ran two cars, with Alan Johnson and Milt Minter at the controls, whilst Bob Hansen and Kendel Noah raced for Bunker-Hansen Racing; the third team was made up of Peter Gregg and Pete Harrison. All of the racers were carefully prepared, with exhaust systems and camshafts sourced from the Carrera 6, crankshafts from the 911T, and pistons specially forged for the job by Mole of Germany.

In the 914/6's inaugural outing at the Phoenix National in March 1970, Alan Johnson took a comfortable Class victory with the car. As will be seen from the advert on page 159, this was a far from isolated result and, by close of season, the six-cylinder machines were Divisional Champions in four of the seven SCCA geographical divisions: Johnson won the Southern Pacific Division, Pete Harrison the South-East,

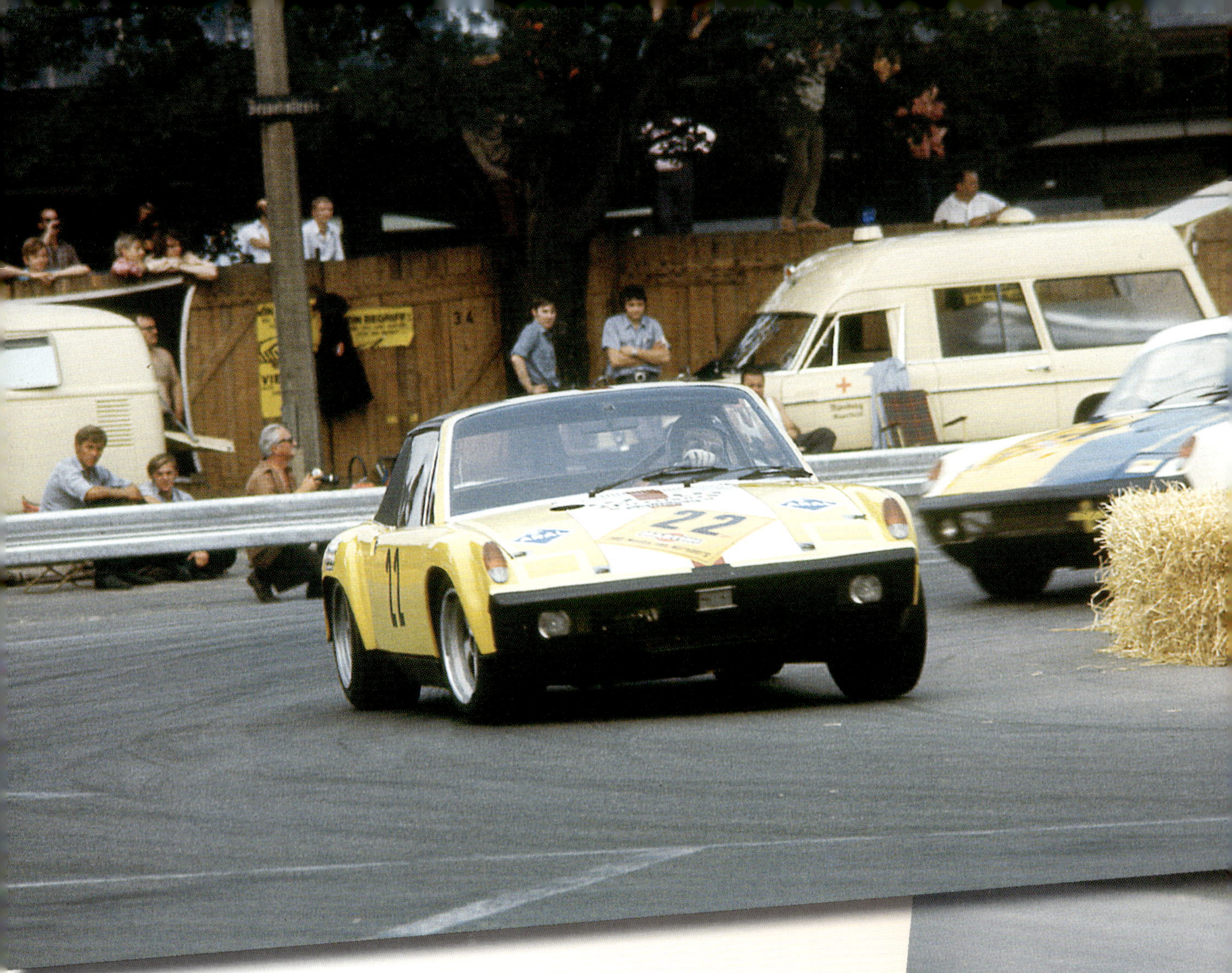
22

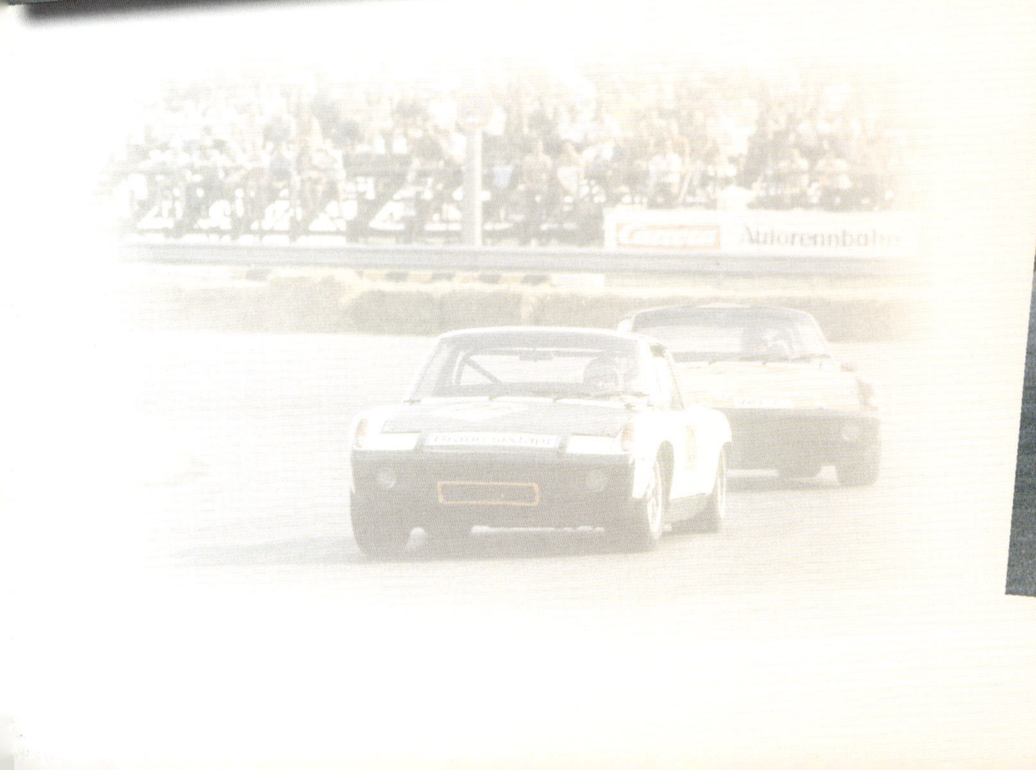
Autorennbahn

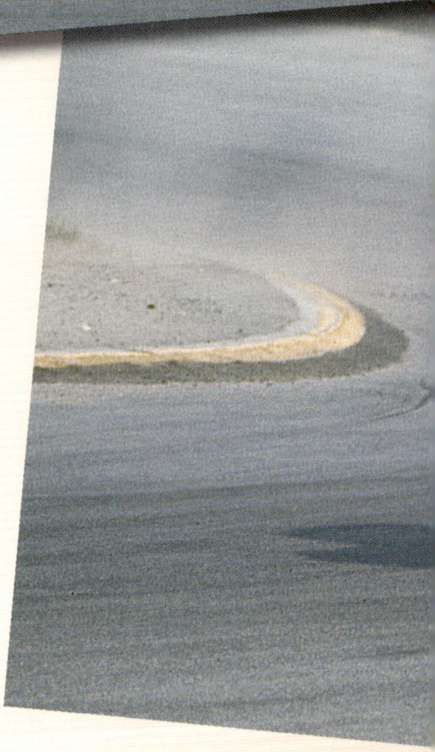

Action from the Norisring in 1971!

The final Targa Florio occurred in 1973. The 914 in the picture was amongst the backmarkers, but at least it did take part. The Porsche to the right of the photograph, driven by Muller and Van Lennep, went on to win the event.

The 914 series was popular in SCCA events during the early 1970s. The 914/6s were very successful, whereas the four-cylinder cars fared less well. This is one of the Class E competitors doing his best against the odds.

Chuck Dietrich the Central, and Bob Hindson took the Mid-West region.

To decide the final overall placings in each Class no less than nine 914/6s qualified for the American Road Race of Champions in November 1970. In addition to the four Divisional Champions, there was Forbes-Robinson, Noah, Gregg, Stephen Behr, and William Stroh. However, the best the Porsches could achieve at Road Atlanta was fourth and fifth (Elliott Forbes-Robinson and Alan Johnson respectively), beaten convincingly by the incredible BRE and Bob Sharp Racing Datsun Z-cars.

The 914/6 GT model was put into Class B when it burst onto the American scene early in 1971, and did not receive the backing of the Porsche+Audi organisation. In fact, although Porsche+Audi withdrew all of its support for the 1971 SCCA season, Bob Hindson nonetheless successfully defended his Mid-West Division title with the 914/6, and Don Parish was declared Central Champion at the end of the year. The American Road Race of Champions was disappointing again, though, with Parish driving home the first Porsche in a lowly seventh place.

When the new two-litre, four-cylinder car arrived in the States it was placed in Class E. Seeing the opportunity to cash in on the chance presented, Porsche+Audi once again enlisted the help of Richie Ginther to prepare a car.

A car was run in the last couple of events of the 1972 season and even qualified for the ARRC at Road

158

American advertising showing the more successful side of the works-supported SCCA Class C campaign with the 914/6.

Partial listing of 1970 Class C Production wins:

Phoenix National	Porsche 914/6	1st
Willow Springs National	Porsche 914/6	1st
Riverside National	Porsche 914/6	1st
Falstaff Classic	Porsche 914/6	1st
Donnybrooke Speedway National	Porsche 914/6	1st
Mid America Raceway National	Porsche 914/6	1st
Olathe National	Porsche 914/6	1st
Continental Division Raceway National	Porsche 914/6	1st
Lake Afton National	Porsche 914/6	1st
Dallas National	Porsche 914/6	1st
Alabama International	Porsche 914/6	1st
Watkins Glen	Porsche 914/6	2nd

You can't win 'em all.

The 914 with a 1.7-liter 4-cylinder engine goes 110 mph, and costs $3,595.* The 914/6 with a 2-liter 6-cylinder engine goes 125 mph, and costs $5,999.* But remember, they're only human.

*Prices are suggested East Coast P.O.E. (West Coast P.O.E. slightly higher.) Local taxes and other dealer delivery charges, if any, additional. Mag wheels and Porsche racing stripe optional, at extra cost. For the Porsche Audi dealer nearest you call 800-553-9550 free. In Iowa, call 319-242-1867 collect.

PORSCHE
Porsche Audi: A division of Volkswagen.

Atlanta. Forbes-Robinson qualified fastest and then went on to win the important race by a considerable margin. However, the car was later disqualified on a technicality and failed to compete in 1973. Instead, Josef Hoppen used it to help produce a booklet to show SCCA racers how to prepare their cars properly, and even put up a $10,000 prize fund for points scorers.

During 1973, the SCCA opened a new category for Showroom Stock Sports Cars, but the rules meant that the two-litre, four-cylinder 914S would not be allowed to compete. However, in an interesting comparison between eight cars of similar performance, the American magazine, *Car & Driver*, drew up a starting grid to show the fastest stock machines over the Ontario Motor Speedway road course. The Fiat 124 was the quickest with a lap time of 2:40.7 (72.5mph, or 116kph, average), with the Triumph GT6 next up, then the Opel GT. The Porsche 914 came in fourth with a 2:42.2 (71.5mph, or 114kph), and then there was a big gap before the MGB in fifth place. It's interesting to note that the slowest car was the Karmann Ghia, averaging just over 65mph (104kph).

Despite encouragement from the Porsche+Audi organisation, and easier Class E grouping, the 914-2.0 was never destined for greatness. A few drivers made it into the field of the American Road Race of Champions in 1973 and 1974, but didn't figure in the results on either occasion.

An American advert showing the Altec/Lansing car prepared for the 1976 IMSA season. It ran in the Camel GT Challenge Series, and certainly attracted a lot of attention.

A final note

The last major competition success for the 914 series (at least while it was still a current model), came in 1976. In 1975, the assault on the Pikes Peak hillclimb in the Colorado Rockies had come to a sudden end for the Garretson tuning concern when its 914/4-based car was destroyed during qualifying. The following year the company returned with a team of 914/6-based machines.

The highly tuned engines were bored out to 2368cc and gave around 200bhp; sufficient to reward the Garretson-Porsches with second, third and fourth places in qualifying. Come race day on 4 July, Rick Mears won the event for the Garretson outfit, posting a time just a few seconds adrift of the record. Of the rest, Garry Kanawyer was the only other finisher, coming home in eighth position.

The car still does well in historic racing today, but it is sad to reflect that, despite numerous victories and even more fine results in competition early in its career, the 914 series never once met its sales target of 30,000 units a year.

The speed of sound.

Because we've been building sound systems for many of the world's great racing circuits, for nearly as long as we've been building them for theatres, recording studios and concert halls—the sound of speed is as familiar to the people at Altec/Lansing as the sound of music.

So, to promote our new line of bookshelf speakers, we've decided to put sound and speed together by campaigning this specially prepared Porsche in the 1976 IMSA/CAMEL GT Challenge Series.

At each event during the series, Altec/Lansing will set up a terrific display where you can check out our car, listen to some great sounds and maybe even win some prizes if you're lucky.

Come out and join in the fun and watch for us as we take wheel and gearshift in hand and go where no speaker company has gone before.

If you can't make it out to the races, stop in and listen to the Bookshelf Family at your authorized Altec/Lansing dealer today.

THE BOOKSHELF FAMILY
Speakers for people from the people at Altec/Lansing

See the Altec/Lansing Porsche in the Camel GT Challenge, Sept. 19 Road Atlanta, Oct. 3 Laguna Seca Raceway, Oct. 24 Mexico City, and Nov. 27 & 28 Daytona Beach.
For more details, send for free catalog: Altec Sound Products, a division of Altec Corporation, 1515 S. Manchester Ave. (Dept. RT), Anaheim, CA 92803.

6
914 specials

Despite a fairly short production run, a number of important specials were based on the 914 series. Some were one-off concept cars without a hope of going into production, whilst others were serious attempts at either trying to improve the styling or performance of the beast.

The 914/8

The 914/8 (sometimes called the 914S just to confuse matters) is without doubt one of the fastest and rarest Porsches ever built. Just two prototypes were constructed, both fitted with three-litre, eight-cylinder racing engines of the 908/03 type. Built during 1969, the first car was for Dr Ferdinand Piech (a 300bhp machine in red), and the second car was a present for Ferry Porsche's 60th birthday.

The Piech car (chassis number 914111) was hardly used at all, but, despite the fact that it was officially for closed circuit work only, it did venture onto German autobahns on more than one occasion, presumably to help develop the road car for Ferry Porsche.

The coachwork was subtly different to a standard 914 in that the wheelarches were slightly flared to allow for wider tyres, and there were wider headlamp covers

The 914/8 built for Ferdinand Piech in 1969. The wider headlamp covers probably look better than those chosen for production, as did the wheelarches filled with fatter tyres. The oval in the centre of the bumper blade concealed an oil cooler.

The power unit in Ferdinand Piech's 914/8, featuring Bosch fuel-injection. The exhaust system gave reduced power compared to the usual racing set-up but 300bhp was still available at 7500rpm

to allow twin headlights to be fitted on each side, a feature seriously considered for production models at the design stage. Other differences included location of the fuel filler cap on the offside of the scuttle, a modified front bumper without foglight grilles, and different indicator lenses at both ends of the car.

The interior was essentially the same as that of an early 914/6; different seats without headrests and some additional switches (to cut the electrics or set off the fire extinguisher system that took up the entire front luggage compartment) were the only notable differences. There was also wood trim around the instrument panel, which was dominated by a 10,000rpm tachometer with non-reflecting glass.

To get the eight-cylinder engine to fit was not as big a job as might be expected, as it's actually less than 150mm (six inches) longer than a standard six-cylinder unit; the extra space was found by encroaching slightly on the rear luggage compartment. Different shock absorbers and springs were fitted to handle the extra power.

The engine, first seen at Monza in 1968 combined with a five-speed racing transaxle, gave the 914/8 a 155mph (248kph) top speed and a 0-60 time of around six seconds. It's interesting to note that the 908 engine provided Porsche with the Manufacturers' Championship title in 1969.

Professor Porsche's car (chassis number 914006, according to Porsche records) was finished in silver, and was much closer to a standard 914/6 in appearance. It did, however, have a number of unique features, such as a steel roof that incorporated a sliding sunroof, the lack of a black vinyl roof covering, and a flush-fitting fuel filler cap located on the bonnet. Like the Piech car, there was an oil cooler under the front bumper, but this 260bhp model was fully road legal and regularly used.

Development costs (in DM) ran into six figures, but it just goes to show how much development potential there was with the 914 chassis. It was this fact that prompted the proposal of a more powerful but practical model that could be put into series production. Fortunately, both of these unique cars have survived.

The Goertz prototype

The 1970 Turin Show saw the debut of two special designs based on the

continued page 167

162

Year	Chassis no	Engine details	Notes
1969	914111	908 3.0 litre unit, 300bhp	Ferdinand Piech car; red
1969	914006	908 3.0 litre unit, 260bhp	Ferry Porsche car; silver

The beautifully prepared front compartment of the Piech car.

Dashboard of the 914/8, dominated by the 10,000rpm tachometer.

Rear view of the Piech machine.

The second 914/8, this one built for Ferry Porsche's 60th birthday. The steel roof was fixed in place to add stiffness to the body.

A contemporary colour shot of the 914/8 given to Ferry Porsche.

Interior of the silver 914/8.

VW-Porsche 914/6; one was perhaps too futuristic to be regarded as anything more than a pure concept car, but the other, styled by Count Albrecht Goertz (a freelance designer with a number of classics, such as the BMW 507, to his name), was considered a possibility for production.

Although the engineering and interior were left as per the standard production model, Goertz made a dramatic change to the 914 bodyshell. The front end was flatter and sharper, rather like a contemporary Maserati, and the roofline continued back, almost to the extent that the vehicle became a sporting estate, or "bread van" as one person put it. Rather oddly, Goertz chose not to add any extra glass in the sides of the car.

Built by Eurostyle of Turin, the Goertz machine was well received by Porsche management (indeed, they gave the go-ahead to make the car road legal), but it was not taken on by the factory. For one thing, it would have had a very limited market and, for another, as the time came to look for a replacement, the mid-engined concept had already been renounced.

Goertz kept the special 914/6 himself for a while before it found its way into a private collection in

The rear end of Professor Porsche's 914/8 hid an engine that gave 260bhp at 7700rpm. This subtle drop in power – which made the car more suitable for road use – was achieved by replacing the fuel-injection system with Weber carburettors, reducing the compression ratio and fitting different camshafts.

A proud Ferry Porsche pictured at Zell-am-See in September 1969 with his birthday present. The car was registered (on Stuttgart plates) for road use, and Ferry clocked up some 6000 miles (10,000km) with the 140mph (225kph) machine before it was retired. Note the hatch on the bonnet – a feature shared with some of the early prototypes.

Left: Count Albrecht Goertz (right, holding the door) talking to Hans Stuck, the legendary racing driver, about his most famous design, the BMW 507.

Germany where it survives in good condition to this day.

The Tapiro

The Tapiro was on the adjoining stand to the Goertz car at the Turin Show, the creation of stylist Giorgetto Giugiaro and made by his Turin-based firm, ItalDesign. The shape of the Tapiro was clearly based on that of the earlier DeTomaso Mangusta: the word Tapiro describes a legendary animal that eats dreams!

Intentionally extreme in the design of its doors and bonnets, it was, to ItalDesign at least, a realistic study with regard to mass production. Although the wheelbase of the 914/6 was retained, height and width were reduced by around 100mm (four inches), whilst length increased by 75mm (three inches).

The doors and engine covers were hinged on a steel backbone, both opening in gullwing fashion. The aggressive lines actually incorporated a number of

170

Left: A contemporary photograph of the Goertz 'Porsche Kombi' by Eurostyle, which was introduced to the public at the 1970 Turin Show.

Designed by Giorgetto Giugiaro, the Tapiro would make a stunning debut at the 1970 Turin Show. Like the Eurostyle-bodied machine, it was based on the 914/6. Sadly, the model was considered too extreme for production, but surely Porsche could have managed to sell at least 3300 – the total sales figure for the 914/6? With such a car, the Stuttgart company could easily have justified it having a high price.

worthwhile features, such as rounded edges near the roof to reduce drag, and a very aerodynamic profile. The designer was also very clever in the way he hid the roll-bar between the doors and engine covers – with the backbone running down the length of the car, this made a very strong structural 'cross'. The luggage compartment at the front was so low that there was only room for the spare wheel and the electrics that controlled the pop-up headlights, but it looked fantastic.

The large areas of glass helped not only give the cockpit a light, airy feel, but also aided visibility, a feature so often lacking in cars of this type. The tasteful leather-trimmed cockpit (finished in a dark tan colour) was dominated by the large central rev counter, something that Giugiaro carried over to his beautiful Alfetta GTV.

Large 8J x 15 rims were used at the front, with 10J x 15s employed at the rear; it should also be noted that adjustable shock absorbers were fitted to improve ride. Bonomelli Tuning provided the finishing touch by boring out and tuning the six-cylinder engine. At 7800rpm, 220bhp was extracted from the 2.4 litre unit, enough to provide the vehicle with ample performance: top speed was said to be in the region of 145mph (230kph).

However, although Porsche could hardly be considered ultra-conservative, the Tapiro was just a little over the top to be accepted as a potential production model. The car was seen at a number of international shows before it apparently disappeared. After many years of neglect, it is now in good hands, and should be restored to its former glory within the next few years.

The Murene

Another special made its debut at the 1970 Paris Salon later in the year. This effort was presented by the Louis Heuliez concern of Cerizay in France, and was the work of Jacques Cooper, a freelance designer of some repute.

Heuliez was well known for its commercial vehicle bodies and coachbuilding activities, so it came as no surprise to find that this was a very professional proposal. Cooper's design was translated into a full-scale model, and from that it took less than three months to build a running prototype based on the 914/6.

Known as the Murene, the mid-engined coupé retained much of the original interior. However, the two-tone coachwork was a complete departure from the 914 series; the bumpers were removed to accentuate the smooth lines and, at the rear, there was a separate luggage compartment with its own lockable lid, and

Right: The Hispano-Aleman pictured on the Frua stand at the 1971 Geneva Show. The slot behind the conventional doors was an air intake for the engine.

172

Left: The Tapiro mysteriously disappeared a few months after the Turin Show and was not seen again until recently, when it was found on a Spanish hillside in a very sorry state. A large number of specials were produced on the 914 chassis, but it was the Tapiro that really caught the public's imagination. At the time of writing, the car was undergoing extensive restoration.

a one-piece tail section that could be moved upward and back to give easy access to the engine bay.

Sadly, the Murene would never go into production, mainly because it arrived too late as the 914's replacement was already being sketched out, and there was no room for a mid-engined car in the proposed new range.

The Hispano-Aleman

First shown on the Frua stand at the Geneva Show in March 1971, the Hispano-Aleman (which literally means Spanish-German) was the victim of an unfortunate disagreement involving its designer and the man who commissioned it.

Verne Ben Heidrich was the Spanish Porsche importer who asked Pietro Frua of Turin to design and build the 914/6-based car in question. For several months, Heidrich worked closely with Frua to come up with a stunning design, although one that was obviously Frua. The beautifully-proportioned, wedge-shaped coupé was very modern-looking, if fairly typical of the supercar breed of the 1970s. One magazine called it "... one of the best-looking mid-engined coupés ever conceived."

Heidrich thought that he could produce a small run of the Hispano-Aleman machine, pricing it at around DM35,000 apiece; about the same as a Jaguar E-type in Germany. Problems only really came to the surface when Heidrich suggested that Porsche (who was very interested in the vehicle) would be welcome to use the design to build the car.

Frua had no intention of letting this happen, presumably because he could see his commission disappearing if Porsche took it on. After the show, the Swiss authorities impounded the car and it wasn't until

The beautiful shape of the Hispano-Aleman drew the admiration of almost everyone who saw it. Sadly, it was destined never to reach production because of several years of legal wrangling about reproduction rights.

1976 that the legal arguments were settled. The car was eventually awarded to Heinrich but, by that time, the days of the 914 were well and truly over anyway.

Although the Hispano-Aleman project came to nothing, Heidrich did at least later make BMW 328 replicas and a basic sports car of his own design, both in limited numbers.

The 916

One particular special, produced by the factory itself, was quite close to reaching the market, and, in fact ten pre-production models were built as a consequence. The machine was the 916 – basically a 914/6 of 1971 vintage, but fitted with a series of larger engines from the contemporary 911s.

Of the 916, *Road & Track* said: "Ever since the Porsche 914 and 914/6s arrived on the automotive scene, much has been rumoured in the way of restyling the controversial lines of the car. One-offs have shown up at a number of the European shows and rumours of a newly revamped car based on the 914 series have been circulating for months. The first indication on the

Of all the specials, the aggressive-looking 916 was the closest to reaching production status, but even this failed to make the final hurdle. This is chassis number 9142330011, the first of the ten pre-production models.

Another view of the car that nearly made it into the 1972 model year line-up – the 916.

CAR GRAPHIC

The 916 featured on the cover of the November 1976 issue of Car Graphic. A number of 916 replicas were built up from official Porsche or aftermarket parts, which shows there was at least some demand for the model.

11 C/G ROAD TEST
メルセデス・ベンツ300D

IMPRESSIONS＝ポルシェ916／ルノー30TS／ホンダ・シビックCVCC
NEW MODEL＝'76 US Cars／ジャガーXJ-S／ニッサン・シルビア
SALON＝イスパノ・スイザ
SPORTS＝ドイツGP／オーストリアGP／富士GC第3戦
STORY＝グレアム・ヒル物語

part of the Porsche works that a new car was being considered came last August when a variation on the 914 was seen at the factory. Reports had it that this car, and several others like it, were 'special order cars for the Paris distributor.' Then, in early October, photos of what was designated the 916 were circulated to all the US distributors. Rather than being a restyled 914 or 914/6 residing in the $3400 to $6000 price bracket, the 916 was a super-luxurious 914/6 at a price rumoured to be in the $14,000 to $15,000 bracket – or, in other words, a 914/6 for the price of a Ferrari Dino."

Development work on the new model was overseen by Ferdinand Piech, and began in mid-1971 in order for the car to be ready for the 1972 model year. Proposed production plans dictated that most of them would receive 911S engines, although the majority of those built had the 2.7 litre Carrera RS flat-six; the Type 915 five-speed transaxle was adapted especially for the vehicle. The 2.4 litre fuel-injected flat-six engine would have achieved a 0-60 time of around seven seconds, and a top speed approaching 145mph (232kph); the Carrera unit should have taken the car nearer to 150mph (240kph). Exhaust emissions were not a problem; indeed, Porsche had already obtained approval for the 2.4 litre-engined 916.

The body was both striking and aggressive-looking. Unique colour-keyed fibreglass bumpers and flared steel wheelarches with blended fibreglass sills (like the 914/6 GT) were the main features. The front bumper moulding incorporated driving lights, an opening for the oil cooler (a feature borrowed from the 914/8s), and a spoiler, while the simple but nonetheless unique tail panel had an exit for the exhaust and recessed area for the number plate. The steel roof was welded in place to add strength to the chassis, and there was also a strengthened floor. In addition, the engine grille was made larger for better cooling.

Fuchs 7J x 15 alloys were fitted on all four corners with 185/70 VR15 tyres, and the front and rear track was increased by the use of spacers. Anti-roll bars (specified for both ends), Bilstein shock absorbers and ventilated disc brakes sourced from the 911S, combined to help keep performance in check.

The luxury interior was predominently trimmed in leather, although the air conditioning compressor location limited movement of the driver's seat, apparently causing Porsche engineers a great deal of concern. An ingenious and novel feature of the 916 model only was that the radio aerial was actually part of the front windscreen.

The cars were prepared for an official launch scheduled to take place at the Paris Salon in October 1971. However, two weeks before the event was due to open, the project was cancelled after just one 914/6-based prototype and ten pre-production prototypes (with chassis numbers running from 9142330011 to 9142330020) were built; six remained with the works, the other five being sold to friends of the company.

Road & Track stated:"With the current money stabilization problems, the duty surcharge on imported cars, and the higher labour costs in manufacturing a low volume car, Porsche decided that the market wasn't large enough to warrant production."

Pricing was the main problem, as the value of the deutschmark had risen consistently since it was floated in May 1971. *Autocar* noted that "... the design was submitted to Porsche's costing department and flatly refused." At $15,000 in America, it would have cost almost $5000 more than the most expensive 911 at that time, so it probably had a point.

Road & Track finished its February 1972 article with the following words: "From a practical standpoint, Porsche's decision to not produce and market the 916 probably was the right one. But the 916 is a mechanical masterpiece, and one can't help but wish that the fortunate few who can afford $15,000 for such a car had been given the chance to own one."

Mike McCarthy was lucky enough to test a 2.7 litre 916 for *Classic & Sportscar* in 1982. Regarding performance, he said: "Use all the revs and that magnificent flat-six simply propels you into middle distance - you're there before you've caught up with yourself. Below about 3500rpm it just feels quite quick, but then the engine comes on cam, the exhaust and engine note changes from that unique beat to an exhilarating, spine-tingling growl, and suddenly you're doing very illegal speeds indeed – we saw 120mph with great ease ... The straight-line performance is, in a word, shattering."

He concluded: "Above all there is the combination of looks and performance that make this a very special car: it would have been a Dino-eater, without a doubt!"

As noted earlier, eleven 916s were built, but the prototype used a production chassis (number 9141430195). Further details of this fascinating model, such as the chassis numbers, original engines and colour schemes, are listed in the accompanying table.

Other specials

Modified 914s are still very popular, particularly in the United States. A Californian company, Beach Boys

Year	Chassis no	Engine details	Notes
1971	9142330011	911S 2.4 litre unit, 190bhp	Canary Yellow
1971	9142330012	911S 2.4 litre unit, 190bhp	Silver Metallic
1971	9142330013	Carrera 2.7 litre unit, 210bhp	Black (later Viper Green)
1971	9142330014	Carrera 2.7 litre unit, 210bhp	Metallic Brown
1971	9142330015	Carrera 2.7 litre unit, 210bhp	Silver Metallic
1971	9142330016	Carrera 2.7 litre unit, 210bhp	Bahia Red
1971	9142330017	Carrera 2.7 litre unit, 210bhp	Gemini Metallic
1971	9142330018	Carrera 2.7 litre unit, 210bhp	Dark Blue
1971	9142330019	Carrera 2.7 litre unit, 210bhp	White (later with 3.2 engine)
1971	9142330020	Carrera 2.7 litre unit, 210bhp	Silver Metallic

A couple of views of a 914 police car.

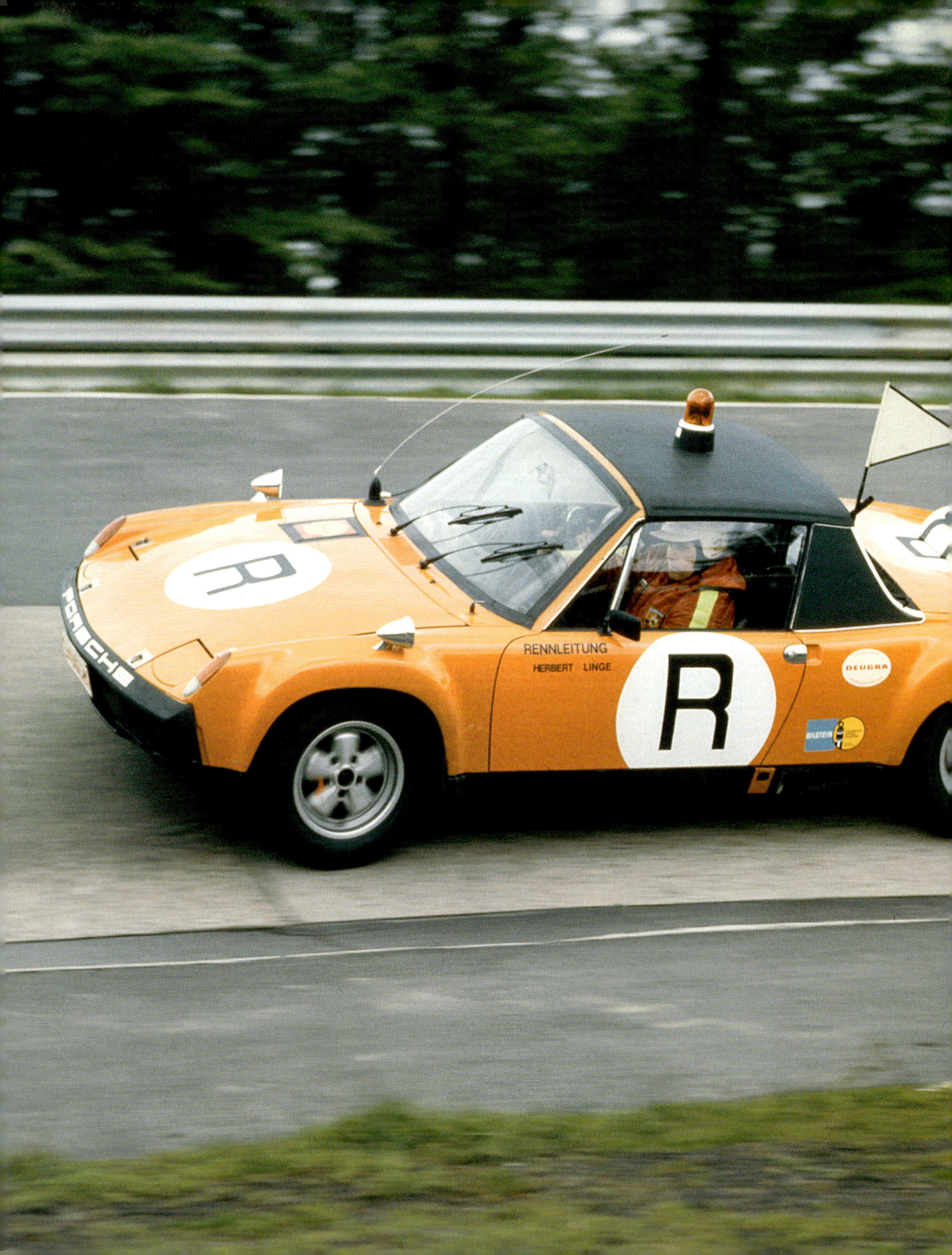
PORSCHE
R
RENNLEITUNG
HERBERT LINGE
R
DEUGRA
BILSTEIN

Racing, offers kits to convert a standard 914 into a speedster or a small pick-up truck, and Corsair Cars once listed a Dune Buggy and a 'Cal-look' conversion. Several other companies offer similar packages, with speedsters, generally, being by far the most elegant and practical.

In Europe, too, there are a number of specialists dealing in conversion kits and accessories, such as Lenner in Germany, but it is perhaps engine swapping that counts as the most popular activity among custom enthusiasts.

In America, there are currently at least five companies supplying either the components or complete kits to allow a Porsche 911 six-cylinder engine to be fitted in place of the 914's four-cylinder unit. Although this conversion is becoming very popular in the States, this book is more concerned with the specials produced when the car was still contemporary.

Back in the early 1970s, Rod Simpson Hybrids of West Los Angeles, California, was offering 914s installed with small block Chevrolet V8 units. Simpson was already well known for similar engine swaps on the 912 model, but the 914 was far better suited to the conversion. A tuned 4.6 litre V8 was shoehorned into the mid-engined Porsche to give a 0-60 time of just 6.3 seconds. The price was approximately $7500 for a finished vehicle.

One of the most interesting conversions was carried out by a Swiss enthusiast who commissioned Franco Sbarro (a racing mechanic who would later build his own rather special cars) to install a Wankel rotary engine from an NSU Ro80 into his 914. *Auto Motor und Sport* actually tried the car in 1971, reporting that it was "a delight to drive such a car." Sadly, Volkswagen never took the hint and the vehicle remained the only one in the world.

Perhaps the somewhat dubious honour of the craziest use of a 914 chassis goes to the German dealer who, in 1972, converted a 914/6 to carry a VW Beetle body and a 2.7 litre Carrera engine. Needless to say, the car was both very quick and unique!

The 914 series also saw official duty. Police forces first began ordering Porsches in the mid-1950s. Germany's and Holland's traffic police had a small

The Type 914/6 GT acting as course car. Later it was converted to carry fire-fighting equipment, making it the fastest fire engine in the world at that time. Over the years, many drivers at the Nürburgring were glad of this ...

The design study produced by ItalDesign for the Karmann Cheetah. The actual car was displayed at the 1971 Geneva Show, but never made it into production.

number of four- and six-cylinder 914s in their fleets, although it was not long before they were replaced by the 911.

The ex-Monte Carlo Rally practice 914/6 GT was used as a course car for the Nürburgring 1000km Race of May 1970, relaying messages to the race organisers via a two-way radio. Later, the 140mph (225kph) machine was kitted out with fire-fighting equipment to make it the world's fastest fire engine: with 220bhp on tap, it was quickly at the scene of an accident anywhere on the lengthy German circuit.

VW Karmann 'Cheetah'

Giugiaro and Karmann co-operation began in 1969, when the Italian firm was asked to style the VW Scirocco (launched at the 1974 Geneva Show). In the meantime, Giugiaro had been asked by Karmann to produce a prototype roadster based on the 1600 Volkswagen Beetle chassis and running gear.

The results, in the author's opinion at least, were fascinating. Here was a vehicle with nearly all of the features of the 914: it had a rear engine, though could just as easily have had a mid-engine layout, but looked strikingly modern, with lines that would no doubt have stood the test of time far better than the 914.

First shown at the 1971 Geneva Show, and with dimensions that could almost certainly have been scaled up without detracting from the crisp, balanced styling, it answered all of the criteria set out by the factory when first deciding to go ahead with the 914 project. Sadly, it remained a one-off prototype. If the Tapiro was a little too extreme for Stuttgart, was this the car that Porsche should have built?

7
After the 914

A final thought

The VW-Porsche 914 series has often been considered a disaster for Porsche and Volkswagen, but this is only true if viewed purely in VW production terms, or financial gain. It should be remembered that the entire Porsche 356 run totalled less than 76,500 units, whilst the Jaguar E-type finished on a total of 72,500. A fairer and perhaps more apposite comparison is to say that 914 production outstripped that of the mid-engined output from Matra, Lotus and Lancia combined – and by quite a considerable margin.

Although sales of nearly 120,000 units can hardly be considered a failure, the 914 range never did as well as envisaged for a number of reasons. The confusion about the model's pedigree (or at least the lack of a strong marque identity in most markets) probably caused the biggest problem. After a great deal of hard work, the Stuttgart company had left the image of Volkswagen far behind, and the last thing many Porsche customers wanted was to be reminded of their treasured possession's heritage. At the other end of the scale, traditional Volkswagen customers found the 914's styling difficult to accept and, besides, for the price of a four-cylinder 914, it was almost possible to buy two standard 1500 Beetles; the Karmann Ghia was also substantially cheaper.

Regarding the 914 model, Ferry Porsche once said: "With hindsight, in my opinion, there were two main unfortunate factors: all 914 bodies were built by Karmann and therefore did not necessarily represent Porsche quality. This was one handicap. The second reason: the inexpensive 914 with Volkswagen engine was even called 'VW-Porsche', which was not exactly conducive to making customers accept it as a genuine Porsche. In addition, it can be said that the installation of a four-cylinder engine and then also a six-cylinder engine led to an engineering concept that was not very fortunate ... there wasn't even enough space for a briefcase behind the seats."

In fact, Ferry Porsche had suggested the possibility of two different rear ends (one for the VW four- and another for the Porsche six-cylinder power unit) so that more space could be engineered into the cabin. These were rejected on the grounds of production cost, highlighting another problem faced by the respective manufacturers.

It has been noted on more than one occasion that maybe the 914 was doomed from the start. The catalogue from early 1970 read: "VW and Porsche present the no-compromise sports car." Despite this, however, there *were* compromises – a lot of them – in order to satisfy too many different requirements from the two parties involved.

The respected author, L J K Setright, put forward his point of view concerning the 914 in a recent *Classic Cars* article. He said: "Profiteering by the dealers and snobbishness among customers killed the 914/6 – yet it was the only Porsche honestly to make available to the public the features that had gained the marque a phenomenal reputation in racing; and it was upon that reputation that the fortunes of the firm were built in modern times."

Early press reports also didn't help. Reading some on the early 914s, it is often difficult to see how any cars were sold at all: according to the various contemporary magazines it was very expensive, didn't perform all that well, wasn't particularly pretty, and early build quality was definitely not what it should have been.

A decade before the 914, Daimler had tried to launch the SP250 in America; it, too, had many problems to overcome initially, but performance at least was excellent for the time. However, it had the wrong name for a sports car and, in five years, just over 1000 Daimler 'Darts' went Stateside. Notwithstanding the superb handling, its questionable how many four-cylinder 914s would have sold in America in the first place without the help of the Porsche badge; perhaps, after all, the manufacturers should breathe a sigh of relief when considering total sales figures ...

It should be remembered, too, that the financial climate was far from ideal during the early 1970s, in addition to which the period in which the 914 was built was one of great political unrest in West Germany: news headlines were dominated by the activities of groups such as Baader-Meinhof, and the bombing at the Munich Olympics. Only when Helmut Schmidt became Chancellor in 1974 did the country stabilise, despite a poor world economy.

Whatever the reasons for its disappointing performance, as far as the dealers were concerned, the 914 series was destined to have a short life, at least by usual Porsche and Volkswagen production standards. The last cars were completed in the Osnabrück works during the early part of 1976, with final sales occurring during June.

The 912E

Ironically, the 912 (the car that the 914 replaced) was re-introduced briefly for the American market during the 1976 model year, and was produced for a while alongside the last of the two-litre 914s, until the all-new 924 got into its stride as far as production was concerned.

Known as the 912E, this model provided dealers with a lower priced machine with which to bridge the gap between the demise of the 914 and the wait for the forthcoming 924. As Road & Track noted: "The 912E will obviously find favour with those who prefer a slightly more practical and tractable Porsche. It's a car with almost all the sporting virtues of the more expensive 911S, yet its simpler pushrod four-cylinder engine should make for better fuel economy and less expensive maintenance than the 911's six."

It was powered by the 923/02 engine; essentially the same as that found in the later two-litre 914 (ie a Volkswagen unit), but with the L-Jetronic fuel-injection system found on 1.8 litre models. Even with just 86bhp on tap, performance was more than respectable: Road & Track recorded a top speed of 115mph (184kph) and a 0-60 time of 11.5 seconds.

Various mechanical aspects of the vehicle were simplified to keep production costs down (such as fitting only a front anti-roll bar, and using solid rather than ventilated disc brakes), as well as a number of features in interior specification. Otherwise, especially if the optional Fuchs alloy wheels were fitted, it was hard to tell a 912E apart from a 911S.

Although shortlived, according to the chassis numbers (which ran from 9126000001 to 9126002099), a total of 2099 912Es were built, all during the 1976 model year, and all destined for American shores. There it sold for $10,845, exactly $3000 cheaper than a 911S coupé, but some $3600 more expensive than the two-litre 914. In the meantime, a totally new Porsche had been launched in Europe.

The 924

The 924 project was originally a design commissioned by Volkswagen under the number EA-425. Almost from the moment the 914 was launched, Volkswagen had been considering the details for its more conventional successor, and the Type 924 was it.

However, at the last minute, just as the machine had reached the pre-production stage, the management at Volkswagen cancelled it. Due to a combination of political wrangling and the energy crisis, the concensus at VW was that it would be too expensive to produce. Porsche was given the opportunity to buy back the design to put it into production, which it did.

The 924 was exactly what Porsche needed in the hard economic times of the 1970s. Sales in general had fallen off considerably, and just 9424 cars were produced in Stuttgart in 1975. However, sales did soon pick up with the introduction of the low-priced 924 in November 1975; at last, Porsche had the entry level machine it had originally been trying for with the 914.

The 924 was a huge departure from traditional Porsche practice. The engine was a water-cooled, 1984cc, four-cylinder unit mounted at the front, with rear-wheel drive through a transaxle system (ie a gearbox combined with the rear axle). With an overhead camshaft and K-Jetronic fuel-injection, the two-litre unit developed a modest 125bhp, but powered the car to 125mph (200kph) and gave excellent fuel economy.

The first prototype 924. Note the heavier rear wing treatment, broken up by vents under the large back window – a prominent feature, even at this early stage.

The elegant body was designed by the Dutchman, Harm Lagaay, under the supervision of Tony Lapine. It was a wedge-shaped 2+2 coupé with smooth lines and a large glass hatch at the rear; even today, it looks surprisingly modern, thanks to some fine detailing.

Naturally, considering that the 924 was going to be part of the VW-Audi range, the vehicle used a large number of parts sourced from that organisation (including the engine block, suspension components, and many interior fittings), and was actually assembled at the old NSU factory.

The 924 made it into America as an early 1977 model year car, superceding the 912E in the spring of 1976. At just $9395, it was some $4600 cheaper than a 911S coupé, and over $1000 cheaper than the shortlived model it replaced. The car was an instant hit, making up more than 13,500 of the 20,000 Porsche sales in the States that year.

For the 1978 model year, a Porsche-designed, five-speed gearbox was made available as a cost option, and the rear suspension and exhaust were modified. A November 1977 article noted: "For the front-engined 924 changes are both engineering and cosmetic. The 1978 models are now quieter and brake pad life has been increased, while anti-roll bars are fitted at both ends for the British market; pile carpet is now used and the rear seats are cloth-trimmed. The 924 now costs £7350 with the 924 Lux, which incorporates a number of previous options – sports wheels, tinted windows, rear wiper and headlamp washers – coming out at £7800." On 24 April 1978, the 50,000th 924 left the works.

The 924 was continually developed and, in November 1978, a 170bhp turbocharged version made its debut, followed a year later by a special lighter and more powerful Carrera GT model. By 1981, over 100,000 924s had been sold, making it one of the most successful Porsche models ever.

The 924 has recently received a lot of good reports from the classic car press. Martin Buckley wrote for *Classic & Sportscar*: "Fifty-fifty weight distribution gives the 924 good, well-balanced handling that allows you to hold deliciously long drifts beyond the limit, though the normal attitude is neutrality with precise, informative and light steering – not unlike that of a 911 – allied to slight roll angles. For the money, it's really a lot of fun."

They last well, too. The author's 1978 example had superb coachwork 20 years after it was built and, even after 150,000 miles (240,000km), still had its factory oil pressure and hardly ever needed topping up; a slightly worn driver's seat was literally the only giveaway of the car's age. Although not quite as exciting to drive, it was a breath of fresh air in so many respects after several years of Alfetta GTV ownership.

The contemporary 911s

The six-cylinder engine of the 911 range was constantly upgraded; from 2.2 litres for 1970, to 2.4 litres for 1972, and on to 2.7 litres for 1974 – the Carrera ultimately became a three-litre unit. The legendary 911 Turbo appeared at the 1974 Paris Salon, taking the world by storm with its electrifying performance. Not only was this the quickest road car to come from the Stuttgart factory during that period, it was also the most

Cutaway drawing of the 924, clearly showing the engine/transmission layout. It also reveals disc brakes at the front, drums at the rear, and a suspension essentially similar to that of a 911.

expensive at nearly twice the price of a 911S coupé.

For the 1976 model year, the European-specification 2687cc units were given more power until the normally-aspirated range was standardized at three litres for 1978. At the same time, the Turbo was endowed with a 3.3 litre six developing a hefty 300bhp. The range had been simplified to allow for the addition of another new car to join the Porsche line-up: the 928.

The 928 and 944

Introduced in February 1977, the 928 was a member of the same family as the 924, with a front-mounted, water-cooled engine and transaxle to give good weight distribution. The engine in this instance, however, was a V8 unit of 4.5 litres designed to tempt customers who traditionally bought from the likes of Jaguar and Mercedes-Benz.

In actual fact, work on the 928 began before the
continued page 189

Pop-up headlights were a 924 feature carried over from the 914.

The interior of the Porsche 924 with manual transmission; a three-speed automatic was also available. Electric windows became an option for the 1978 model year, as did a new Porsche-designed five-speed gearbox.

The clean lines of the 924 rear have stood the test of time well. The rubber strip along the waistline was added shortly after production began, but the alloy wheels were a cost option.

Part of the 911 range for 1976 (from left to right): the three-litre Carrera Targa; the 2.7 litre 911 (the 912E looked virtually the same), and the mighty 260bhp Porsche Turbo.

The V8-engined 928 was a true Grand Tourer, and Porsche's answer to competition from the Jaguar XJ-S and the Mercedes-Benz SL/SLC series.

The Porsche 944 was powered by a 2.5 litre, four-cylinder engine (not a six like most manufacturers adopt once a two litre capacity has been reached). The body was essentially that of a 924 with flared wheelarches.

After the 914, it was not until the mid-1990s that Porsche again tried its hand at a mid-engined production car. It was more expensive than was hoped but the purposeful-looking Boxster survived into the 21st century, and has recently received a face-lift. This is the production model for the 1997 model year.

924 project, as at one point it was suggested as the possible successor to the 911 range. However, when the Type 924 passed to Porsche ownership, because the need for a cheaper car was greater, it was the smaller-engined model that ended up going into production first.

The 928, being a luxury Grand Tourer, was not cheap by any standard. In America, its largest market, it cost $28,500 on introduction. This compares to $11,995 for a 924, or $19,500 for a 911SC coupé – only the 911 Turbo was more expensive. The 155mph (248kph) 928S was added to the range in August 1979, with the engine bored out to give 4.7 litres and 300bhp.

The gap between the 924 and 928 was narrowed for the 1982 model year by the appearance of the 2.5 litre, four-cylinder 944. Although clearly based on the 924, both mechanically and visually, the 944 used less VW-Audi sourced parts and was much quicker. Porsche launched a turbocharged version capable of 152mph (243kph) four years later.

The new generation of Porsches proved highly successful in terms of sales. There also followed another glorious period of competition victories in endurance events, and the marque entered the Formula One arena again by supplying McLaren with engines from 1983: fortunately, with far greater success than the company's first venture into the world of F1.

Appendix I
Concise buyer's guide

It appears that most of the troubles experienced with the 914 range today are actually the same as those encountered when the cars were contemporary. Fortunately, most problems were gradually ironed out as the model was developed, so later cars appear to be the best to go for (for a number of reasons, as will be explained later). Twenty years on from when production ended, rust is, of course, another factor to take into account.

Body
Unlike its successor (which has a fine reputation for resistance to corrosion), comparitively speaking, the 914s do rust quite badly. Extensive double-skinning on panels has not particularly helped the situation, and the cost of replacement body panels is high. However, it must be said that the 914 is certainly no worse than most and fares substantially better than contemporary Italian cars, for instance.

Like all old cars, the door bottoms and sills should be inspected (door skins are available, but they are

Check front and rear extremities for signs of corrosion, as well as the area around the headlamp wells, bumper mountings and – well, just about everywhere. Sadly, VW-Porsche 914 bodies have a reputation for rust ...

Originality is important on any collectible car. The main text of the book will help define what is and isn't correct for your particular vehicle. This is an American-spec 914/4 from the 1973 model year.

very expensive). Properly checking the box section on each side of the car involves removal of the outer sill covering, but a good idea of condition can be gauged by prodding each end of the sill to see if there is any sign of rust. Lift the carpets inside to look at the inner sills/sill steps. Sills were always painted matt black (except on Limited Edition cars) and, unless the vehicle was fitted with the M471 kit, or is a real GT or 916, they should be steel rather than glassfibre.

914s generally have some rot in the engine compartment, with the battery box often being the first and most obvious area to fall victim to rust, especially on earlier cars, which either didn't have a battery cover, or had one which was too small (later cars had a full-size cover for the top). Battery acid and the elements entering through the engine grille were a lethal combination for the metal underneath.

Excessive body rot in the area of the battery box can often cause the rear suspension mounting to collapse, eventually leading to the offside wheel disappearing under the bodywork – a disastrous situation. Whereas most common bodywork problems can be fixed quite easily, the only cost-effective remedy, when faced with this scenario, is to buy a replacement rolling chassis.

Four-cylinder cars tend not to suffer as badly as they had a tray under the engine grille to prevent ingress of the worst of the weather.

Both front and rear extremities of the car should be checked. Foam was injected into the panels to prevent rust but, unfortunately, the idea backfired as the foam holds moisture and therefore promotes corrosion: VW-Porsche was not alone in learning too late about this problem. Rot is also quite common around the torsion bar mounting.

The area behind the front bumpers is a common rust spot, the front scuttle often has a small amount of rust near the windscreen, and both luggage compartments should be inspected, especially the floors. The front luggage compartment lid is prone to rot at both rear corners and the leading edge where the lock is located. Also check the rear compartment hinges and mechanism.

The door handles are prone to metal fatigue, regardless of year. Unfortunately, as with most cars from the period, cheap material was used to reduce production costs.

Contemporary problems mentioned by the majority of owners concerned body parts. *Road & Track* expanded on that broad statement with the following: "The general term 'body parts' covers a lot of things, but 914s had a lot of problems. There were no major mechanical complications with the body, just careless workmanship. Locks froze [seized] on doors and trunks, bumper guards and door handles fell off and headlights wouldn't pop up. Many owners griped about the thin sheet metal in the 914. Although a thin skin helps make a lighter car, the 914's long flat body panels are very tender when it's parked in close quarters."

There were a multitude of bumper, lighting and other options depending on the market, as well as different badges and decals – refer to the text for guidance. Most parts are still readily available from specialists, and the 914 now has such a loyal band of followers that, as parts go out of circulation, they are rapidly remanufactured.

The wings, floorpan, headlamp wells and the area around the door strike panel are also known to rot, and should be carefully inspected for previous repairs. Of lesser importance, the Targa roof has an annoying habit of squeaking as the body flexes. This can usually be cured by a liberal dose of silicone spray, but the roof also has something of a reputation for leaking, and the clips that hold it in place in the rear compartment are renowned for breaking. It should also be remembered that only the 914/6 had underseal applied as standard; it was an option on the four-cylinder cars.

Chassis numbers are located in the front luggage compartment, either stamped into the offside wheelarch, on a plate attached to the casing of the offside headlamp (up to the 1974 MY), or on a plate fixed to the front bulkhead (1975 model year on). American-specification 914s also have the chassis number mounted on a small plate on the nearside windscreen pillar. The coachbuilder's plate is situated on the inside of the nearside door post and carries paint details.

Exterior trim
Although the black vinyl covering on the roll-bar looks good, the aluminium trim running along the bottom of the bar is often the source of corrosion, with rain getting in underneath it. A quick check is to run a finger across the top of the trim to see whether the metal under the vinyl is lumpy (ie rusty), or smooth as it should be. A proper repair is an expensive job.

Engine
For a mid-engined vehicle, access is quite good, though obviously nowhere near as convenient as a front- or rear-engined machine. Generally speaking, the four-cylinder 914s uphold Volkswagen's fine reputation for reliability, and almost every part on the 1.7 and 1.8 litre models is interchangeable with the standard 411/412 unit. Not many 411/412 items will fit the larger two-litre engines, however, these being unique to the 914 and the later VW Transporter range.

Of the few known mechanical problems in the VW-powered cars, the most common is valves dropping – something found on all air-cooled VW units, not just those used in the 914s. This usually results in a holed piston.

Contemporary reports note that the starter solenoid used to be a constant source of grief when the engine was hot. Distributor problems were listed in *Road & Track*, as were Bosch sparkplug maladies; the best remedy for the latter is apparently to fit NGKs instead!

The fuel-injection system on four-cylinder cars is reasonably reliable but, like all fuel-injection set-ups, can be expensive to fix if it does develop a problem: a

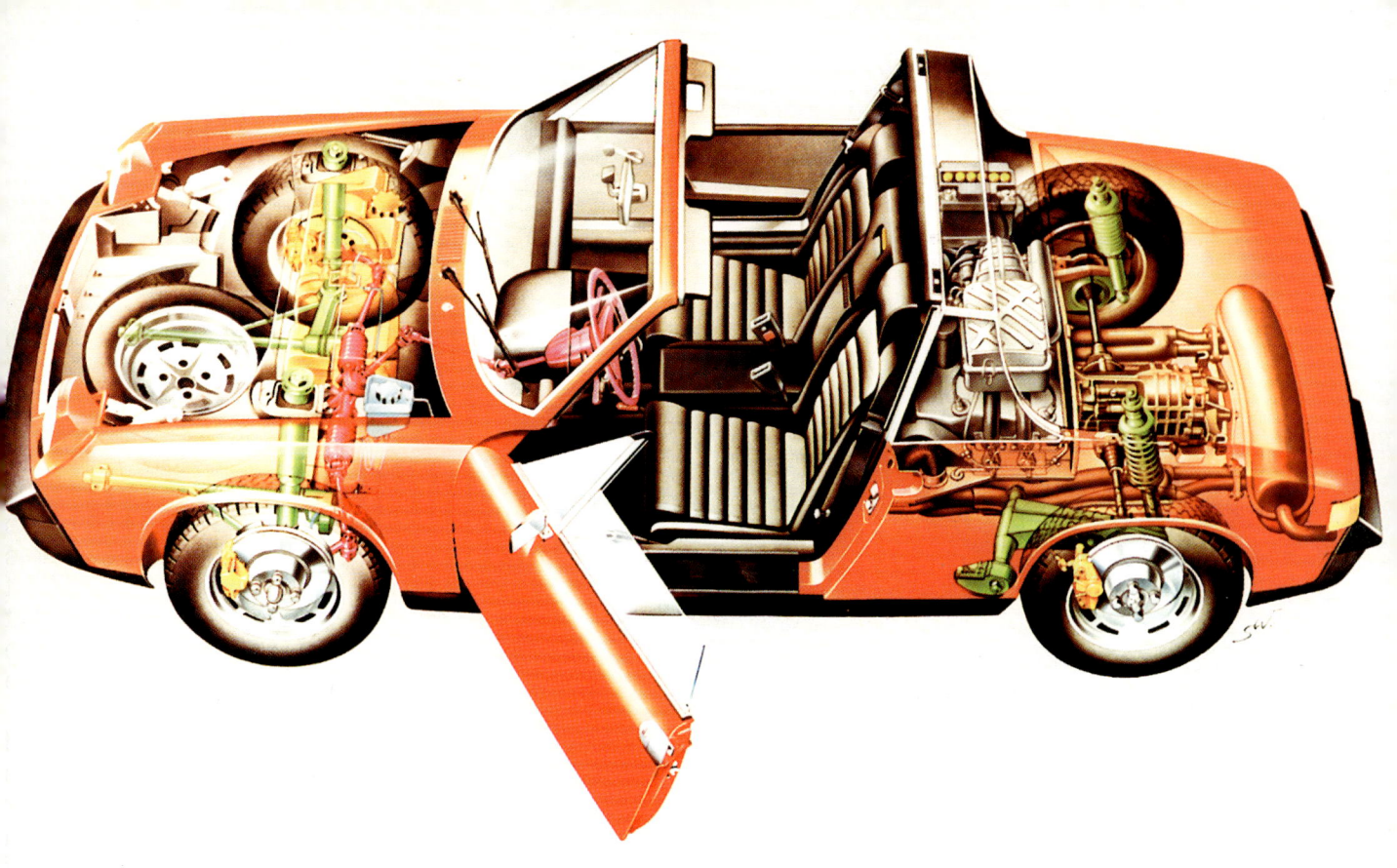

This cutaway drawing of the 914-2.0 shows all of the major components in their correct places, and should help to identify and locate any of the items mentioned in this chapter, including body panels and specific areas.

number of owners have converted their engines to run on carburettors.

The rubber fuel pipes that connect the injectors to the rest of the system should be checked, as they have been known to perish through a leaking battery, sending fuel at high pressure in the direction of the distributor. As a contemporary survey listed the fuel pump and fuel lines as common problem areas while the cars were still relatively new, they are well worth careful inspection. In this respect, an improvement was made from 1972 model year vehicles.

Exhaust systems tend not to have very long lives, especially on cars that aren't used all that often. The exhaust systems vary for the four-cylinder variants and – naturally – for the six-cylinder machine. They are quite expensive but readily available, although many owners have changed to specialist exhausts, like those produced by Ansa.

The six-cylinder Porsche engines are very strong, but it is worth checking valve guide and chain tensioner condition. Worn valve guides can usually be diagnosed quite easily by looking at the exhaust, as the engine smokes badly when on the over-run or under hard acceleration. If the chains rattle, there is probably a tensioner problem that needs to be sorted quickly – both jobs can be expensive to rectify. The remote oil tank for the 914/6 is located under the nearside rear wing.

Transmission

The gear linkage on earlier cars had a very poor reputation, although was improved with the introduction of the Type 914/12 transmission for the 1973 model year. In any case, as one owner put it: "A bit of careful adjusting and lubricating turned a car with a reputation for sloppy shifting into a car with an enjoyable linkage."

Very early 914s (ie 1970 and 1971 models) were renowned for synchromesh problems, particularly on first and second gears, but also on third. Something

This picture shows the rear suspension and drive shafts on a 1973 model year car. The suspension mounting area should be checked for body corrosion (especially on the offside, underneath the battery box), and drive shafts often give trouble.

else that came to light in the *Road & Track* survey was that "... 13% of the owners reported [clutch cable] breakages, on some occasions more than once. It is not the fault of the cable, but of the nylon pulley that guides it. It should, according to one owner, be cleaned every 600 miles [1000km] to avoid rapid cable deterioration, but that's asking a lot of an owner."

Another common problem is the stretch bolt on the final drive shaft coming undone inside the gearbox, but this can be avoided by using Loctite once it is tightened properly. Driveshafts often fail but are easy to obtain (being the same as those used on the 911s).

Suspension, steering & braking system

The suspension and steering have no special problems to speak of, and parts are easy to obtain for both Volkswagen and Porsche-powered machines.

Because of the mid-engined layout, with the suspension correctly set, the 914 handles very well. When Lotus had one to evaluate, Graham Arnold, the company's sales chief at the time, was so impressed that he actually considered buying it. It will be remembered that the Lotus Elan was extremely accomplished in the handling department, so this is praise indeed.

Apart from looking for the usual signs of wear or lack of maintenance, it should be borne in mind that the rear brake calipers often seize. They can be reconditioned easily and cheaply, but if replacements are needed, because they incorporate the handbrake they are quite complex and therefore very expensive.

Another common problem is a seized or sticking brake pedal, caused by corrosion locking up the pedal assembly. Stripping and cleaning the assembly, then adding a new nylon bush, cures the fault. Brakes on four-cylinder models are sourced from Volkswagen, whilst those for six-cylinder cars come from Porsche.

The 914 series was fitted with a bewildering number of wheel and tyre options. Standard steel 4.5J wheels came from the VW range, although the 5.5J version was unique. Pedrini, Mahle and Fuchs wheels were also specially made. Six-cylinder cars shared all wheel options with the 911 range, including the standard steel items. All equivalent tyre size options are still available today.

Interiors generally last well, although expect cracks in plastic components if the car has come from a hot climate. This 914/6 had the Beetle-sourced window winders that are often apt to fail. Note also the trim on top of the rear wing, a common spot for corrosion; to eradicate the rust completely would mean removing the wing which, like the front wing, is welded in place to add rigidity to the chassis.

Interior

Generally speaking, 914 interiors last quite well. The main problem with the interior has always been the glue used by the factory to secure the dashboard, door panels, roof headliner, and so on, which after several months in service, rapidly lost effectiveness, forcing owners to use something stronger.

Windows also gave trouble, even while the car was contemporary, as the Beetle window winders found on the early cars failed. When they did work there was often an insufficient seal at the front and rear of the glass; the window has also been known to come free of its runners. The design of the side window was changed in 1973, but niggly faults endured.

Clear laminated windscreens were standard on the 914/6, the 914-2.0, and all cars destined for America, Canada and Sweden: tinted laminated screens were an option. On the smaller-engined machines, clear tempered glass was the norm, with either of the two laminated screens as options. The rear screen was never offered in tinted glass, but could be purchased with a heater element.

According to *Road & Track*: "Speedometers and tachometers failed completely or sporadically; drive cables broke, bevel gears failed." In actual fact, instrument failure was listed as one of the most common problems with the series. The speedometer problem is often linked with the stretch bolt inside the gearbox. Instruments were sourced from either the VW or Porsche parts bin, depending on which engine was used, though all came from VDO originally.

Heating system

One of the main problems cited in the 1974 *Road & Track* survey was unsatisfactory heating and ventilation: "As in our previous Porsche owner survey, the heater was a continual trouble spot (13% mentioned it), although we can add air-blower ventilation problems for the 914. It simply didn't work well enough most of the time, and it also stopped working, rotted and smelled."

The most serious heating problems can usually be traced to the heat exchangers; it is not unusual to lose the outer shrouding, thus rendering the heater totally ineffective.

Spares today

The German rule that requires spares be manufactured for ten years after a model's production run has ended has ensured that most mechanical components are available, with the VW-engined cars being particularly well catered for.

Porsche and Volkswagen dealers/specialists can usually supply any necessary parts. The harder to obtain items will almost certainly be available (either new or second-hand) from the small but growing number of dedicated specialists in Germany and the United States. As the more popular parts run out, it's become increasingly common for specialists to remanufacture them, thanks in no small part to the increased value of the 914 series.

Membership of a Porsche Club will reap benefits in the long-term, as most specialists advertise in club magazines, and club members can offer advice and provide valuable contacts.

The best buy?

The 914 series used to be the poor relation in the Porsche family; indeed, the author can remember being offered one for just £600 by a trader friend in the mid-1980s! But prices have risen dramatically over the past decade. So much so, that they have now caught up with the lower end of the 911 market, which would have seemed impossible a few years ago.

As most of the production went to America, not surprisingly, this is where the vast majority of vehicles are concentrated today. A number of specialists deal with the 914 in Europe, but most cars still originate from the States. However, as many have learnt, it is probably well worth avoiding the temptation to save a few pounds by importing sight unseen.

Which is the best to buy? Of course, this all depends on personal preference and budget. The rare and desirable 914/6 will cost more to buy in the first place, more to run and, indeed, more to maintain. But if it is the beautiful sound of the classic six-cylinder Porsche engine that appeals the most, then there is no other option.

However, if it is just the 914 concept that is important, the European-spec, two-litre, four-cylinder models were not far behind the Porsche-engined model on power. They are naturally more plentiful, making them cheaper to buy initially; spares are a lot less expensive, and, with most of the improvements to the 914 series occuring on, or after, the 1973 model year range, it is probably this model that offers the best value for money.

www.veloce.co.uk

Appendix II
Engine specifications

The following tables list all of the engines that were used in the 914 series, complete with main specifications:

Type W80
Production (MY)........... 1970-1972
Main market .... All
Cylinders .... Four
Bore & stroke .... 90 x 66mm
Cubic capacity............. 1679cc
Compression ratio 8.2:1
Fuel system .... D-Jetronic MPC fuel-injection
Hp (DIN) @ rpm .... 80bhp @ 4900
Torque @ rpm.............. 100lbft @ 3500

Type 901/36
Production (MY)........... 1970-1972
Main market .... All
Cylinders .... Six
Bore & stroke .... 80 x 66mm
Cubic capacity............. 1991cc
Compression ratio 8.6:1
Fuel system .... 2 x triple-choke Weber carburettors
Hp (DIN) @ rpm .... 110bhp @ 5800
Torque @ rpm.............. 116lbft @ 4200

Type EA80
Production (MY)........... 1972-1973
Main market .... All
Cylinders .... Four
Bore & stroke .... 90 x 66mm
Cubic capacity............. 1679cc
Compression ratio 8.2:1
Fuel system .... D-Jetronic MPC fuel-injection
Hp (DIN) @ rpm .... 80bhp @ 4900
Torque @ rpm.............. 99lbft @ 2700

Type EB72
Production (MY)........... 1973
Main market .... USA
Cylinders .... Four
Bore & stroke .... 90 x 66mm
Cubic capacity............. 1679cc
Compression ratio 7.3:1
Fuel system .... D-Jetronic MPC fuel-injection
Hp (DIN) @ rpm .... 72bhp @ 5000
Torque @ rpm.............. 90lbft @ 3700

Type GA95
Production (MY)........... 1973-1974
Main market .... USA
Cylinders .... Four
Bore & stroke .... 94 x 71mm
Cubic capacity............. 1971cc
Compression ratio 7.6:1
Fuel system .... D-Jetronic MPC fuel-injection
Hp (DIN) @ rpm .... 95bhp @ 4900
Torque @ rpm.............. 109lbft @ 3500

Type GB100
Production (MY) 1973-1975
Main market .... Europe
Cylinders .... Four
Bore & stroke .... 94 x 71mm
Cubic capacity............. 1971cc
Compression ratio 8.0:1
Fuel system .... D-Jetronic MPC fuel-injection
Hp (DIN) @ rpm .... 100bhp @ 5000
Torque @ rpm.............. 115lbft @ 3500

Type EC76
Production (MY)........... 1974
Main market .... USA
Cylinders .... Four
Bore & stroke .... 93 x 66mm
Cubic capacity............. 1795cc
Compression ratio 7.3:1
Fuel system .... L-Jetronic AFC fuel-injection
Hp (DIN) @ rpm .... 76bhp @ 4800
Torque @ rpm.............. 94lbft @ 3400

Type AN85
Production (MY)........... 1974-1975
Main market .... Europe
Cylinders .... Four
Bore & stroke .... 93 x 66mm
Cubic capacity............. 1795cc
Compression ratio 8.6:1
Fuel system .... 2 x twin-choke Weber carburettors
Hp (DIN) @ rpm .... 85bhp @ 5000
Torque @ rpm.............. 105lbft @ 3500

Type EC76
Production (MY)........... 1975
Main market .... USA
Cylinders .... Four
Bore & stroke .... 93 x 66mm
Cubic capacity............. 1795cc
Compression ratio 7.3:1
Fuel system .... L-Jetronic AFC fuel-injection
Hp (DIN) @ rpm .... 76bhp @ 4900
Torque @ rpm.............. 89lbft @ 4000

Type GC88
Production (MY)........... 1975-1976
Main market .... USA
Cylinders .... Four
Bore & stroke .... 94 x 71mm
Cubic capacity............. 1971cc
Compression ratio 7.6:1
Fuel system .... D-Jetronic MPC fuel-injection
Hp (DIN) @ rpm .... 88bhp @ 4900
Torque @ rpm.............. 105lbft @ 3500

Appendix III
Chassis specifications

Brief specifications of all the 914 Porsches arranged in chronological/engine size order (to be used in conjunction with powerplant details in Appendix II):

Porsche 914/4
Production (MY)	1970-1972
Engine types	W80
	EA80
Cylinders	Four
Cylinder capacity	1.7 litres (102cu. in.)
Transmission type	914/11
0-60 time	12.4 secs
Top speed	110mph (176kph)
Weight	900kg (1980lb)

Porsche 914/6
Production (MY)	1970-1972
Engine type	901/36
Cylinders	Six
Cylinder capacity	2.0 litres (121cu. in.)
Transmission type	914/01
0-60 time	8.8 secs
Top speed	123mph (197kph)
Weight	940kg (2070lb)

Porsche 914-1.7
Production (MY)	1973
Engine types	EA80
	EB72
Cylinders	Four
Cylinder capacity	1.7 litres (102cu. in.)
Transmission type	914/12
0-60 time	12.4 secs
Top speed	110mph (176kph)
Weight	900kg (1980lb)

Porsche 914-2.0
Production (MY)	1973-1976
Engine types	GA95
	GB100
	GC88
Cylinders	Four
Cylinder capacity	2.0 litres (120cu. in.)
Transmission type	914/12
0-60 time	10.5 secs
Top speed	116mph (186kph)
Weight	923kg (2030lb)

Porsche 914-1.8
Production (MY)	1974-1975
Engine types	AN85
	EC76
Cylinders	Four
Cylinder capacity	1.8 litres (109cu. in.)
Transmission type	914/12
0-60 time	12.1 secs
Top speed	112mph (179kph)
Weight	910kg (2000lb)

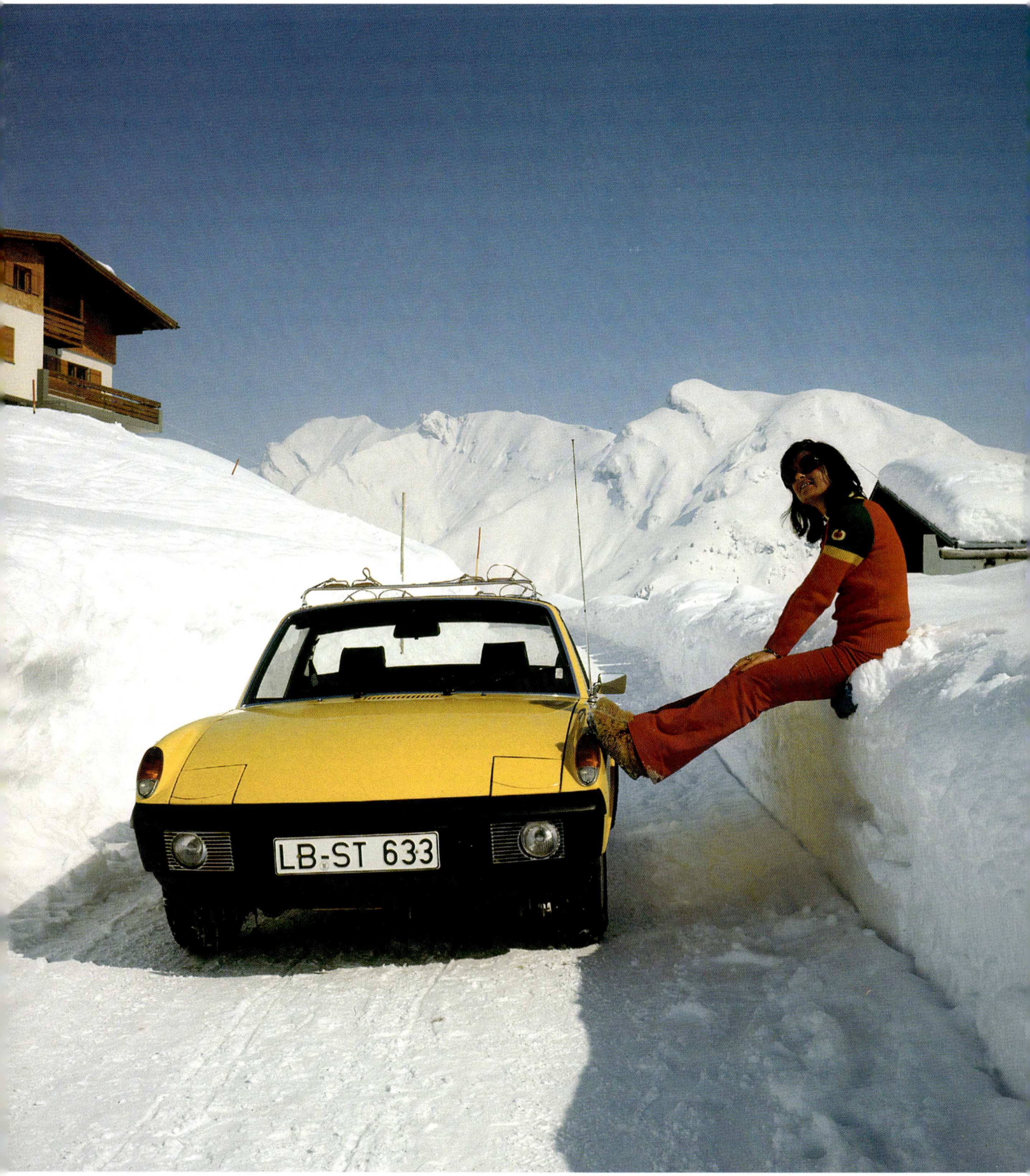
LB-ST 633

Appendix IV
Production details

A complete breakdown of 914 production, including chassis numbers, engines (type, size and number of cylinders), and yearly build numbers:

	Chassis numbers	Engines	Size	No built
1970 MY (built 1969/70)				
914/4	4702900001-4702913312	W80	1.7 (4)	13,312
914/6	9140430011-9140432668	901/36	2.0 (6)	2657
914/8	914006-914111	908/03	3.0 (8)	2
1971 MY (built 1970/71)				
914/4	4712900001-4712916231	W80	1.7 (4)	16,231
916/6	9141430011-9141430443	901/36	2.0 (6)	432
1972 MY (built 1971/72)				
914/4	4722900001-4722921580	W80	1.7 (4)	
		EA80	1.7 (4)	21,580
916	9142330011-9142330020	911/53	2.4 (6)	
		911/83	2.7 (6)	10
914/6	9142430011-9142430260	901/36	2.0 (6)	229
1973 MY (built 1972/73)				
914-1.7	4732900001-4732927660	EA80	1.7 (4)	
		EB72	1.7 (4)	
914-2.0		GA95	2.0 (4)	
		GB100	2.0 (4)	27,660

1974 MY (built 1973/74)

914-1.8	4742900001-4742921370	AN85	1.8 (4)	
		EC76	1.8 (4)	
914-2.0		GA95	2.0 (4)	
		GB100	2.0 (4)	21,370

1975 MY (built 1974/75)

914-1.8	4752900001-4752911369	AN85	1.8 (4)	
		EC76	1.8 (4)	
914-2.0		GC88	2.0 (4)	
		GB100	2.0 (4)	11,369

1976 MY (built 1975/76)

914-2.0	4762900001-4762904075	GC88	2.0 (4)	4075

Total production

Standard four-cylinder 914 series cars 115,597
Standard six-cylinder 914 series cars 3318
Number of special factory-built cars 12
Grand total of 914 series cars built 118,927

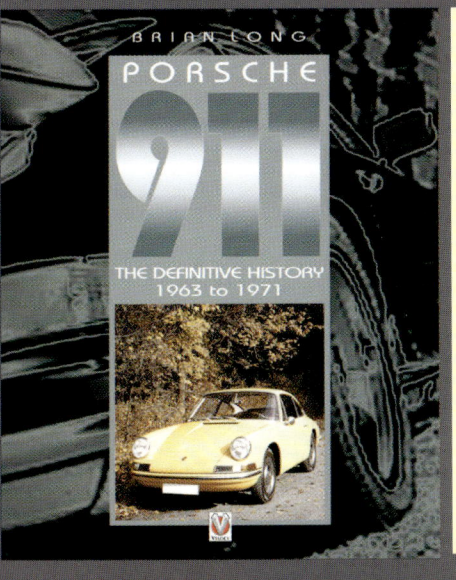

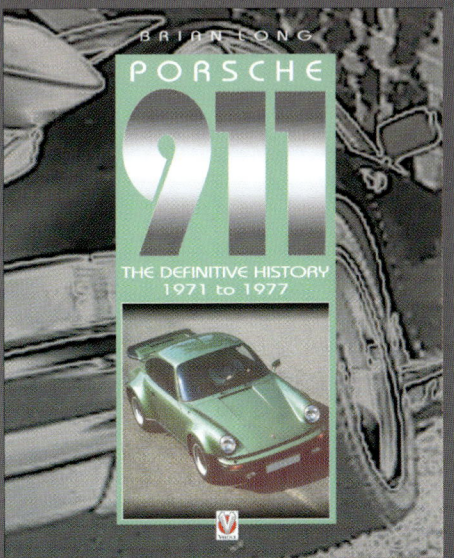

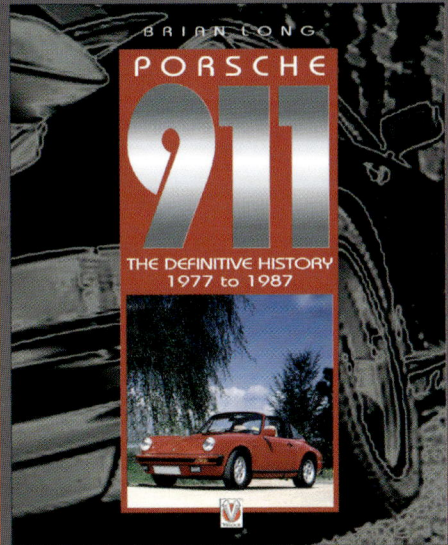

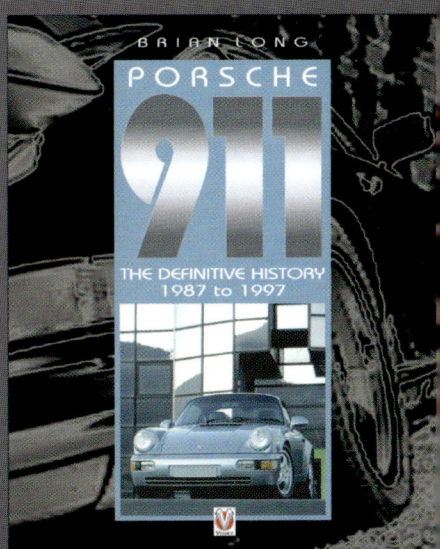

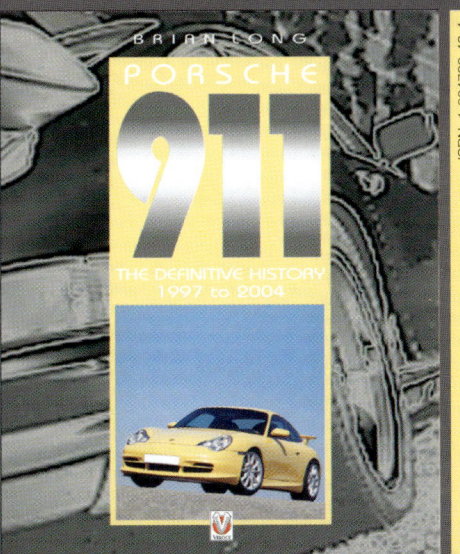

The definitive, in-depth history of the evergreen Porsche 911

192-208 pages • over 230 mainly colour illustrations each volume • 25x20.7cm • £29.99-£34.99

Post & packing extra: please call 01305 260068 or e-mail info@veloce.co.uk for details

Another great Porsche book from Veloce!

Porsche 911 3.2 Carrera
The last of the Evolution

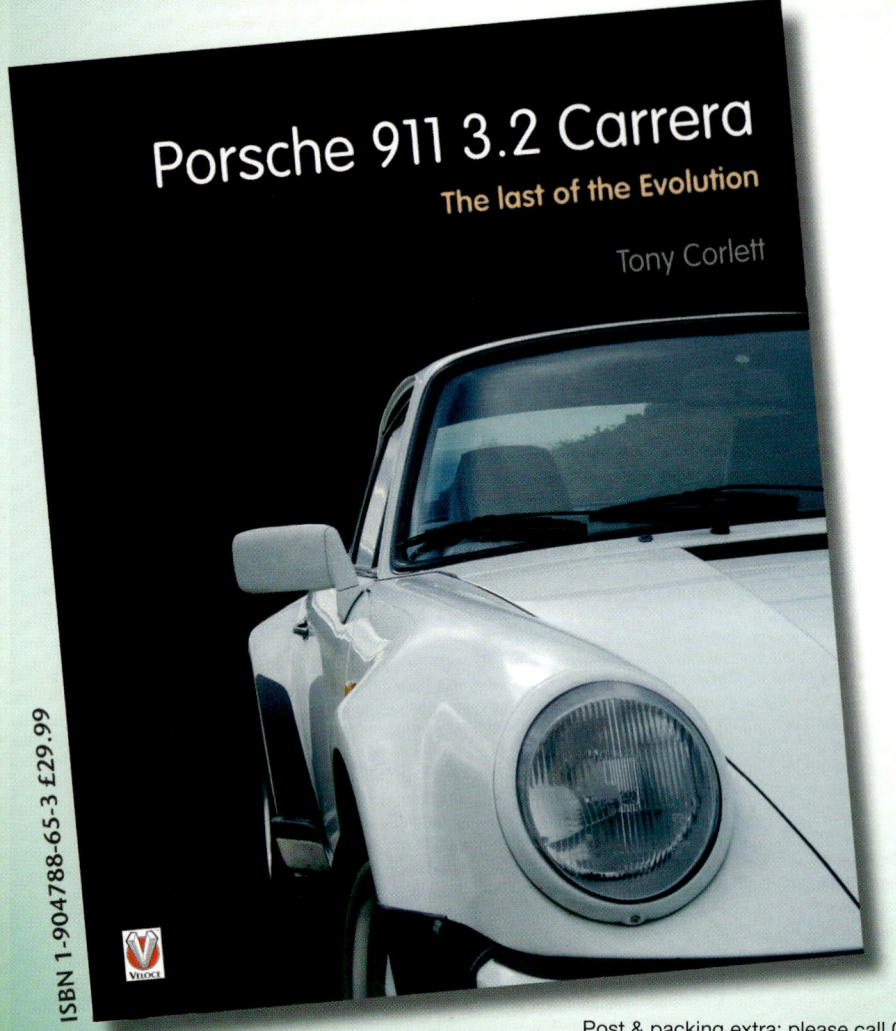

ISBN 1-904788-65-3 £29.99

Post & packing extra: please call 01305 260068 or e-mail info@veloce.co.uk for details

The complete enthusiast's guide to the Porsche 911 3.2 Carrera, written by the 911 3.2 Register Secretary of the Porsche Club Great Britain

NEW FROM VELOCE!

STOP!

Don't buy a Porsche 928 without buying this book first!

Having this book is just like having a marque expert by your side. Benefit from David Hemmings' years of ownership experience; learn how to spot a bad car quickly, and how to assess a promising car like a professional. This is the COMPLETE GUIDE to choosing, assessing and buying your dream car

Paperback • 195x139mm • 64 pages • 100 colour pictures
ISBN 1-904788-70-X • £9.99

The Essential Buyer's Guide — PORSCHE 928 — Your marque expert: David Hemmings

Other published titles cover the Volkswagen Beetle and Alfa Romeo Giulia GT, with many more planned - call for details: 01305 260068

Post & packing extra: please call 01305 260068 or e-mail info@veloce.co.uk for details

Seriously BIG Porsche books!

Porsche 993 The Essential Companion

by Adrian Streather
26.5 x 21cm • 688 pages • 1300 illustrations • £49.99

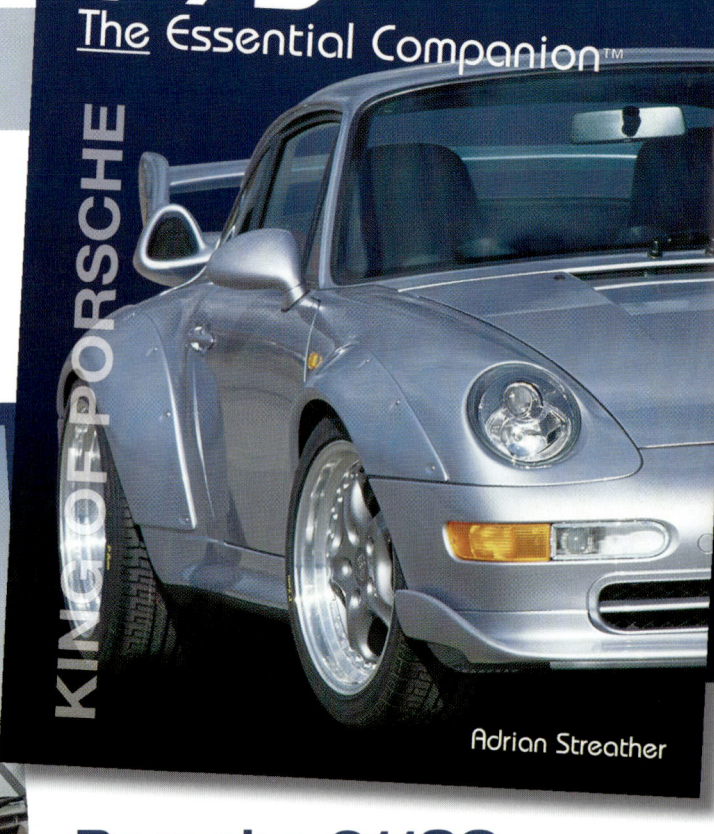

Porsche 911SC The Essential Companion

by Adrian Streather
26.5 x 21cm • 432 pages • 1180 illustrations • £34.99

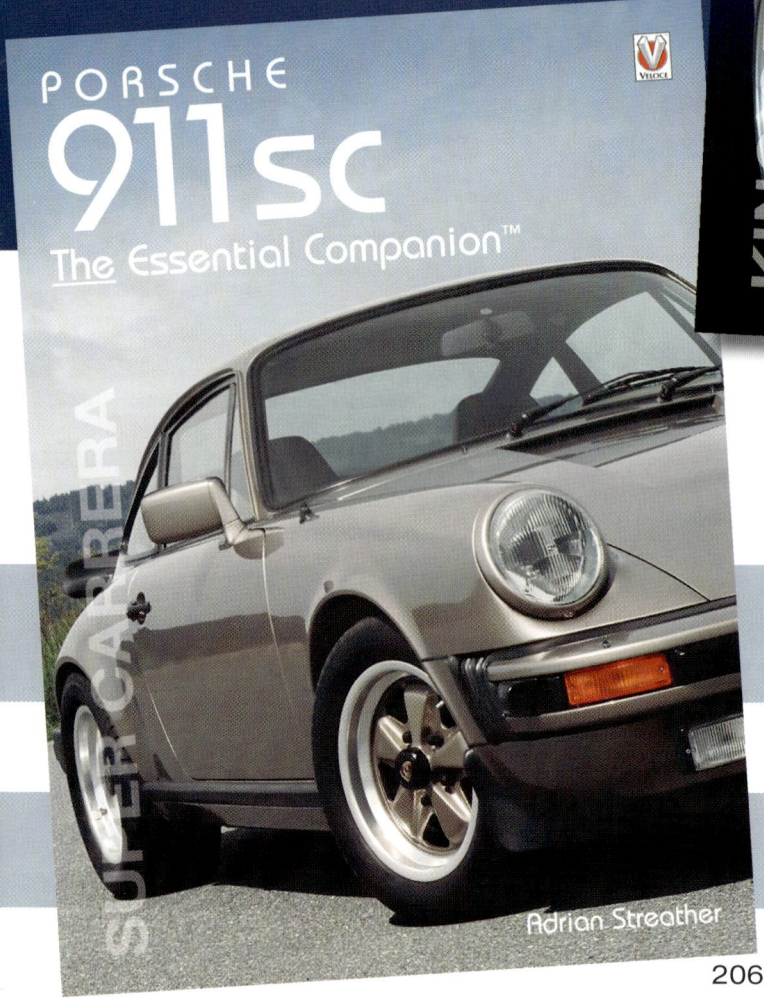

Index

Behr, Stephen 158
Bertone 28
BMW 21, 28, 72, 102, 167, 169, 173
Bob Sharp Racing 158
Boddy, William 47
Bonnier, Jo 15
Bonomelli Tuning 171
Borgward 11
Bott, Helmuth 59, 88
Brandt, Willy 38
Branitzki, Heinz 88
BRE 155, 158
Broadley, Eric 27
Brock, Pete 155
Buckley, Martin 183
Bunker-Hansen Racing 155

Camel 160
Car 69
Car & Driver 56, 159
Car Graphic 175
Cars & Car Conversions 62
Cars Are My Life 127
Carl Zeiss 88
Carrera Panamericana 11, 22
Chasseuil, Guy 140, 146
Chevrolet 179
Christmann, Mr 141
Chrysler 23, 123
Cisitalia 8
Classic & Sportscar 176, 183
Classic Cars 91, 181
Club Porsche Roman 150
Connaught 12
Cooper, Jacques 171
Corsair Cars 179
Crayford Auto Dev. 69
CSI 15

Daimler (Britain) 182
Daimler (Germany) 7
Daimler-Benz 7, 21, 24
Datsun (Nissan) 56, 146, 155, 158
Davis, Colin 20
Davis, Hubert 46-47
Daytona 72, 137, 148, 151
De La Pena, Mr 22
DeTomaso 27, 169
Dietrich, Chuck 155
DKW 21-22
Drauz 13
Dusio, Piero 8
Duval, J 151

Earls Court Show 12, 47
Eiffelrennen 11
Elford, Vic 140, 153
Erhard, Ludwig 38
European Grand Prix 8
Eurostyle 167, 171
Everett, Mr 148
Exner, Virgil 23

Fagan, Dave 62

Abarth 14
Abarth, Carlo 8, 146
Adler 22
AFN 12, 47, 51, 53, 62, 123
Ahrens, Kurt 140
Alfa Romeo 14, 35, 51, 102, 171, 183
Alpine 146
Altec 160
Andersson, Ake 146
Andersson, Ove 146
Andruet, Jean-Claude 146
Arnold, Graham 194
Attwood, Richard 140
Audi 24, 32, 37-38, 43, 88, 108, 127, 130, 148, 159, 183, 189
Austrian Alpine Rally 125, 140
Austro-Daimler 7
Auto Motor und Sport 179
Auto Union 7-8, 21, 24, 28, 37
Autocar 55, 62, 65, 176
Autohaus Max Moritz 148, 152, 155, 158
A-Z of Sports Cars 123

Bailey, B 151
Ballot-Lena, Claude 140, 145-146
Balzarini, Mr 20
Barth, Edgar 15
Bayer-Werke 28
Beach Boys Racing 176
Bean, B 151

Falk, Peter 19
Fall, Tony 125
Ferrari 27, 87, 176
FIA 14, 16, 137, 140
Fiat 25, 27-28, 56, 102, 146, 159
Filius, Otto 32
Firestone 120
Floridia, P 152
Forbes-Robinson, E 158-159
Ford 21, 24-25, 27, 134
Frankfurt Show 11-14, 18, 20, 23, 36-38, 44, 59
Frazer-Nash 12
French Grand Prix 16
Frua 172-173
Frua, Pietro 173
Fuhrmann, Dr Ernst 11, 88

Garretson 160
Geneva Show 9, 16, 172-173, 180
Ghia 22-23, 25, 29, 56, 125, 127, 159, 181
Ginther, Richie 155, 158
Giugiaro, Giorgetto 127, 169, 171, 180
Goertz, Albrecht 162, 167, 169, 171
Goetze Werk 88
Gregg, Peter 148, 155, 158
Gretener, John 146
Gugelot Design 28-29
Gugelot, Hans 28
Gulf 139
Gurney, Dan 16

Haldi, Claude 145-146
Hansen, Bob 155
Harrison, Pete 155
Hart, E W 7
Heidrich, Verne 173
Herrmann, Hans 11, 140
Heuliez 171
Heuliez, Louis 171
Hill, Graham 15
Hindson, Bob 158
Hispano-Aleman 172-173
Hitler, Adolf 7, 21
Hockenheim 44
Hoffman, Max 10-12
Holste, Werner 32
Hoppen, Josef 155, 159
Horrell, Paul 72
Huhn, Robert 141
Huslein, Otto 8

IMSA 148, 160
ItalDesign 169, 180

Jaguar 13, 28, 72, 90, 102, 173, 181, 184, 187
Jenkinson, Denis 27, 87
Johnson, Alan 155, 158
Jurgensen, Christian 150, 155

Kaiser, Mr 140
Kalkbrenner, K 88

207

Kanawyer, Garry 160
Karmann 12, 14, 21-23, 25, 29, 36, 43, 51, 56, 123, 125, 127, 159, 180-181
Karmann, Wilhelm 22
Karmann, Wilhelm Jr 22-23
Kastner, Kas 155
Keller, Mr 150
Kersten, Mr 153
Kiesinger, Kurt 38
Klie, Heinrich 29
Kling, Karl 11
Komenda, Erwin 12, 18
Koob, Mr 145
Krumm, Dietrich 150, 152
Kurtz, H 88

Lagaay, Harm 183
Lamborghini 27-28
Lancia 78, 102, 146, 181
Lansing 160
Lapine, Tony 183
Larrousse, Gerard 145-146, 153
Lawrence, Mike 123
Le Mans 11, 14, 31, 140-141, 148, 150
Le Mans 148
Leiding, Rudolf 88, 127, 134
Lenner 179
Liège-Rome-Liège Rally (Marathon de la Route) 11, 13, 142, 144-146
Linge, Herbert 11, 15, 19-20
Locke, Mr 148
Lohner 7
Lohner-Porsche 7
Lola 27
Lotus 14, 27, 97, 102, 181, 194
Lotz, Kurt 29, 33, 38, 88, 127

Marko, Helmut 145, 148
Maserati 87, 167
Matra 27, 102, 123, 181
McCarthy, Mike 176
McLaren 189
McQueen, Steve 142
Meaney, R 151
Mears, Rick 160
Mercedes (-Benz) 7, 36, 97, 102, 187, 189
MG 72, 102, 136, 159
Mille Miglia 11, 13, 32
Minter, Milt 155
Modern Motor 134
Monte Carlo Rally 19, 25, 127, 140, 146, 150, 180
Monza 150, 162
Moritz, Max 150
Moss, Stirling 15
Motor 62, 65
Motor Trend 37, 56, 87, 91, 107-108, 136
MotorSport 33, 47, 87

Muller, Herbert 152, 158
Murene 171, 173

Nicholas, G 151
Noah, Kendel 155, 158
Nolte, Mr 141
Nordhoff, Heinz 21-25, 29, 32, 127
Norisring 156
NSU 24, 32, 38, 88, 179, 183
Nürburgring 11, 14-15, 140-141, 146, 152-153, 179-180

Ontario 159
Opel 21, 24, 43, 56, 88, 102, 123, 159
Österreichring 146, 150, 153

Palmer, Brian 91
Paris Salon 10-11, 123, 171, 176, 183
Parish, Don 158
Peugeot 18
Phoenix 155
Piech, Anton 8
Piech, Ferdinand 20, 33, 59, 88, 127, 161-163, 165, 176
Piech, Louise 8, 20, 88
Pikes Peak 160
Pininfarina 27-28
Polensky, Helmut 11
Popular Imported Cars 46
Porsche, Butzi 18, 20, 28-29, 88
Porsche, Ferdinand 7-8, 10, 21, 89
Porsche, Ferry 7-9, 11, 14-15, 18, 20-21, 25, 29, 32, 38, 88, 127, 130, 161-163, 166, 168-169, 181
Porsche Design 88
Pucci, Antonio 20

Quist, Gerd 150, 152

RAC Rally 146
Redman, Brian 140
Reilly, John 37
Renault 7, 27, 146
Reutter 8-11
Road & Track 36, 56, 59, 65, 87, 130, 136, 173, 176, 182, 192-193, 196
Road Atlanta 158
Road Test 27, 33, 56, 112, 127
Rod Simpson Hybrids 179

Sage, Mr 150
Sbarro, Franco 179
SCCA 87, 152, 155, 158-159
Schickentanz, C 153
Schmid, D 152
Schmidt, Helmut 182
Schmidt, L 88
Schneider, Klaus 32
Schmucker, Tony 134
Schwarz, Gunther 141

Sebring 14, 20, 148
Segre, Luigi 22
Seidel, Wolfgang 15
Setright, L J K 181
Siffert, Jo 140
Simca 123
Sonauto 141-142, 146
Spa 150
Sports & GT Cars 134
Steckkonig, Gunther 140, 145-146
Steyr 7
Strahle, Paul 150
Stroh, William 158
Stuck, Hans 169
Supercar Classics 72

Targa Florio 13-15, 20, 140, 152, 158
Therier, Jean-Luc 146
Thorszelius, Hans 146, 150
Tomala, Hans 18, 35
Tour de France Auto 11
Tourist Trophy 11
Toyota 72
Toyota Team Europe 146
Triumph 69, 102, 155, 159
Tullius, Bob 155
Turin Show 162, 169, 171, 173

Van Lennep, Gijs 148, 152, 158
Veuillet, Auguste 146
Volkswagen 7-9, 21-25, 28-29, 32-33, 35-38, 43, 45-48, 51, 53, 55-56, 59, 62, 65, 67, 69, 82, 87-90, 93, 95, 97, 102, 110, 112-113, 117, 123, 125, 127, 130, 134, 167, 179-183, 189, 192, 194-196
Volvo 102
Von Hanstein, H 15, 32
Von Hohenzollern, Prince 146
Von Neumann, John 12
Von Senger, R 9
VW-Porsche 32, 36-38, 43, 67, 85, 88, 90, 117, 122, 127, 181, 190-191

Waldegaard, Bjorn 25, 140, 146, 150
Walker, Rob 15
Walter, Heini 15
Wendler 11, 14
Wheels 47, 89
World Car Guide 46
Wright, G 151
Wyer, John 139

Zagato 14
Zeltweg 137

The Porsche company, its subsidiaries and products are mentioned throughout the book.

www.veloce.co.uk